BEYOND METAPHYSICS?

Contemporary Studies in Philosophy and the Human Sciences

Series editor: John Sallis
Associate editors: Hugh J. Silverman and David Farrell Krell

* Also available in paperback

BEYOND METAPHYSICS?

THE HERMENEUTIC CIRCLE IN CONTEMPORARY CONTINENTAL PHILOSOPHY

by
John Llewelyn

Humanities Press International, Inc.
Atlantic Highlands, NJ

First published in 1985. Reprinted in paperback 1989 by
HUMANITIES PRESS INTERNATIONAL, INC.,
Atlantic Highlands, NJ 07716.

Library of Congress Cataloging-in-Publication Data

Llewelyn, John.
  Beyond metaphysics?

  (Contemporary studies in philosophy and the human sciences)
  Includes bibliographical references.
  1. Philosophy, Modern—20th century. 2. Philosophy—Europe—
History—20th century. I. Title. II. Series.
B804.L55   1984   110   84-4638

ISBN 0-391-03115-5
ISBN 0-391-03619-X (Pbk.)

Printed in the United States of America

TO MY PARENTS AND MAGGIE AND JACKY

Le plus haut point de la raison est-il de constater ce glissement du sol sous nos pas, de nommer pompeusement interrogation un état de stupeur continuée, recherche un cheminement en cercle, Etre ce qui n'est jamais tout à fait?

Maurice Merleau–Ponty

CONTENTS

ACKNOWLEDGMENTS

For comments on ancestors of chapters of this book or for discussion of questions arising in them I thank Robert Bernasconi, Roy Bhaskar, George Davie, Stanley Eveling, Anthony Giddens, Fergus Kerr, Magda King, Alan Montefiore, Basil O'Neill, Timothy Sprigge, David Wood, "Richard" (W. H.) Walsh (without his encouragement the book would never have been started) and David Farrell Krell (without his encouragement it would never have been—I also thank him for this word: finnished). I am obliged to Mrs Judith A. Camlin of Humanities Press for her patience and advice. I am indebted to Mrs Maureen Wallace for the carefulness of her typing. I am especially beholden to my wife for her care also as midwife.

For permission to use in chapters 3 and 4 material published in The *Journal of the British Society for Phenomenology* I am grateful to the editor, Wolfe Mays. I am grateful to the following publishers of works to which they own rights as indicated:

GEORGE ALLEN & UNWIN LTD.; for permission to quote from Edmund Husserl, *Ideas* (1931).

L'ARC; for permission to quote from *L'Arc: Jacques Derrida* (1973).

BEACON PRESS; for permission to quote from Maurice Merleau-Ponty, *The Structure of Behaviour* (1963).

BASIL BLACKWELL LTD.; for permission to quote from Martin Heidegger, *Being and Time* (1962), Ludwig Wittgenstein, *Notebooks 1914–1916* (1961), Wittgenstein, *On Certainty* (1969), Wittgenstein, *Philosophical Investigations* (1967), Wittgenstein, *Philosophische Bemerkungen* (1964).

THE UNIVERSITY OF CALIFORNIA PRESS; for permission to quote from Hans-Georg Gadamer, *Philosophical Hermeneutics* (1976).

CAMBRIDGE UNIVERSITY PRESS; for permission to quote from Edo Pivčević, ed., *Phenomenology and Philosophical Understanding* (1975).

JONATHAN CAPE LTD.; for permission to quote from Roland Barthes, *Elements of Semiology* (1967), Claude Lévi–Strauss, *From Honey to Ashes* (1973), Lévi–Strauss, *The Raw and the Cooked* (1970), Lévi–Strauss, *Tristes Tropiques* (1973).

THE UNIVERSITY OF CHICAGO PRESS; for permission to quote from Jacques Derrida, *Writing and Difference* (1978), Claude Lévi–Strauss, *The Savage Mind* (1966).

THE CROSSROAD PUBLISHING COMPANY and THE CONTINUUM PUBLISHING CORPORATION; for permission to quote from Hans–Georg Gadamer, *Truth and Method* (1975).

EDITIONS GALLIMARD; for permission to quote from Jean–Paul Sartre, *Critique de la raison dialectique* (1960), Sartre, *L'Etre et le néant* (1943).

HARPER & ROW; for permission to quote from Martin Heidegger, *The End of Philosophy* (1973), Heidegger, *Identity and Difference* (1969), Heidegger, *On Time and Being* (1972), Heidegger, *On the Way to Language* (1971), Heidegger, *Poetry, Language, and Thought* (1950), Heidegger, *What is Called Thinking?* (1968).

INDIANA UNIVERSITY PRESS; for permission to quote from Martin Heidegger, *Kant and the Problem of Metaphysics* (1962), Heidegger, *The Piety of Thinking* (1976).

THE JOHNS HOPKINS UNIVERSITY PRESS; for permission to quote from Jacques Derrida, *Of Grammatology* (1974, 1976).

METHUEN & CO. LTD.; for permission to quote from Jean–Paul Sartre, *Being and Nothingness* (1969), Sartre, *Existentialism and Humanism* (1948), Sartre, *The Problem of Method* (1964).

EDITIONS NAGEL; for permission to quote from Jean–Paul Sartre, *L'Existentialisme est un humanisme* (1946).

NEW LEFT BOOKS LTD.; for permission to quote from Paul Feyerabend, *Against Method* (1975), Jean–Paul Sartre, *Critique of Dialectical Reason* (1976).

MAX NIEMEYER VERLAG; for permission to quote from Martin Heidegger, *Sein und Zeit* (1972).

MARTINUS NIJHOFF; for permission to quote from Edmund Husserl, *Cartesian Meditations* (1960), Husserl, *Formal and Transcendental Logic* (1969), Emmanuel Levinas, *Otherwise than Being or Beyond Essence* (1981), Levinas, *Totality and Infinity* (1969).

THE NORTHWESTERN UNIVERSITY PRESS; for permission to quote from Maurice Merleau–Ponty, *Consciousness and the Acquisition of Language* (1973), Merleau–Ponty, *Signs* (1964), Merleau–Ponty, *The Visible and the Invisible* (1968).

THE PHILOSOPHICAL LIBRARY INC.; for permission to quote from Jean–Paul Sartre, *Being and Nothingness* (1969), Ferdinand de Saussure, *Course in General Linguistics* (1959).

PRESSES UNIVERSITAIRES DE FRANCE; for permission to quote from Gaston Bachelard, *La Dialectique de la durée* (1936), Bachelard, *Le Matérialisme rationnel* (1963), Bachelard, *Le Nouvel esprit scientifique* (1934), Bachelard, *La Philosophie du non* (1940).

ROUTLEDGE & KEGAN PAUL LTD.; for permission to quote from Josef Bleicher, *Contemporary Hermeneutics* (1980), Jacques Derrida, *Writing and Difference* (1978), Edmund Husserl, *Logical Investigations* (1970), Maurice Merleau–Ponty, *The Phenomenology of Perception* (1962), F. P. Ramsey, *The Foundations of Mathematics* (1931).

SHEED & WARD LTD.; for permission to quote from Hans-Georg Gadamer, *Truth and Method* (1975).

VISION PRESS LTD.; for permission to quote from Martin Heidegger, *Existence and Being* (1949).

LIBRAIRIE PHILOSOPHIQUE J. VRIN; for permission to quote from Gaston Bachelard, *La Valeur inductive de la science* (1929), Emmanuel Levinas, *En Découvrant l'existence avec Husserl et Heidegger* (1982).

GEORGE WEIDENFELD AND NICOLSON LTD.; for permission to quote from Claude Lévi–Strauss, *The Savage Mind* (1966).

YALE UNIVERSITY PRESS INC.; for permission to quote from Hans-Georg Gadamer, *Hegel's Dialectic* (1976), Martin Heidegger, *An Introduction to Metaphysics* (1959).

FOREWORD

In the dialogue named after him, Meno faces Socrates with this dilemma:

> How will you inquire, Socrates, into that which you do not know? What will you put forth as the subject of your inquiry? And if you find what you want, how will you ever know that this is what you did not know?

The Platonic solution is to admit that we have prior knowledge at least of the forms that the answers to questions must take, but this knowledge may be in need of recollection, *anamnesis*. The forms of knowledge are what Aristotle, Kant, and Hegel call categories. Aristotle's categories are the structures of scientific knowledge of what is and metaphysical knowledge of what it is to be, epistemological and ontological armatures corresponding to the various kinds of interrogative pronouns, adjectives and adverbs: what, why, how, how many, where, when, etc. Kant and Hegel modify the Aristotelian doctrine in important ways, but their own doctrines retain much from his, and from Plato's theory of forms they retain the epistemological circularity of what he calls *anamnesis*, what Kant calls the *a priori*, and what Hegel calls *Erinnerung*.

The following chapters describe why some contemporary Continental thinkers agree and why others disagree with Heidegger's idea that the categories of scientific knowledge presuppose a pre-scientific understanding whose structures are what he calls existentials. These "fore-structures" of understanding are described in chapter 1. They give rise to a hermeneutic circle which encompasses the epistemological circle. The hermeneutic circle, according to Heidegger, is a circle beyond metaphysics in so far as epistemology is equated, as he equates it, with the metaphysics of beings regarded as objects presented to subjects.[1] The hermeneutic circle is also a circle beyond traditional ontology in so far as this is equated, as he equates it, with metaphysics regarded as the theory of the beingness (*Seiendheit*) of beings in distinction from fundamental ontology which asks after the meaning of being (*Sein*). "Metaphysics ... tells us what what-is is by conceptualizing the 'is-ness' of what-is."[2] It is when metaphysics is understood in this sense that parts one and two of this book are covered by its title.

Chapter 2 explains how the Husserlian transcendental phenomenological reduction suspends some questions of traditional metaphysics but falls short of fundamental ontology because it fails to suspend the correlation of noetic consciousness and noematic objectivity.

Chapter 3 argues that although *Being and Nothingness*, like *Being and Time*, styles itself fundamental phenomenological ontology, Sartre forsakes the transcendental standpoint of phenomenology for the transcendent supernatural standpoint of the God he deposes in order to indulge in the rationalistic metaphysics of Olympian survey. Although he sets out to disclose the meaning of being, his ontology relapses into an ontology of the beingness of beings predicated on a correlativity conceived in such a way as to lead to a vicious regress or vicious circle. Chapter 4 argues that the *Critique of Dialectical Reason* supplies no way out of this predicament. Although Sartre's aim is, like Heidegger's, to show how the epistemological circle of categorial science is inscribed *sub specie temporalitatis* within the hermeneutic circle of pre-scientific existential understanding, the innocuous hermeneutic circle finds itself encompassed within a vicious circle which has its origin in Sartre's failure to resist the blandishments of a metaphysics that purports to be a super-science *sub specie aeternitatis*.

If, notwithstanding his debt to Heidegger, Sartre fulfills Heidegger's project no more than Husserl anticipates it, the philosophy outlined in chapter 5 is as remote from that project as can be imagined. With Bachelard, metaphysics as super-science comes into its own again, and his teaching that there is an "epistemological break" between the scientific and the pre-scientific is incompatible with the idea that reflective knowledge and epistemology are earthed in a hermeneutic circle of pre-reflective understanding.

With Bachelard's epistemology representing the polar opposite of Heidegger's endeavor to demonstrate that the hermeneutic circle takes us beyond traditional, that is, in Heidegger's view, epistemological, metaphysics, the issues at stake in this opposition acquire sharper focus when in chapter 6 a return is made to some of the proposals aired in chapter 1 in order to see how they are applied by Gadamer and how his philosophical hermeneutics holds up not only against the critique implicit in Bachelard's theories but against objections from realist critics like E. D. Hirsch and Emilio Betti and the "critical" theory of Habermas. This debate between the scientific objectivists on the one hand and the hermeneutic humanists on the other is continued in the account of the relations between Merleau–Ponty and Saussure given in chapter 7 and of the discussions between Ricoeur and Lévi–Strauss reported in chapter 8.

The previously noted interconnectedness of the topics referred to in the title and subtitle of this study is reflected in the relationship between part one and part two. Part one is concerned mainly with the ontological questions introduced in chapter 1. These are posed again in the first chapter of part two, but part two is largely a consideration of particular applications of the main topic of part one to the interpretation of material in the fields of law, scriptural exegesis, linguistics, history, social anthropology,and other humanities or human sciences. Each of its three chapters appraises moves made from one side or the other to reduce the extent of disagreement between the parties to the controversies reviewed. Part three begins with a short chapter written in the same spirit of conciliation and optimism. The reason the title of the book has a question mark begins to come to light in a final chapter on the work of Levinas and Derrida. The reader is advised that it will not become clear before this chapter why certain topics are raised in the chapters that precede. Admittedly, this is a nuisance, but it is an inevitable consequence of the generic hermeneutical circularity of which "the hermeneutic circle in contemporary Continental philosophy" is a specific manifestation: a consequence of the fact that an understanding of the parts is dependent on an understanding of the whole, and vice versa. It will be convenient to follow the practice of reserving the adjectives "hermeneutical" and "hermeneutic" for, respectively, the generic and the specific circularity. Josef Bleicher defines the hermeneutic circle as the "ontological condition of understanding" which "proceeds from a communality that binds us to tradition in general and that of our object of interpretation in particular" and which "provides the link between finality and universality, and between theory and praxis." Of the hermeneutical circle he says that it is a "methodological device in interpretation which considers a whole in relation to its parts, and vice versa."[3] I accept this way of marking the distinction, except I prefer to regard the hermeneutical circle as what makes the methodological device necessary.

This study is primarily exegetical. It has two interlinked themes, but no attempt is made to argue a general thesis. The particular points at which it is argumentative are probably points at which its author is having difficulty reaching a clear view of what is going on in the works he is aiming to expound. May the reader reach a clear enough view of what is going on in this work for it to be of some assistance in the difficulties he has with the others.

PART ONE

META-METAPHYSICAL
ONTOLOGY

CHAPTER ONE
HEIDEGGER: BEYOND THE
CATEGORIES OF BEING

The origin of the concept of being and of the remaining cate-
gories does not lie in the realm of sense-perception.
                                                    —Edmund Husserl

1. *Categories and existentials*

It will do Heidegger an injustice if this chapter nowhere sounds extremely strange. One reason for this is implicit in Heidegger's remark
that his lecture "What is Metaphysics?" cannot but "remain equivocal
in an essential sense" because the thinking it calls for must be at the
same time metaphysical yet nonmetaphysical.[1] It must think the ontological difference between being and beings.

Heidegger records that among the experiences that led his thinking
toward the question of the ontological difference were his reading of
Husserl's *Logical Investigations*, particularly Investigation 6, of Brentano's thesis "On the Manifold Meaning of Being According to Aristotle," and of Carl Braig's manual "On Being: An Outline of Ontology."[2]
This last, a volume of a series by Braig on the foundations of philosophy, includes a compendium of texts and references that could not have
failed to excite Heidegger and has section headings that anticipate
themes that were to occupy him throughout his life; for example, "The
ontological meaning of the concept of space," "The ontological meaning of the concept of time," "The ground of beings," and "The being of
beings and being thought."

Braig was a professor on the faculty of theology at Freiburg when
Heidegger was himself a student of theology there. Although Heidegger
soon concentrated his attention on philosophy, it was from conversa-
tions with Braig that he first became aware of the impact the writings of

Schelling and Hegel had in the field of speculative theology. He was later to say that his thinking would never have taken the path it did had it not been for his theological background.[3] It would, however, be dangerous to see Heidegger's lifework as a secularized theology.[4] And it would be erroneous to see it as an espousal of either theism or atheism or indifferentism.[5] The question he is asking is more fundamental than any of these. Hence he suggests to an audience of theologians at Drew University in 1964[6] and to an audience that included many scientists on the occasion of his inaugural address at Freiburg in 1929[7] that their respective subjects, along with metaphysics, have in their preoccupation with questions about beings been led astray from the question of the meaning of being.[8] This absorption in ontics and an onto-theo-logical metaphysics at the expense of fundamental ontology is never condemned as a mistake by Heidegger. He frequently allows that the positions advocated are correct. And he does not see it as his business to refute any of them. His so-called destruction of them consists in taking them apart in order to make manifest how they are inclined to arise. This inclination has some resemblance to what Kant called transcendental illusion and to the predicament illustrated by the myth of the cave, which Heidegger himself discusses in *Plato's Doctrine of Truth*.[9] Among many other theories of illusion and self-deception with which comparison might be made are those of Bergson, Nietzsche and Wittgenstein. And *Being and Time* could be called an ontopathology of everyday life, except that what Heidegger names inauthenticity is not a disease but the normal condition of man. However, it is especially important with Heidegger to go back in the beginning to the things themselves, *zu den Sachen selbst*. That is where he himself begins in *Being and Time*, with a description of the phenomena of the everyday world (27–28).

Having challenged the assumption that, because the concept of being is self-evidently intelligible or because it is indefinable or because it is the most universal concept, the question about the meaning of being is one that it is superfluous to raise, Heidegger proceeds to claim that the only ontology fitted to this question must be phenomenological in a sense derived from that given to the word by Husserl, a sense of which the introduction to *Being and Time* produces an outline. This outline is a preliminary to developments it undergoes more than three hundred pages later (357). Yet it blazes a trail for the style of writing to which Heidegger turns after only two of the projected six divisions of *Being and Time* are published. For instance, the reading of the later writings casts new light on the earlier remark that "whenever a phenomenological concept and principle is drawn from primordial sources, there is a possibility that it may degenerate if communicated in the form of an assertion" (36). But that assertion itself and the style of the later writings are vindicated by the phenomenological descriptions carried out within *Being and Time*. And in view of that assertion it is understandable why Heidegger should stop calling what he is doing phenomenology. The reason is "not—as is often thought—in order to deny the significance of phenomenology, but in order to abandon my own path of thinking to namelessness."[10]

Care needs to be taken not to misconstrue what Heidegger means by phenomenology when he does use that term for what he practices. He is not using it for description of phenomena if by that is intended the immediate data of perception, what reveals itself to the senses. The phenomena that Heideggerian phenomenology describes are usually not given. They conceal themselves. Phenomena regarded as whatever offer themselves to immediate sensuous or nonsensuous intuition are. They have being. This, it would seem, goes without saying. And because the concept of being has to be used in an attempt at an elucidation of that concept, it has been concluded that there can be no elucidation of it. Any proposed elucidation would be circular. Hence the question of the meaning of the concept gets left unasked and the concept gets concealed. Hence the need for fundamental ontology, which, since its subject matter is concealed, is phenomenology, a description of the phenomena in Heidegger's meaning of that term. It is clear from this that fundamental ontology must be phenomenological. It is less clear that every kind of ontology must be phenomenological. Heidegger's claim that "only as phenomenology is ontology possible" (35) is acceptable only if we allow that every ontology is incomplete until supplemented by what he calls fundamental ontology, an elucidation of the meaning of being. Does what he says in the introduction provide grounds for confidence in the feasibility of such elucidation? We could simply wait and see how the program is carried out before deciding whether there could be a feasible program. This is a procedure we should be ready to adopt. For it may be that we are ourselves in the same position as the proponents of traditional metaphysical ontology to whom Heidegger refers. How, if that were so, could we hope to reach a point from which to survey that position by tugging at our own metaphysical bootlaces? This hope, according to *Being and Time*, is not vain. The first step toward the realization of this fact is taken when we appreciate that it is not the fundamental ontologist but the antifundamentalist who is begging the question. The question is begged in the assumption that because the concept of being is used in any definition, the attempt to elucidate the meaning of being is viciously circular. If the antifundamentalist were reminded of definition in use, of the logical theory that to be is to be the value of a bound variable and of the metaphysico-epistemological theory that to be is to be perceived, he would doubtless say that these theories and devices do embody a circularity. Whether they do or not, and whether, if they do, that circularity would be vicious, it should be noted that they emanate from the fields of propositional or predicate logic, metaphysics and epistemology. But Heidegger is asking why we should take it for granted that being is confined to these fields. Admittedly, he refers to being as a concept, *Begriff*. This is an aspect of the previously mentioned difficulty confessed to, nay welcomed, in *What is Metaphysics?*. That difficulty is compounded by his finding himself called upon to work phenomeno*logically*, that is, to give an explication, a conceptualized analysis, yet an analysis of a unique kind, *eine eigene Begrifflichkeit* (6),[11] in that the analysandum is not, any more than it was for Kant, a predicate or property, nor is it an object or a subject.

That it is not remains to be shown. How *Being and Time* begins to show this can only be adumbrated here. (We return to this question in part three.) Perhaps the beginning of the beginning is the recognition that to assert or deny anything of being and to inquire or wonder about it at all presupposes at least an undeveloped and in that sense preontological, that is, pretheoretical, understanding of being. "We must know in advance what 'free' means in order to be able to seek and find the particulars. Likewise with 'being.'"[12] But this is a presupposition not only of the pursuit of ontology, whether fundamental or not. It is a presupposition also of the pursuit of any science. "As ways in which man behaves, sciences have the manner of being which this entity—man himself—possesses. This entity we denote by the term '*Dasein*'" (11). Scientific research, philosophy, theology, and golf are pursuits to which you and I choose to devote our time. We see them as possibilities. And when we find ourselves brought up to live in one particular way, we see alternative ways of living as possibilities even if they are not ones it is in practice possible for us to pursue. We see what we do under the rubric of what does or does not matter. This is so, too, when we do what we do simply because we like it. There is indeed an etymological connection between *Möglichkeit*, "possibility," and *mögen*, "to like," "desire," or "be willing." In this sense even drifting is something one chooses to do.

What distinguishes human beings from other beings, according to
Heidegger, is that the human being sees himself as faced with the choice
to be or not to be. If all Heidegger were aiming at was a mark by which
to distinguish man from other beings it would have been enough to say,
on analogy with Kant's statement about *cogito*, that it must be *possible*
for man to see himself as faced with this choice, to think *sum* or *ich bin*,
that is, according to the etymological speculations on page 54 of *Being
and Time*, to think "I dwell."[13] It would also have been enough to describe this as a choice between being this and not being this, an appli-
cant, for instance, for a particular post. What Heidegger says in fact is
that "Dasein always understands itself in terms of its existence—in
terms of a possibility of itself: to be itself or not itself" (12). The con-
cluding phrase here is an anticipation of what is to be said further on
about authenticity. Comment on that would be out of place at this stage.
But a brief comment on "Dasein" and "existence" is required here.

Heidegger sometimes uses the word Dasein to mean a being, a man,
and sometimes as a substitute for "man." On certain occasions, however, the word functions as a gerund, and even when it functions as a
name of an entity of a special sort it is meant to express that entity's
manner of being, *als reiner Seinsausdruck* (12). *Da-sein* is to be present,
adesse. Moreover, if a particular Dasein sees itself to be faced with a
choice it is in a situation in which there is a choice to be made. It is
confronted. And if, as Heidegger maintains, it is of the essence of
Dasein that each particular Dasein "has its being to be, and has it as its
own," then its essence is its existence, that is, to ex-sist, and *Sein* conveys the gerundival meaning "called to be existed." The published fragment of *Being and Time* is taken up with the analysis of the senses in
which Dasein stands outside itself, ahead of itself, toward beings of a
different kind from itself and with beings of its own kind. That existential analytic is embarked upon because if we are to elucidate the meaning of being in general that elucidation must apply to the particular manner of being of Dasein.

A reading of *Being and Time* would err from the start, however, if it
were insensitive to the way in which the elucidation must apply to the
particular manner of being of each particular Dasein; insensitive, that is,
to the force of Heidegger's statement that

> the roots of the existential analytic, on its part, are ultimately
> *existentiell*, that is, *ontical*. Only if the inquiry of philosophi-
> cal research is itself seized upon in an existentiell manner as a

possibility of the being of each existing Dasein, does it become at all possible to disclose the existentiality of existence and to undertake an adequately founded ontological problematic. (13)

Philosophical inquiry is singled out for mention here because that is the pursuit in which his reader is presumed to be engaged, and it is up to the reader himself to prove upon his own pulses whether the findings of the existential analytic tally with his own experience (*Erfahrung*). It is from this that the reader must set out if he is to travel the path of Heidegger's "radically individuating" (38) existential analytic, somewhat as the transcendental analytic of the *Critique of Pure Reason* can be followed only in the light of one's experience of temporal succession and as Kant's moral analytic can be followed only by someone who is conscious of a difference between the sense of moral obligation on the one hand and prudential necessity on the other.[14]

But Heidegger's existential analytic purports to be an exposure of the foundations that underlie both a metaphysic of cognitive experience and a metaphysic of morals. Whereas Kant's objective is to exhibit the formal concepts without which intuition is blind, Heidegger's objective is to exhibit the transcendental "concept," the "pure and simple *transcendens*" (38), being, without which the formal concepts or categories of the understanding and the so-called fundamental principles of any metaphysic of practice would be the blind leading the blind (11). Theoretical activities are activities. They, like moral, technological, artistic, religious, or any other kind of behavior, are ways in which Dasein chooses to be in the world. The existential analytic is a disclosure of the precategorial structures, the existentials, which define what it is to be in a world. These structures are continually being overlooked by philosophers and nonphilosophers alike, though it seems to be Heidegger's belief that they err in different directions. The ontology of Descartes typifies the philosophical tendency to construe the world as a totality of substantive entities present at hand (*vorhanden*) to one another, each a bearer of present at hand properties, each related externally to the others. Even Dasein gets construed as such a free-floating, worldless, present at hand Self. But this is to view Dasein as a postlapsarian Humpty Dumpty. All the philosophers who take this view could never put Dasein together again. Against this view Heidegger holds that Dasein is irreducibly being-in-the-world, and that the everyday way of being-in-the-world is not a neutral awareness of property-sustaining entities or stuff like matter in motion, nor does that way consist in the making of judgments about states of affairs. Our world presents that face to us only when there is something missing from it or amiss in it, as when the handle of a hammer breaks and we see hickory as the kind of wood (in French: *essence*) with the properties requisite for the repair. Only then do we regard the wood as stuff and the split haft before us as an object possessing certain characteristics. They had those characteristics before they presented themselves to us in this way (71). But until then the thought that they did was precluded by our absorbed involvement (*Bewandtnis*) with a tool with which to get on with the job in hand. For us in that context the hammer was something ready to hand (*zuhanden*) through which, without its being the focus of our thought, we were trying to achieve the end in view. And when it is broken we are caught up at once in the problem of what is to be done to effect a repair. We still do not inhabit a world of neutral "things"; "The fact that observation is a kind of concern is just as primordial as the fact that action has its own kind of sight" (69). We inhabit a world of circumspective concern, *umsichtige Besorgen*, with what does not have the mode of being of Dasein and of solicitude or minding, *Fürsorge*, with what does. The *um* of *umsichtige* represents the fact that to be in the everyday world is to be there "in order to ...". That world is an *Um-welt*. It is not a totality of things. It is not a totality of facts. It is a referential totality of assignments, a *Verweisungsganzheit*.

Concern and solicitude, or mindfulness, are existentials. They are expressions of care, *Sorge*, the most basic existential. *Besorgen, Fürsorge*, and *Sorge* are used by Heidegger as technical terms. This becomes evident as soon as we see that they all also cover their deficient and indifferent modes. Thus, ignoring is a form of minding or solicitude, and neglect a form of concern.[15] It is important that Heidegger should provide for these indifferent modes of concern and solicitude. Without the indifferent mode of concern, for instance, we should have no slot other than presence at hand for the unlit desklamp at our elbow as we write by broad daylight.

Heidegger himself stresses the need to find room for indifferent modes of solicitude (121). If he did not do this, he would appear to be committed to allowing that in the everyday world Dasein may be present at hand. Whereas his contention seems to be, rather, that the treatment of Dasein as present at hand is not a feature of our everyday being with others but a feature of some ontological interpretations of our being with others, the Cartesian one already referred to, for instance. If this distinction is not overlooked it may be possible to defend Heidegger against the charge that he himself does not escape a certain confusion he attributes to everyday existence. In support of this charge, W. B. Macomber invokes some passages (239, 289, 333, 387–88) where Heidegger says Dasein regards itself as ready to hand and other passages (59, 114, 130, 201, 225) where he says Dasein regards itself as present at hand.[16] A comparison of the passages in question reveals, however, that the first view is said to be one attributed to itself by Dasein in everyday life, while the second view is Dasein's ontological interpretation of itself. That the distinction between these two views is crucial for the interpretation of *Being and Time* receives confirmation from the following words taken from its last page:

> It has long been known that ancient ontology works with "Thing-concepts" and that there is a danger of "reifying consciousness." But what does this reifying signify? Where does it arise? Why does being get "conceived" "proximally" in terms of the present at hand *and not* in terms of the ready to hand, which indeed lies closer to us?

"Proximally" (*zunächst*) is put in quotation marks in the last sentence of this passage because, as the sentence goes on to make clear, readiness to hand rather than presence at hand is the category through which we commonly deal with our tasks and with one another. It is the ancient ontological interpretation that reverses the order of priority.

Should we agree with Heidegger that ontological interpretations in the tradition of Western metaphysics have reified the self or the nonhuman environment but *never* "instrumentalized" them? Whether or not we do, it must be acknowledged that although, by appealing to the distinction between the everyday outlook and a metaphysical or ontological outlook, we have removed an obstacle from the path of Macomber's argument that according to Heidegger the everyday outlook takes Dasein instrumentally, there remains on Heidegger's path the difficulty of explaining why understanding and interpretation at the level of theoretical ontology tend to be reifying, whereas at the level of everydayness Dasein sees itself instrumentally, in spite of the fact that it is itself pretheoretically ontological, that is, has an interpretative understanding of being (12). Heidegger concedes at the end of the published portion of *Being and Time* that he has still not answered this question. "Do the answers to these questions lie along the way?" he asks (437). At least some pertinent pointers have been set up along the part of the route he has already traversed, especially in his discussion of language, truth, and logic.

2. *Language and the structure of care*

In considering how discourse (*Rede, logos*), which is one of Heidegger's existentials, fits into the structure that his existential analytic begins to lay bare, it must be remembered that readiness to hand and presence at hand are categories applicable to entities other than Dasein and are therefore not existentials. This makes a difference as to what can be legitimately inferred from the statement, "Perhaps even readiness to hand and equipment have nothing to contribute as ontological clues in Interpreting the primitive world; and certainly the ontology of Thinghood does even less" (82). If the everyday world of primitive Dasein is different from ours, then if we can understand it at all it will only be by imagining variations on the general formal structure we discover in our own. This may hold too for our attempts to understand an Oriental world.[17] Should not Heidegger say the same about his existential analysis of Dasein? Might not that be merely local? Instead of applying his ontology of Dasein to men whose worlds are radically different from ours, should he not say about them something parallel to what he says about animals, which have environment but not world,[18] that "the basic ontological state of 'living' ... can be tackled only reductively and privately in terms of an ontology of Dasein" (194)?

That he ought to answer these questions in the affirmative is implied by his emphasis at the beginning of the book on the existentiell basis of the existential analysis and his emphasis toward the end of the book on the *Geschicklichkeit* of Dasein, its belonging to a generation with a communal destiny (384). Whatever the explanation may be for the way in which the Greeks came to see *logos* predominantly as assertion, the fact that they did does not commit Dasein in general to a metaphysical ontology centered on presence at hand. Nor can it be taken for granted that Dasein in general is committed to a nonmetaphysical ontology, a fundamental ontology, of the sort Heidegger begins to describe in *Being and Time*. Perhaps he himself came to think this, and that may be one reason why his manner of addressing himself to the question of the meaning of being underwent a change. More will be said about that change in the third section of this chapter. But let it be conceded immediately that it is difficult to understand how, given Heidegger's account of assertion, there could be a metaphysical ontology not centered on presence at hand. For such an ontology is presumably a body of theoretical assertions. These, on his account, substitute what he calls an apophantical "as" for what he calls the existential-hermeneutical "as" of circumspective concern in a referential totality of assignments. The apophantical "as" is the "as" of the qua-lities or, more generally, of the properties for which predicate logic is tailored, and the formal relations, *Beziehungen*, of that logic have their ontological source in circumspective orientation (*Verweisung*) (77). Heidegger adopts the label "existential-hermeneutical 'as'" to avoid the risks of suggesting that our involvement in a referential totality, a *Verweisungsganzheit*, involves representing our circumstance predicatively. The label is misleading in that assertion is also hermeneutic, if by that we mean that an interpretation is made. Assertions make their own kind of explicit interpretation. This goes, too, for the various kinds of statement intermediate between circumspective interpretation and theoretical assertion.

> Between the kind of interpretation which is still wholly wrapped up in concernful understanding and the extreme opposite case of a theoretical assertion about something present at hand, there are many intermediate gradations: assertions about occurrences in the environment, accounts of the ready to hand, "reports on the Situation," the recording and fixing of the "facts of the case," the description of a state of affairs, the narration of events in which someone has been involved. We cannot reduce these "statements" to theoretical assertions without fundamentally distorting their sense. Like the theoretical assertions themselves, they have their "source" in circumspective interpretation. (158)

This reminder of the spectrum of speech-acts we tend to lump together as "statements" or "propositions" is very much in the spirit of Wittgenstein's reminder of "how many different kinds of things are called 'descriptions.'"[19] And Wittgenstein's reminder of the multiplicity of language-games in paragraph 23 of the *Philosophical Investigations* is very much in the spirit of Heidegger's remark that "being-with-one-another is discursive as assenting or refusing, as demanding or warning, as pronouncing, consulting, or interceding, as 'making assertions,' and as talking in the form of 'giving a talk'" (161).

It would be profitable to plot the similarities and differences between

Wittgenstein's phenomenology of "seeing as" and Heidegger's treatment of the temptation to overlook the pre-predicative "something as something" under the impact of developments of Aristotelian logic. One thing they share is a concern to remove the urge to picture perception as an "interpretation" of something neutrally there in itself, as though one might apply a coat of paint to something that as yet has no color. Heidegger writes:

> In interpreting, we do not, so to speak, throw a "signification" over some naked thing which is present at hand, we do not stick a value on it; but when something within-the-world is encountered as such, the thing in question already has an involvement which is disclosed in our understanding of the world, and this involvement is one which gets laid out by the interpretation. (150)

The so-called "in itself," Heidegger submits, is the equipmental complex in which we are circumspectively concerned, and the "sight" of circumspection is not to be confused with re-presentation (*Vorstellung*). Further, the interpretation (*Auslegung*) appropriate to circumspective concern requires no synthesis of present at hand representations and no copulation of subjects and predicates.

> Prior to all analysis, logic has already understood "logically" what it takes as a theme under the heading of the categorical statement—for instance, "The hammer is heavy." It takes it for granted that the "meaning" of the sentence is: This thing—a hammer—has the property of heaviness. In concernful circumspection there are no such assertions "first of all." But such circumspection has of course its specific ways of interpreting, and these, as compared with the "theoretical judgement" just mentioned, may take some such form as "The hammer is too heavy," or rather just "Too heavy!", "Hand me the other hammer!". Interpretation is carried out primordially not in a theoretical statement but in an action of circumspective concern—laying aside the unsuitable tool, or exchanging it, "without wasting words." From the fact that words are absent, it may not be concluded that interpretation is absent. (157)

The "sight" (*Sicht*) of both predicative and pre-predicative interpretation is fore-sight (*Vorsicht*), seeing something in advance. All interpretation is also based on having something in advance (*Vorhabe*) and grasping something in advance (*Vorgriff*). This doctrine is not worked out by Heidegger in as much detail as one would like, but it is clear enough that it is an attempt to distinguish the different ways in which for there to be interpretation there must be something "understood," assumed to go without saying, at least provisionally. The situation of Dasein is a hermeneutic circle. What Heidegger, and after him Gadamer, says in effect is that the interpreter is prepossessed or had a priori by language. The interpreter's fore-sight or pre-view is the prima facie appearance the thing to be interpreted presents to him. This provisional view can be conceptualized, but this does not require that assertions about the subject matter have to be made. This complex forestructure applies to our practical involvement with our environment where our having a particular concern means that there is something occupying our attention which we are predisposed to see as having a certain instrumental or detrimental bearing on the realization of the object or our concern. We may or may not grasp this relevance correctly. The preconceptions that get expressed in our behavior may be misconceptions. And when we express them in assertions these preconceptions will include the logical forms built into the foundations of the language we are accustomed to, as illustrated in "The hammer is heavy," "Heaviness belongs to the hammer," "The hammer has the property of heaviness." These forestructures bring out the fact that interpretation is particularly closely related to the future, as too is understanding (*Verstehen*), Dasein's being toward possibilities. Interpretation is grounded in understanding. It is the articulation of understanding's disclosures (156).

Understanding is an existential, and it is one that is especially expressive of Dasein's ex-sistence, of its being ahead of itself, project (*Entwurf*). But Dasein is a thrown (*geworfene*) project. It finds itself already in the world. Heidegger calls this existential *Befindlichkeit*, "state" or "state of mind," "condition." This ontologico-existential structure is exemplified ontically in *Stimmung*, "mood" or "temper," how we find ourselves, for example joyful, bored, or in a state of despair. "Temper" has overtones of its use in the phrase "well-tempered clavichord" to refer to Bach's prototype of the "prepared" piano. It may also help to grasp what Heidegger means if we take notice that a mood is a condition in which we may already find ourselves when we wake, how the world as a whole waxes and wanes for us. State and mood are expressive of Dasein's facticity. They are precognitive and preconative disclosures of the burden of Dasein's gerundive state that it is and has to be its there (135–36), like it or lump it.

The world in which Dasein finds itself is one in which it is fallen among entities with which it is concerned or of whom it is mindful (in Heidegger's extremely broad senses of *Besorgen* and *Fürsorge*), beings that are over against it. Consequently, falling (*Verfallen*) has a special relationship with the present (*Gegen-wart*). But, as the second division of *Being and Time* goes on to show, the temporal ecstases of present, future, and past are inextricably interconnected, as too are the existentials falling, understanding, and state. These three existentials are articulated in discourse (*Rede*). Everyday conventional discourse (*Gerede*) is sunk in our dealings with people and objects that surround us here and now. It has a special relationship with falling, the manner of our sociality, our *Mitsein*. But Dasein exists as factically thrown falling (367). In Dasein existence, facticity and falling are inseparable. Together they constitute the structure of care. Care is the matrix existential.

The temporal character of care has begun to emerge. The second division of *Being and Time* reconsiders some of the structures of care already considered in the first division and endeavors to show in what sense temporality is the ontological meaning (*Sinn*) of care (323). Heidegger also says of temporality that "it first showed itself in anticipatory resoluteness [*vorlaufenden Entschlossenheit*]. This is the authentic mode of disclosedness, though disclosedness [*Erschlossenheit*] maintains itself for the most part in the inauthenticity [*Uneigentlichkeit*] with which the 'they' fallingly interprets itself" (331). In falling Dasein looses itself in the anonymous and impersonal "they" or "one," *das Man*, whose medium is the institutions of daily public life. The institution dominantly responsible for Dasein's forgetfulness of its own responsibility is everyday language with its tendency to mask the ontological significance of Dasein's mortality by talking of death as something that "comes to all of us," where the "us" is the indefinite, impersonal, strictly third personal one that hides the definite, first personal me (253). In this state of decadence death is something we fear or face with courage. But Dasein's fear (*Furcht*) and courage in the face of the ontic fact (*Tatsache*) of death are equally attempts to escape anxiety (*Angst*), the mood in which it finds itself facing the ontological fact (*Faktum*) (56) of Dasein's finitude. An ontological fact is not an ontic fact, but an ontic fact may stand to an ontological one in the character of something like what Kant calls a Typic,[20] a reminder. The memento of finitude is death. Our very fear in the face of it and our turning away are themselves ways in which we live our being *toward* our end. It is irrelevant whether death is ontically a phenomenal fact of life that we shall all experience, *erleben*.[21] Also irrelevant is the question whether anyone is ontically, factually, immortal. Ontologically and phenomenologically death is a *possibility* and Dasein's being factically thrown toward it is the ultimate realization of that being ahead of itself which is one of the structures of care. It is the possibility beyond which there is no possibility since there there is no "there is." When Dasein reaches its wholeness in death, it simultaneously loses the being of its "there." "Das Erreichen der Gänze des Daseins im Tode ist zugleich Verlust des Seins des Da" (237). Phenomenologically and ontologically, death is the possibility of the absolute impossibility of all being there, *da sein* (250), not the reality (*Wirklichkeit*) or fact (*Tatsache*) of this impossibility, since ontological possibility is more basic not only than logical possibility but than ontic reality and metaphysical fact. This is why Heidegger's connection of death with authenticity cannot be a mere echo of the sentiment expressed by Dr. Johnson, "When a man knows he is to be hanged in a fortnight, it concentrates his mind wonderfully." And it explains why phenomenologically death is not the great leveler but the great individualizer. Heidegger is not saying simply that my death is what individuates me, in that it is what distinguishes me from others since others cannot die my death. If this were what he meant it would be fair comment that others cannot sneeze my sneezes either and that my birth individuates me no less. But the statement that my birth or my birthmark is something that individuates me and makes me unique among men is quite compatible with Heidegger's claim (251) that being toward death is what distinguishes Dasein from all other beings, including animals, which because they do not have a world but only a life to lose, do not die, but perish (*verenden*) (240). That statement is likewise compatible with Heidegger's claim that the anxiety of being toward death individualizes Dasein, that is, sets it free from the "they." For this is an existentiell possibility open to every Dasein. The inauthenticity of everyday falling into the anonymous "they," where Dasein forgets its own name, is one possibility open to it. But the choice of that possibility itself serves to demonstrate that Dasein can choose to be authentic. There is yet another parallel here with Kant, namely with his statement that a good will and freedom must be counted a possibility, although we never know whether that possibility has been realized. And reminiscent of Kant's treatment of the sense of respect for the moral law is, *mutatis mutandis*, Heidegger's statement that the mood of anxiety brings Dasein face to face with its being free for the authenticity of its being (88). He also refers to authenticity as a response to the call of conscience and says that the understanding of this call reveals itself as our wanting to have a conscience (*Gewissen-haben-wollen*) (288).

In light of Heidegger's admiration for Kant's writings in the metaphysics of experience, evidenced by the fact that as well as lectures at least three books on the sage of Königsberg were written by the sage of Todtnauberg,[22] it is to be expected that he would be stimulated too by Kant's writings in ethics. Nevertheless, the surface similarities must not be allowed to hide the fact that Heidegger sees himself to be working on a stratum of bedrock on which Kant hit only sporadically. One should not forget the difference between Heidegger's distinction of resolute authenticity from irresolute inauthenticity and Kant's distinction of autonomy from heteronomy. The former ontological distinction, according to Heidegger, founds the latter ontic distinction of practical reason. To forget these differences would be to fall into the philosophical "tranquillity" (177) against which he warns us and himself of thinking we have nothing new to learn, that it has all been said before.

Nor should we read voluntaristic "existentialism" or subjective individualism into what Heidegger calls resoluteness. At the end of *The Essence of Reasons* he says: "Only in its Dasein with others [*Mitsein*] can Dasein surrender its subjective individuality [*Ichheit*] in order to win itself as an authentic self."[23] He does not deny that the authentic man is self-possessed, stands on his own feet, and is self-constant (*selbstständig*), "self-constancy" being the ontological translation he gives for the word that in the metaphysical tradition from which he adapts it means "substantiality" (322). But, as in the sentences from page 331 of *Being and Time* quoted above, although *Entschlossenheit* does mean "resoluteness," Heidegger obviously intends his readers to see it as cognate with *Erschlossenheit*, "disclosedness." This is confirmed by the statement in "The Origin of the Work of Art" that "the resoluteness intended in *Being and Time* is not the deliberate action of a subject, but the freeing of Dasein from its captivity by beings into the openness of being."[24] We are close to the way "resolution" is used in optics, and we are meant to think of *Entschlossenheit* in terms of a clearing in a wood (*Lichtung*), of light and of sight.[25] But this is not merely the sight of cognitive perception. That is why, borrowing another word from Kierkegaard, he calls the moment of resolution and truth an *Augenblick*, the "twinkling of an eye," the "moment of vision."

Augenblick is a focal word in Heidegger because it concentrates the notions not only of light and sight but also of temporality. The authentic moment of vision is contrasted with the atomistic now, the *Jetzt*, of the inauthentic time whose fallenness weds Dasein to the present. The present, as was noted above, is the existential meaning of falling (346) and anxiety, like any other state of mind or mood, has its existential meaning in thrownness (*Geworfenheit*) and having been (*Gewesenheit*). But anxiety is distinguished by its power to bring Dasein back to its thrownness as something that it is possible to retrieve. Retrieval or repetition (*Wiederholung*) is not replication but projection, carrying forward. Every mood goes along with an understanding, and every understanding goes along with a mood. The future is the existential meaning of understanding. Anxiety discloses to Dasein its potentiality for the moment of vision, which is a forward-looking retrieval (*zukünftige, vorlaufende-wiederholende Augenblick* (391, 397), a hermeneutic circularity.

3. *What is* Ereignis?[26]

In addition to collecting notions of sight and temporality, the spectrum of the word *Augenblick* is widened by Heidegger's bringing the word together with what he calls *Ereignis*. The moment of vision, he says, is an authentic present (*Gegen-wart*) which enables us to encounter for the first time what can be "in a time" as ready to hand or present at hand. But as against the "now" in which something comes to be, is present, and passes away, " 'in the moment of vision' nothing can occur [*vorkommen*]" (338).

The word *Ereignis* commonly means "occurrence." But when it is introduced in works that Heidegger wrote after *Being and Time*, he warns his readers that although what it points to can be discerned thanks to the kind of saying that shows (*im Zeigen der Sage erblickt*), it cannot be represented (*vorgestellt*) as an occurrence or event. It can only be experienced (*erfahren*) as *das Gewährende*, "a giving." It follows that in spite of its association with the notion of appropriation, *Ereignis* cannot be translated simply as "appropriation," for that puts the accent on the idea of taking. *Ereignis* is at least both give and take.[27] Heidegger also plays on what he sees as an etymological connection between *ereignen* and *er-äugen*, the latter being a verb formed on *Auge*, "eye." Whether or not it has this etymological root, Heidegger clearly intends his use of the word *Ereignis* to convey the idea of disclosure. As just mentioned, he wishes to rely also on the fact that the idea of appropriation and appropriateness is carried by various members of the family of words based on *eigen*, "own," "proper," for example, *eigenst*, "ownmost," *aneignen*, "to appropriate," *geeignet*, "suited," *Eigentum*, "belongings," and its inauthentic counterpart *Eigenschaft*, "property." The fact that the words for "inauthentic" (*uneigentlich*) and "authentic" are themselves members of this family supports our earlier observation that "resoluteness" is to be understood with the help of the idea of disclosure or opening (*Erschlossenheit*), which expresses the meaning of the "there" (the *Da*) of Dasein, the being (the *Sein*) of which is the being that is an issue and at stake for this being in its very being (132–33).

How then is *Ereignis* to be translated? We should no more expect to be able to find a synonym for it, Heidegger says, than for *logos* or *Tao*. He admits that where he uses the word in the "Letter on Humanism" it is employed with a studied ambiguity.[28] Perhaps something of the ambiguous structure of this complex word is expressed by the phrases "mutually appropriative disclosure" or "mutually disclosive appropriation." Both of these phrases are needed, we shall find, since being and truth as *a-letheia*—hence also language—are inseparable in *Ereignis*. (Compare "realization" as used by Sartre. See below, chapter 3, first section.)

There is, it was noted previously, a difficulty in principle with any attempt to fix what *Ereignis* stands for. This difficulty is that *Ereignis* cannot be represented, and there is nothing from which it could be derived or in terms of which it could be explained (*erklärt*).[29] There is a constant danger of assuming it can be understood in terms of "being" as employed in metaphysics. But *Ereignis* is richer than the metaphysical concept of being. It is the latter that has to be thought through the former. Only through *Ereignis* can we reach the nonmetaphysical sense of being that *Being and Time* ultimately intended to bring out.[30] No doubt it was because of the risk of confusing this nonmetaphysical being with its metaphysical antitype that, as Heidegger says in the lecture "The Way to Language" delivered in 1959, he had for the preceding twenty-five years used the word *Ereignis*.[31]

More than thirty-two years before giving that lecture, at the outset of *Being and Time*, he asks why we should infer that what being means is not an open question from the fact that, because being is not a being, it cannot be defined conceptually and verbally by genus and differentiating property. Heidegger's admission that being cannot be given a conceptual or verbal definition does not settle that it cannot be ostensively defined, and his reader might reasonably inquire why he does not consider whether that sort of definition of being is possible. Paradoxically, it is something like an ostensive definition of being that Heidegger goes on to give after *Being and Time*. Not, of course, an ostensive definition such as might be given of a color predicate. That has been ruled out by Heidegger's denial that being is a concept or an entity. Being is not something whose meaning can be grasped in an *Erlebnis*, an "impression" or "idea of sensation or reflection." It can only be glimpsed in the thinking that experiences (*erfährt*). And it can only be said in the Saying, *Sagen* or *Sagan*, which shows (*zeigt*). When one says "it" one is already in danger of sinking into a metaphysical onto-theo-logical representation of being as a being, albeit a very special sort of being perhaps: the ground of all beings. To conceive being in this fashion is to fall back on "telling stories" (6), like the one about the Indian, retailed by Locke, according to which the earth is supported by an elephant supported by a tortoise.[32] If any story can be told about being, it will be more like the one about the Irishman told by James Joyce, which finnishes back where it began. And the manner of its telling will be told by *sagan*, the Old Norse word meaning "to show" from which "saga" is derived. The vehicle for this monstrative telling to which Heidegger resorts in his later thinking is, in a wide sense of the term, poetry, *Dichtung*. His thinking is *dichtendes Denken*, "condensation," *dicht* meaning "compact," "thick" or "dense." The density of Heidegger's later thinking is undeniable. That thinking is at its most concentrated in the gnomic lines of *Aus der Erfahrung des Denkens* and *Gedachtes*.[33] But we have seen that already in *Being and Time* there is frequent appeal to—though not in my view reliance on—etymological overlap, whether fictive or factive, and there are invocations of the *etymon*, the true word at its source. Nearest to that source are the poets and poetic thinkers like Heraclitus and Parmenides.[34]

It is particularly to Parmenides' sayings "chre to legein te noein t'eon emmenai" and "to gar auto noein estin te kai einae" that Heidegger returns again and again in his questioning of being and *Ereignis*. The most insistent reflection (*Wiederholung*, *Erwiderung*) on the first of these fragments is the series of lectures *Was heisst Denken?* (*What is Called Thinking?* or *What Calls for Thinking?*). Parmenides' words are usually translated, "It is necessary to say and think that the being is." Heidegger elicits from them, "Called for is the letting lie before us so also the caring for the twofold: beings in their being [*Seiendes seiend*]." *Eon*, described as the participle of participles, is also interpreted "what is present in its presencing [*Anwesendes anwesend*]." No less provocative is the version given in these lectures, in the essay "Moira," in *Identity and Difference*, and elsewhere of the second of these two fragments, which he had already quoted in *Being and Time* (171) and which is usually translated, "For it is the same thing to think and to be." Interpreted thus, it is in the spirit of the Hegelian dialectic. But when Heidegger returns to the source of Parmenides' saying he draws out, "For caring, taking to heart [*In-die-Acht-nehmen*], and the presencing of what is present are the same (belong together)." Thinking is thankful remembrance (*Andenken*).

In *Identity and Difference* Heidegger uses Parmenides' words and the principle (*Satz*) of identity as a springboard for placing (*erörtern*) *Ereignis* in the context of *belonging* together, as opposed to that of belonging *together*. The principle of identity as understood by Antisthenes, for example, sees identity as a property belonging to the being of beings. In so far as the principle is a logical one to the effect that "*A* is *A*" or "if *p* then *p*," it is correct. But it depends upon the more basic truth that being belongs to identity. That is to say, the presence of beings in the world is earthed in and emerges from the reciprocally appropriative disclosure of being and being there. The German idealists, Kant, Fichte, Schelling, and Hegel, were on the way to perceiving this when they held that judgment involves synthesis. But their thinking, whether categorial or dialectical or both, did not break away sufficiently from representation (*Vorstellung*) and the concept. That is why they and their opponents supposed that the appropriative belonging together of man and being was grounded idealistically in the one or realistically in the other.[35] The truth is that "a belonging to being prevails [*waltet*] within man, a belonging [*Gehören*] which listens [*hört*] to being because it lends its ear to and is appropriated [*über-eignet*] to being."[36] The belonging calls for listening, as was already hinted in what was said in *Being and Time* about wanting to hear the voice of conscience. There what Dasein had to listen to was itself. This still holds. But it becomes more evident now that this involves listening to language. Only through listening to language can there be authentic mutually disclosive belonging together of *Dasein* and *Sein*.[37]

Does this mean that since language and being are said to be what has to be listened to, language and being are one? How could language and being be one if, as Heidegger often says, language is *the house of* being? This is a problem for anyone wishing to argue that Heidegger does mean to say that language and being are one. Three ways of solving that problem might be proposed. First, we could be told to bear in mind that Heidegger himself says that the phrase "house of being" is a rather clumsy one.[38] Second, we could be asked to consider whether a solution might not be arrived at if the "of" of this phrase were read as a genitive of definition. This would mean that being *is* the house and hence that being is language. And perhaps this inference is strengthened by a simile employed in the final paragraph of the "Letter on Humanism": "Thought gathers language in simple monstrative saying [*Sagen*]. Language [*Die Sprache*] is thus the language of being, as the clouds are the clouds of the sky."[39] Third, and more complicatedly, it might be suggested that if (a) we are justified in the earlier inference that what man has to listen to is both language and himself, and (b) we assume that what has to be listened to is not plural, and (c) we take it that according to Heidegger man has to listen to being, then we shall have to conclude that man and being cannot be separated. But this conclusion, the argument might continue, is in line with what we have found Heidegger saying about the authentic mutually disclosive letting belong together, in a word *Ereignis*, of *Dasein* and *Sein*. And if (d) we are entitled to treat "of" in "the house of being" as expressing a genitive of definition, the same conclusion may be derivable from the statement in the "Letter on Humanism" that "language is at once the house of being and the dwelling of mankind [*Menschenwesens*],"[40] a thought familiar from the interpretation of being in terms of dwelling (*bin*) proposed in *Being and Time* and developed in *An Introduction to Metaphysics* and in "Building, Dwelling and Thinking."[41]

These defenses of the view that for Heidegger language and being are one are vulnerable to several objections. The supplementary defense just cited is obviously unacceptable since it attempts to facilitate the conclusion that language and being are one by showing that man and being are one, but in this attempt it begs the issue by using the premise that in the phrase "house of being" the "of" represents a genitive of definition. To grant that premise is to grant immediately that language and being are one. And there are a number of reasons why this should not be granted. First, the hypothesis (b) that what has to be listened to is not plural is challengeable on the grounds that listening to language may be the way of our hearing and belonging to being. Second, the hypothesis (a) that what has to be listened to is both language and man himself is in conflict with Heidegger's metaphor of language as the shepherd of being, for a shepherd does not shepherd himself. Third, Heidegger says of language and *Ereignis* that they are each "the relation of relations."[42] This implies that they are one, and that implies that language and being are not one, since, unless our interpretation has gone awry, *Ereignis* is the name or unname for the metarelational mutually disclosive letting belong together of man and being.

In connection with this last point it should be added that in the lecture "Time and Being" delivered in 1962 Heidegger says that time and being belong together in mutually disclosive appropriation or mutually appropriative disclosure: "Zeit und Sein ereignet im Ereignis,"[43] where the singular verb ending is not a misprint, but an attempt to signal that verb's tie with *es gibt*, "there is," as in the clauses "Sofern es Sein und Zeit nur gibt im Ereignen,"[44] where in any case, according to Heidegger, the *und* of coordination misrepresents the belonging together of being and time.[45] We shall return at the end of the chapter to this tie between *Ereignen* and "there is."

In *Being and Time* being and truth were shown to belong to each other. In the addendum to "The Origin of the Work of Art" the intimacy of this belonging is underlined by the phrase "of truth, that is, of being."[46] In "Time and Being" *Ereignis* is said to be what lies hidden beneath the name *a-letheia*, "truth."[47] In *Being and Time* the discovering or uncovering of the truth of propositions is said to be *Entdeckendsein*. In spite of the lower case initial for *sein* here the translators express a preference for translating the composite word by "Being-uncovering," thereby forging a link between it and the verbal noun *Sein* to which they give an upper case initial throughout their translation (218). They also put "Being-true" for *Wahrsein* although there is no hyphen in the German and at this stage the author is talking about the truth of propositions, not about primordial truth. This is not a trivial mistranslation, since *entdecken* is the verb Heidegger uses for the discovery of beings, entities within the world. Where he is treating of being (or Being) he uses the verb *erschliessen*, "to disclose." Without the primordial truth of what shows itself there can be no truth or falsity of what is said in assertion. The truth of what is said, that is, discovered, is secondary to the truth of Dasein's discovering. But the latter, for example the discovering of scientific truths, is itself rooted in the disclosure of Dasein's world (220–21). On pages 223 and following Heidegger spells out the genesis of the correspondence theory of truth, and his own view of the derivativeness of this theory is supported by his existential analytic as a whole. He denies that his account of truth is merely lexicography. And he warns that even when our thinking is of an elemental word like *aletheia* as used by Heraclitus,[48] we must be alert to the risks of esotericism (220).

Although Heidegger goes back to the world of the ancient Greeks for hints (*Winke, Leitfaden*) that guide his thinking, he also finds clues in our everyday world and the world of modern technology.[49] Indeed, the "step back" is not archaism, he says, but a step "into the *essence* of modern technology which is still to be thought."[50] "To repeat," *Wiederholen*, is "reciprocal rejoinder," *Erwiderung*; what we shall find Gadamer calling the fusing of horizons. And it is *zukünftig*, "anticipatory." "Origin always comes to meet us from the future,"[51] "the present ... springs from the mutual calling to each other of origin and future."[52] This is what Heidegger had been trying to show in the second division of *Being and Time*. It is therefore understandable that he should regard the charge of archaism as a superficial judgment of how he regards the task of the philosopher.[53] But he concedes that this judgment has some truth in so far as he sees the task of philosophy, or at any rate of thinking, as being "to think what the Greeks have thought in a more Greek way than they did themselves";[54] for instance, to elicit the truth about truth that gets hidden in Plato and Aristotle, and to show how the insight of Aristotle's *peri hermeneias* into the sign (*semeion*) as something that shows, was lost when the Stoics conceived it as a signifier.[55] This work is what Heidegger has in mind when he says, "The ultimate business of philosophy is to preserve the *force of the most elemental words* in which Dasein expresses itself, and to keep the common understanding from levelling them off to that unintelligibility which functions in turn as a source of pseudo-problems" (220). These pseudo-problems and dilemmas determine what goes onto the philosopher's agenda, and their dissolution is one of the tests of whether the business has been properly conducted. The business will never be definitely concluded, however, since the common understanding and therefore the philosopher have an ineradicable inclination to misinterpret themselves. Somewhat, but only somewhat, as for John Austin, everyday language is not the end-all but only the begin-all for the dissolution of philosophical dilemmas,[56] so for Heidegger the language of the ancient Greeks—which was everyday language for them—carried within it the seed of its own decline and fall. This is not on account of adventitious pollution simply. But because Dasein is *ontologically* falling. This is a feature of Dasein's finitude. It is limited by the conventions of its social *Mitsein* so that the truth to which it has access is always truth in a given language with a certain forestructure, truth in a particular universe of discourse. Because Dasein is disclosure it is also shut out. Because it is in the truth it is in untruth (222). By this is meant not merely that Dasein makes mistakes and believes false propositions. The falsity and also the truth of a proposition is possible only on the basis of primordial error (*Irre*). Primordial error is coincident with disclosure because man feels at home with what he discovers in his world and becomes accustomed to its face. This familiarization is oriented (*ausgerichtete*) proximation and de-severance (*Entfernung*) (105–10).[57] It is precisely this familiarity with his world that hides from Dasein that it has forgotten what it is to be in a world. Its snugness (*Heimlichkeit*) distracts it from the awesomeness (*Unheimlichkeit*) and mystery (*Geheimnis*) of *Ereignis*.[58]

An exploration of that mystery, we have discovered, will be an exploration of language, of primordial language, not idle talk (*Gerede*), not assertion, not anything that has to be spoken, but what in *Being and Time* is called discourse (*Rede*) and what in his later works Heidegger calls *Sage* and *Sagan*, monstrative saying. Because *Ereignis* and language, as we also discovered, are the meaning (*Sinn*) of being, truth, and time, the exploration of any one of these is the exploration of them all, the exploration of a hermeneutic circle. The way into this circle is what already in *Being and Time* is called experience, *Erfahrung*, which has reverberations of *fahren*, "to go" or "transgress," and which is the word Hegel used when he said his *Phenomenology* presented a "science of the experience of consciousness."[59] This must not be confused with *Erlebnis*, which is the word Dilthey used for the experience of reliving historical events, and which is the word used for our consciousness of phenomena and facts. "Language is a proto-phenomenon whose peculiarity [*Eigenes*] cannot be demonstrated by means of facts and lets itself be glimpsed only in an unprejudiced experience of language [*in einer unvoreingenommenen Spracherfahrung*]."[60] Heidegger is not in this last phrase going back on the claim made in *Being and Time*, and later made so much of by Gadamer, that all understanding is interpretation, which brings with it forehaving, foresight, and foreconception. The prejudices he is alluding to are those of metaphysics and the flat world of people in general, *das Man*. But although we live with one foot in this familiar world, we live with the other foot more venturesomely in the strange (*fremd*)[61] world of the hermeneutic circle. "Man dwells poetically",[62] but "we do not dwell enough where we already are."[63] Dwelling is a poetical thinking that builds the language that shows where the mutually disclosive belonging together of being and man takes place.

The reading of Anaximander, Parmenides, Heraclitus, Hölderlin, Trakl, Rilke, George, and other composers of *Gedichte*, poesy, is one way to an experience of condensed (*gedichtete*) language. But the word *Dichtung* is used in a broad sense by Heidegger to include *any* projective saying (*entwerfende Sagen*)[64] and pure or distilled speaking (*rein Gesprochenes*).[65] In contrast with such authentic poetry, everyday language is a forgotten and used-up poem.[66] But everyday language itself can be projectively retrieved, and one point of departure for a depth analysis of it is, "curiously enough, when we cannot find the right word for something that concerns us, carries us away, oppresses or excites us."[67] As when the hammer fails us.[68] "Then we leave unspoken what we have in mind and, without directing our attention to the matter, achieve moments of insight [*Augenblicke*] in which language itself has fleetingly and from afar touched us with its essential nature."[69]

Since the experience of the nature of language and *Ereignis* is experience of the meaning of being, we can also expect only momentary flashes of the latter, no more than provocative hints which escape capture by concepts. This is something that can be read between the lines of *Being and Time*. The planned third division of the first part of *Being and Time*, to have been called "Time and Being," never appeared as such. In reply to a letter from Jean Beaufret, Heidegger explains that this was because his language was still too metaphysical. But he is aware that the newer words he makes use of run the same risks as their predecessors. The way to language and an experience (*Erfahrung*) of the meaning of being is dangerous (*gefährlich*). That is why Heidegger comes to talk of bringing to light (*phainesthai*) instead of phenomena, then , as we saw at the beginning of this chapter, ceases to use the word phenomenology. He ceases to talk about hermeneutics and the hermeneutic circle, considering such talk superficial.[70] Instead of *Rede* and *Sprache* he begins to use the word *Sage* and is apprehensive that it may get corrupted to signify a concept.[71] Philosophizing through concepts is to give way to phenomenology and phenomenology is to give way to thinking which listens for hints (*Winke*), but even "hinting" runs the risk of becoming a catchword for a cut-and-dried concept.[72] No wonder that the reader who looks back over Heidegger's lifework finds himself with a string of basic words and is sometimes not clear whether a given pair tells one bead or two of the hermeneutic rosary. Perhaps if only we were experienced enough we should reconcile ourselves to saying, as Heidegger sometimes says, *das Ereignis ereignet*, language languages, the world worlds, time times, space spaces, and (notoriously) nothing noths. A rose is a rose is a rose. Or, as Angelus Silesius wrote in words that anticipate those of Gertrude Stein and which Heidegger more than once quotes: "The rose raises no question why. It flowers because it flowers." It is in the nature of Heidegger's question that we should be kept on the hop like this, as is hinted when in saying that *Ereignis* and language are the relation of relations he writes *Ver-hältnis*, "relation" or "ratio," with a hyphen to point up the connection with *verhalten*, "to hold back," and with *halten*, "to hold in trust," "keep" or "shepherd." He gives a very good reason for thinking of *Ereignis* and language in this way. We cannot see language in the round and state the nature of language in language precisely because we are in language and because, at its purest, language is monstrance, showing, *Sage*. The question of the essence of language has to be consigned to the silence in which new paths in language are opened up (*be-wëgt*).[73] Hankering after a conceptual grasp of the essence of language as a whole is an aspect of Dasein's inauthentic yearning for a wholeness that denies his finitude, for a presence to truth that is a truth of language in general without being a truth in a particular language, for a hermetic closing of the hermeneutic circle of his existence. But Dasein is always *on the way* to language, just as Dasein is always *toward* its end, death, and can never experience its death as a fulfillment and its life as a closed book (sections 45ff.).

Referring to the heralded but unpublished division of the first part of *Being and Time*, Heidegger writes to Beaufret that the turn from Being and Time to Time and Being was not a turning away from the standpoint of *Being and Time* and that in the lecture "On the Essence of Truth" delivered three years after the publication of *Being and Time*, "the essayed thinking reaches for the first time the place of the dimension [*die Ortshaft der Dimension*] from which Being and Time is experienced and indeed experienced out of the basic experience of the oblivion of being."[74] According to some of the most recent of Heidegger's publications, the bridges, jugs, boots, and other things that occupy the locus of the dimension (that is to say, the place where Dasein and being meet between heaven and earth) are the playground of the *Ereignis*, the crisscrossing square dance of the fourfold (*Geviert*): earth, sky, gods, and mortals.[75] This is what is indicated by *Sein* when written with a superimposed Saint Andrew's cross, as Heidegger writes it, for instance, in *The Question of Being*. Although this may be a retractation rather than a retraction of what is said in *Being and Time*, it is interesting to note that in "Time and Being" Heidegger mentions one significant respect in which he sees himself to have diverged from the path he followed in *Being and Time*. He says that he no longer holds by the attempt he made in section 70 of that book to derive spatiality from temporality. Assuming he is right to think that he was making such an attempt, his declaration that he has renounced it proves that he now wishes to emphasize the importance of spatiality. The shift of emphasis could, with profit but also with risk, be compared to the shift of emphasis that takes place between Kant's Schematism and his Refutation of Idealism. Whereas, however, Kant does not introduce space into his analysis of the schemata of pure concepts of the understanding, but only into his prefatory reference to the schemata of nontranscendental concepts, Heidegger in *Being and Time* anticipates later pieces like "The Nature of Language," "Building, Dwelling and Thinking," etc., by giving detailed analyses of spatial notions such as place, dimension, and region. What Heidegger says about the region (*Gegend*, from *gegen*, "toward") suggests that it is the protological framework, presupposed by the logical and technological framework he calls *Ge-stell*,[76] in which the mutually appropriative disclosure of Dasein and *Sein*, man and being, takes place.

Ereignis then is a move (*Be-wëgung*) on the chessboard of protological space, an interplay in the *Spielraum* where the word and the world are one flesh. Though when we say *Ereignis* is this we should be as reluctant to suppose we are giving a definition as Plato was reluctant to define the word good. When we say *Ereignis* is this the word "is" should be placed, as Derrida puts it, *sous rature*, "crossed out," "crucified." *Ereignis* lies beyond what obtains in the logical space of facts or states of affairs and lies hidden under the pseudorelation between words and the world which, in the *Tractatus Logico-Philosophicus*, Wittgenstein ventured to whistle.[77] Preoccupied, like the audience at Heidegger's inaugural lecture "What is Metaphysics?", with that which fits the framework of propositional logic, Wittgenstein, although on the way, was further than he thought from what Heidegger was alluding to in speaking, just five months earlier in 1929, of the uncanny experience a man may have of the meaning of those simple complex words "there is," of what it is for there to be something, when he wonders why there is anything at all rather than nothing.[78] With reference to Augustine's remark about the question What is time? Wittgenstein comments: "Something that we know when no one asks us, but no longer know when we are supposed to give an account of it, is something that we need to *remind* ourselves of [*sich* besinnen]."[79] Heidegger would say that when I face the question why there is something and not rather no thing, as also when in anxiety I face toward my death, I am making an anamnetic return to the question of the meaning (*Sinn*) of being which is already understood, if usually overlooked, when I inquire scientifically and metaphysically about beings. This question comes to remembrance, *Besinnung*. For the being, Dasein, who is factically thrown-project, the being for whom the end is in the beginning and the beginning in the end, the being whose being is hermeneuticly circular, phenomenological archaeology and phenomenological eschatology are mutually implicated in being beyond the categorial beingness of metaphysical factuality, beyond "the *concept* of being" investigated by Husserl.[80]

CHAPTER TWO
HUSSERL: ESSENTIALIST PHENOMENOLOGY AND THE CHANCE OF METAPHYSICAL NEUTRALITY

For this is what disputes between Idealists, Solipsists and Realists look like. The one party attack the normal form of expression as if they were attacking a statement; the others defend it, as if they were stating facts recognized by every human being.

—Ludwig Wittgenstein

This chapter proposes a hypothesis as to what may be one of Edmund Husserl's intentions. Only in its final paragraphs does it comment on his chances of carrying this intention out. There, too, a comment is made on the bearing this chapter has on the intentions attributed to Heidegger in the first chapter of part one and the intentions attributed to Gadamer in the first chapter of part two.

I argue that Husserl's method of reduction, if pursued consistently, should enable him to remain on neutral ground with respect to the alternatives of metaphysical realism and metaphysical idealism where these are understood as putative factual statements of what there is. It may be thought that my interpretation of Husserl is inspired more by Wittgenstein than by Husserl, but I hope the parallel I draw is shown to be well enough supported by what Husserl says to make it worth consideration. However, parallel lines do not meet, or meet only at infinity. Thus, although Wittgenstein and Ryle share Husserl's antipathy for psychologism, they would say that Husserl himself is often too psychologistic. Further, although the method of varying perspectives in imagination, which Husserl refers to in *Ideas* and elsewhere, foreshadows the method of substitution within a sentence-frame which Ryle uses to map the bounds of sense, there is already an ancient anticipation of this latter technique in Aristotle, for example in his observation that whereas a state of affairs may come to be coming to be cannot come to be. In addition, although Husserl's pure logical grammar, particularly as expounded in *Formal and Transcendental Logic*, has at least a strong family resemblance to Wittgenstein's linguistic phenomenology, although both writers say they are describing concepts, and although Wittgenstein says, "*Essence* is expressed by grammar," Husserl's intuition of essences cannot be identified with the style of conceptual analysis or logical geography practiced by Wittgenstein and by Ryle, notwithstanding that the latter admired the *Logical Investigations* enough to offer lectures on it and to seek an audience with its author in Freiburg.

1.   *Transcendental eidetic reduction*

In the *Cartesian Meditations* and elsewhere Husserl proposes a method that, although akin to the procedure of hyperbolic doubt practiced by Descartes in the *Discourse on Method* and the *Metaphysical Meditations*, appears to differ from this procedure in not being employed to establish the certainty of metaphysical assertions of existence. The philosopher is to disengage himself from all epistemological attitudes toward the world, including doubt. This disengagement is to be a suspension of judgment about all matters of fact, including the philosopher's own empirical and metaphysical self. Husserl calls this inhibitory exercise transcendental reduction because it permits only the philosopher's transcendental consciousness to be investigated. But the transcendental consciousness is no more than a field of meanings, *Sinne*. It is as though by surveying these meanings we could remind ourselves of what goes without saying and is prior to any saying. One might expect that having disengaged himself from the world of fact the philosopher could regain the world and its inhabitants only by putting the engine back into gear so that the transcendental field of meanings is once more engaged with the physical and social environment. But this is not how Husserl proceeds. It is not as though he first performs the transcendental reduction and then, having conducted the investigations facilitated by the engine's idling state, lets in the clutch and thereby reconstitutes the world. According to Husserl, the world is rediscovered during and within the transcendental reduction.

One reason why Descartes and Husserl call their books meditations is that in them they purport to be soliloquizing. Admittedly, Husserl's First Meditation seems initially to be a joint undertaking. "Let us consider. As radically meditating philosophers, we now have neither a science that we accept nor a world that exists for us" (59).[1] But Husserl immediately concedes that this first person plural mode of address ought strictly to be eschewed at the beginning of transcendental phenomenological reflection. He corrects himself, referring to "what we (or, to speak more precisely, what I, the one who is meditating) acquire" (60). Yet by the time he reaches the Fifth Meditation the plural is allegedly legitimized. How?

This question cannot be answered until some explanation has been given of what Husserl means by the expression "transcendental ego." He uses this as an expression of what may be referred to as the thinker and his thoughts, these being regarded as inseparable. The reader of Descartes' Second Meditation may well be taken aback by the abruptness of Descartes' move from the question of the thinker's existence to the question of the thinker's essence or nature. The reader of Husserl's Second Meditation is given a more explicit warning of this transition. The transcendental phenomenological reduction reveals a concrete ego: not merely "the bare identity of the 'I am'" (67), but the complex *ego cogito-cogitatum* (*qua cogitatum*) (74). This is the first and most basic scheme of consciousness. The field of transcendental subjectivity studied under the phenomenological reduction is noetic-noematic. A study may be made of the structures of the different modes of consciousness, for example perception, memory, imagination, judging, valuing, loving. And a study may be made of the structures of the objects of these mental acts or attitudes. But the noetic and the noematic are correlative. This is the point that is being made when it is said that consciousness is intentional or that consciousness is always consciousness of something. As Husserl himself says, "The word intentionality signifies nothing else than this universal fundamental property of consciousness: to be consciousness *of* something; as a *cogito*, to bear within itself its *cogitatum*" (72). He acknowledges indebtedness to Brentano for stressing the importance of this insight. Brentano himself acknowledges indebtedness to Scholastic philosophy for this doctrine of the referentiality of all consciousness.[2] The doctrine reappears in more than one British admirer of the work of Brentano, for instance in G. E. Moore's papers "The Subject-Matter of Psychology"[3] and "The Refutation of Idealism."[4] Although the doctrine is sometimes called a doctrine of correlativity, the fact that Moore can make use of it in a refutation of idealism suffices to show that the correlativity involved is not such as to beg the question against realism by flatly denying there can be things of which no one is conscious. Both realism and idealism take up positions about what there is. But metaphysical ontology of any sort is extraneous to transcendental phenomenological reduction. This is why when Husserl mentions the *cogitatum* he sometimes adds the phrase *qua cogitatum*. The noema is an *Objekt*, not a *Gegenstand* like a tree or a house. It is never a physical object but always a thing as appearance, setting aside the question whether there is, for example, a house empirically there in space and time. As appearance or phenomenon it is inseparable from the consciousness to which it appears. No more than that is meant by Husserl's remark that the *cogitatum* is something that the *cogito* bears within itself. This, he therefore claims, is not dogmatic metaphysical idealism. It is metaphysically neutral.

Because in opting for phenomenological reduction the phenomenologist is opting for metaphysical neutrality, phenomenology is not metaphysically reductive. It is not a form of metaphysical phenomenalism. It is a study of phenomena in their appearing and evidence. Husserlian phenomenology is not directed at the phenomenal peculiarities of particular things. These are the concern of, among others, the artist and optician. Although the phenomenologist may begin his study by examining how a particular tree, tower, or triangle appears to him, he may equally well begin with an imagined thing. Husserl would have applied to himself Wittgenstein's statement that "we are not doing natural science, nor yet natural history—since we can also invent fictitious natural history for our purposes."[5] Whatever the phenomenologist's starting point, it is merely the theme on which variations are performed by way of a thought experiment aimed at the achievement of a progressively clearer idea of what is necessary for a thing to be an instance of its sort. The search is for invariants and for apodictic and, where possible, adequate evidence.

One outcome of this search is the discovery of the "first descriptive generality" already mentioned, namely, the correlativity of *cogito* and *cogitatum* (77). This is disclosed by the meditating philosopher's reflection on his own particular transcendental ego. But the phenomenologist is not interested in what are only features of his own particular ego. That, too, is to be regarded *qua cogitatum*, as an instance of the eidos ego, any ego whatsoever. I am to ask what remains invariant through the various selves I imagine myself to be. The eidetic insights I thereby

obtain are achieved within the transcendental phenomenological suspension and therefore involve no stance with regard to the existence or
nonexistence of selves other than myself (106).

2. *Abstractive reduction*

If what has just been said is true, it may seem surprising that in the
Fifth Meditation Husserl should invoke what he calls an abstractive
epoche, since on the face of it this duplicates the transcendental eidetic
reduction already ·carried out. The former is introduced as though it
were an egological reduction. But the latter has already been so described (106). Husserl states unambiguously that the former is a new
kind of epoche although it is carried out within the framework of the
latter. The status of this abstractive epoche is in some respects similar to
that of a quotation within a quotation. This comparison should not be
allowed to conceal the fact that, according to Husserl, the abstractive
reduction reaches down to the founding stratum of my experience (127).
What this abstractive reduction leaves aside is not merely existential
judgment about what is other than myself. The very *concepts* of what is
other than myself are dispensed with. Abstraction is made from the
cultural, the scientific, the public: from what Hegel calls objective spirit,
a phrase that Husserl himself uses in the Fifth Meditation (162). Husserl's aim in effecting this abstraction is to demonstrate that although it
divides the transcendental ego's field of experience into what is alien
and what is non-alien, the very consciousness of the former is part of the
latter (131).

As we shall see, it is significant that Husserl's discussion is cast in
terms of concepts. But that long discussion is obviously intended to demonstrate something more than that the concept of the non-other presupposes the concept of the other. If that were all Husserl wished to
show there would be no need for him to undertake, as he does in section
46, a positive analysis of what is meant by "my own," for which the
verbal opposition of "alien" and "non-alien" serves as at most a clue
(140). The difficulty is to decide what more Husserl is saying beyond
"my ideas are mine" when he writes:

> Whatever the transcendental ego constitutes in that *first* stra-
> tum, whatever he constitutes as non-other, as his "peculiarly
> own"—that indeed belongs to him as *a component of his
> concrete essence* (as we shall show); it is inseparable from his

concrete being. Within and by means of this ownness the transcendental ego constitutes, however, the "Objective" word, as a universe of being that is other than himself—and constitutes, at the first level, the other in the mode: alter ego. (131)

The difficulty with this passage stems from the ambiguity of the word "constitution." We are told that it is the transcendental ego that does the constituting. Earlier in the same section and elsewhere we are told that to constitute is to synthesize. And what is constituted is the outcome of my transcendental ego's acts of putting together, everything that is Objective (*Objektiv*) for me as well as my identical ego itself. Constitution is responsible for the idea that the perceiver and the perceived are unities and that they are already given prior to any perception—though perhaps we should say more strictly that they are already given or could be so given, in order to cover cases where a physical object, for instance, comes into existence at the moment it is perceived.

This already-thereness is implied in the idea of the intentionality of consciousness and it is part of what Husserl means by transcendence. There is always more to be discovered about a thing, always further views that can be had of it; its potentialities are never exhausted. But I regard these discoveries as ones that in principle I could make or have evidence of. In so far as through abstractive reduction I regard my experience as my stream of consciousness transcendence is immanent.

Immanent transcendence is primordial, according to Husserl. He now faces the task of explaining how it can function as the basis for what he describes as proper though constitutionally secondary Objective transcendence (136).

3. *Others and Objective transcendence*

Although it is a world that is my world that is left to me after the abstractive reduction, and although Husserl describes it as primordial, he does not mean that it is temporally the first world I experience. That this is not so follows from my having to perform the abstractive reduction in order to reach it. The same has to be said for the intersubjective world I constitute when I go beyond the level of the primordial egological world by admitting the idea of other egos but do not yet go so far as to admit the idea of an Objective nature. According to Husserl, "The intrinsically first other (the first 'non-Ego') is the other Ego" (137).[6] He goes on to say that "the other Ego makes constitutionally possible a new infinite domain of what is 'other': an *Objective Nature* and a whole Objective world, to which all other Egos and I myself belong." Does this mean that whereas other egos of some sort are in some sense necessary conditions for there being an Objective world (or, as some philosophers would prefer to say, that whereas the concept of other egos is necessary for the concept of a world), the conditionality is not reciprocal? The other Egos that make an Objective world possible are said to be pure others. This suggests that Husserl is not ruling out as inconceivable a world in which there were only Egos. But this would still be an Objective world of Egos, even if there were in it no other entities with which to contrast the inhabitants of it. In any case, such a world is not one that could be founded on the primordial stratum of our experience in our world. For that experience is of a psychophysical person at the subjective level and of "psychophysical men as worldly Objects" at the intersubjective level (137).

It is worth repeating that the experiences just referred to are made possible by means of an inhibitive thought experiment. Although they are the bedrock of phenomenology, they are not elements with which the phenomenologist builds up the complex world. Husserl denies that phenomenology is constructive. Notwithstanding this employment of Leibnizian terms like monadology and harmony, he denies that his method is metaphysical, speculative, or deductive. It does not, for example, begin with an axiom like the *ego cogito* and deduce consequences from it. He makes no use of the principle of sufficient reason and condemns the use made of it by Leibniz and Descartes. Husserl's aim is nondeductive clarification (118, 138).

The way Husserl describes the starting point of his analysis in section 48 suggests that his procedure shares at least one feature with the transcendental procedure followed by Kant, for in both cases the point of departure is a fact, in Husserl's case "the fact of experience of something alien (something that is not I)."

Husserl himself says that it is *concepts* that have to be clarified. If, as he also says, the concept of an Objective world is the concept of a public world, that is, a concept dependent on the concept of other selves, then the latter concept is in special need of intentional clarification. This clarification uncovers what he calls appresentation. This is said to be an analogical apperception and to involve a mediate intentionality (138). It might be concluded from this that he is producing an argument from analogy. But this would be to attribute to him what he has criticized in Descartes and other metaphysicians. His analogical apperception is not an inference (141) and hence not an inference to the existence of other egos. The place occupied by the idea of the alter ego is analogous to that occupied by the unseen sides of a physical thing, which are the horizon of my actual perceptions, except that whereas I can in principle put myself in a position to see a previously unseen side, I cannot in principle have someone else's perceivings. Pairing (*Paarung*) of my self with another self is analogous also to the relation between my present perception of a thing and previous perceptions of that thing. The horizon of the past is "co-determinant for an understanding of the present itself" (160), as also is the horizon of the future. The role of retention and protention is described in detail in Husserl's the *Phenomenology of Internal Time Consciousness* of 1905. But the following passage from the *Cartesian Meditations* summarizes Husserl's view of the connection between retention and protention and the analogical apperception of others. It deserves quoting at length not only for the light it throws on what Husserl says, but also because it illuminates what is said by Heidegger, Sartre, Merleau–Ponty, and other philosophers who look back to him.

> Apperception is not inference, not a thinking act. *Every* apperception in which we apprehend at a glance, and noticingly grasp, objects given beforehand—for example, the already-given everyday world—every apperception in which we understand their sense and its horizons forthwith, points back to a "*primal instituting*," in which an object with a similar sense became constituted for the first time. Even the physical things of this world that are unknown to us are, to speak generally, known in respect of their type. We have already seen like things before, though not precisely this thing here. Thus *each everyday experience* involves an *analogizing transfer* of an originally instituted objective sense to a new case, with its anticipative apprehension of the object as having a similar sense. To the extent that there is givenness beforehand, there is such a transfer. At the same time, that sense-component in further experience which proves to be actually new may function in turn as institutive and found a pregivenness that has a richer sense. The child who already sees physical things understands, let us say, for the first time

the instrumental sense [*Zwecksinn*] of scissors; and from now on he sees scissors at the first glance *as* scissors—but naturally not in an explicit reproducing, comparing and inferring. Yet the manner in which apperceptions arise—and consequently in themselves, by their sense and sense-horizon, point back to their genesis—varies greatly. There are different levels of apperception, corresponding to different layers of objective sense. Ultimately we always get back to the *radical differentiation of apperceptions* into those that, according to their genesis, belong purely to the *primordial sphere* and those that present themselves *with the sense "alter ego"* and, *upon* this sense, have built a new one—thanks to a genesis at a higher level. (141)

This passage illustrates what Husserl calls the law or lawfulness (*Gesetzmässigkeit*) of oriented constitution. What does this amount to? It might seem from this passage that the law of oriented constitution implies that a child's world is a world of merely physical things which only later present themselves to him as, for instance, tools. But earlier in the *Cartesian Meditations* Husserl notes that a tool presents itself to us as a mere physical thing only when we *disregard* the spiritual or cultural characteristics (112). He also says that it is the developed ego that sees things as mere substrates whose predicates remain to be discovered (113). Although Husserl uses examples from child psychology here and elsewhere as clues leading to phenomenological discoveries, his talk of history (*Geschichte*) and genesis is intended to make the transcendental logical point that whatever we discover has already waiting for it a logical place or formal concept under which it will be subsumed: "What we call unknown has, nevertheless, a known structural form: the form 'object' and more particularly the form 'spatial thing,' 'cultural object,' 'tool' and so forth" (113). This is a point Heidegger might have brought out by writing the German word for history as *Ge-schichte* to signal a relationship with *Schichten*, "strata" (an artifice that is rather more effective than would be that of writing "hi-story" or "hi-storey").

It would, however, be wrong to suppose that in his remarks about history Husserl is making a logical point as opposed to a temporal one. What he understands by transcendental logic embraces primordial, pre-chronological, temporality.[7] And genesis is synthesis, a temporal process. Although many of the analyses carried out in the *Cartesian Meditations* are cast in terms of a static use of the distinction between form and

matter predominant in his *Logical Investigations*, analysis cannot proceed far before a dynamic version of the hylomorphic model has to be
employed. By means of this model, for example, passive synthesis furnishes the "material" to be worked up by the active synthesis involved
in learning to see the world as a manifestation of Objective Spirit.

Genetic phenomenology is a kind of archaeology of experience. It
probes back from a given stratum to the strata underlying it. Its investigations are of four main kinds. First there are studies of subjective
processes, the primordial temporal life of the abstractively reduced
world. Specimens of such subjective genetic investigation are most
abundant in the *Phenomenology of Internal Time Consciousness*, *Experience and Judgment*, and the papers on active and passive synthesis
published in Husserliana 11. Second, what may be called intersubjective
genetic investigations are conducted in, for example, the *Cartesian
Meditations*, *Ideas* 2 and the papers published in Husserliana 13–15.
Third, in *Ideas* 2 and 3 and to some extent the discussions on space and
time in Husserliana 16, a genetic phenomenology of material nature is
undertaken. Fourth, the *Cartesian Meditations* adumbrates a program of
cultural genetic investigations and this program is pursued further in the
Crisis. Intersubjective genetic phenomenology refers back to the primordial in the sense of absolutely first stratum of subjectivity, but it and
the phenomenology of the natural and the cultural worlds also investigate what is relatively primordial or prior. In the *Cartesian Meditations*
both of these notions of primordiality occur. The higher strata are
founded on the prior strata and ultimately on the primordial living present (161), a topic to which we shall return before this chapter concludes.

4.   *Phenomenology and metaphysics*

Husserl considers that by the time he has reached the end of the
Cartesian Meditations he has established that "positive science is a science lost in the world. I must lose the world by epoche, in order to regain it by a universal self-examination" (183). The world cannot be
regained, he argues, unless I am not condemned to solitary confinement
within it, unless solipsism is untenable. He attempts to show that solipsism is untenable by showing that any tenable philosophy must be a
phenomenological transcendental idealism. A traditional way of refut-
ing solipsism has been to argue for metaphysical realism. For Husserl,
as for Berkeley, metaphysical realism is a nonsense (*Unsinn*).

> The attempt to conceive the universe of true being as some-
> thing lying outside the universe of possible consciousness,
> possible knowledge, possible evidence, the two being related
> to one another merely externally by a rigid law, is nonsensi-
> cal. They belong together essentially; and, as belonging
> together essentially, they are also concretely one, one in the
> only absolute concretion: transcendental subjectivity. (117)

But it is not Husserl's intention to replace metaphysical realism by
metaphysical subjective idealism. Both of these standpoints are metaphysical theories that culminate in an existential assertion or counter-
assertion. They are nonsensical in the sense that they go beyond what is
disclosed solely by an explication of sense (*Seinsinn*), by an analysis of
the world that is left to me after the enactment of the eidetic and abstractive reductions. I find that the quality of life I experience after the
enactment of these reductions presupposes the concept of what is not
mine. In the third section of this chapter a comparison was made with
Kant's procedure on the grounds that in one place Husserl describes his
own method as the explication of the presuppositions of a fact. The fact
he alludes to is the fact of experience of something that is not I. This fact
plays a role to some extent comparable with the part played by the fact
of objective Newtonian science as the point of departure for Kant's
transcendental deduction of the categories of the understanding. But
Kant also takes a different point of departure, the fact that our experience is temporally successive. And there is a parallel for this too in
Husserl's really primordial starting point, the stream of consciousness of
the abstractively reduced de-alienated ego. In Husserl's eyes Kant spoils
everything by not acknowledging the absurdity of the thing-in-itself.
That apart, there is a considerable degree of similarity between their
philosophical procedures. Especially striking is the importance they
both give to a proper understanding of what Husserl calls *Seinsinn*, "the
notion of existence or being." But even Kant's view of the thing-in-itself
as a mere limiting concept is in Husserl's view nonsensical (118).
"Transcendence in every form is an immanent existential characteristic
constituted within the ego" (117); "everything existing for me must derive its existential sense [*Seinsinn*] exclusively from me myself" (176).
As we noted above, one must resist the temptation to think that Husserl
means no more by these statements than that no one else can do my
believing. They make allusion to the law of oriented constitution which
lays down a theory of types of existence according to which the superior

stories of the hierarchic structure are founded in the living present of the
ego's intentionally motivated stream of consciousness.

And here another temptation must be resisted. Husserl is not producing an ontological argument from concepts leading to the conclusion,
"Therefore others exist." He repeats over and over that the making of
existential claims is not possible within the phenomenological suspension. This may incline one to conclude that he is not speaking as a phenomenologist when in *Ideas* 3 he says it is completely beyond doubt that
the world exists.[8] But this statement and his characterization of solipsism as an illusion would perhaps be consistently phenomenological if
they were regarded as categorial, or synthetic a priori. That they cannot
be both phenomenological and lexicographical remarks is clear from
Husserl's insistence, in line with views he held as early as the *Logical
Investigations*, that transcendental phenomenology is eidetic. For

> the eidos itself is a beheld or beholdable universal, one that is
> pure, "unconditioned"—that is to say: according to its own
> intuitional sense, a universal not conditioned by any fact. It is
> *prior to all "concepts,"* in the sense of verbal significations;
> indeed, as pure concepts, these must be made to fit the eidos.
> (105)

It is this resort to eidetic intuition that stands in the way of aligning
phenomenological analysis with conceptual analysis regarded as the explication of the meanings of words. But I see no reason why it should
not be described as conceptual analysis regarded as a discipline that
issues categorial reminders and aims to show what cannot be said. If the
Husserlian practices sketched in this chapter make him a phenomenologist, that title can be awarded with equal justification to the author of
the *Tractatus Logico-Philosophicus*, the *Philosophical Remarks*, and the
Philosophical Investigations. Both Husserl and Wittgenstein are investigating "the 'possibilities' of phenomena."[9] And as Wittgenstein holds
that his philosophical investigation "leaves everything as it is,"[10] so Husserl holds that his "does nothing but *explicate the sense this world has for
us all, prior to any philosophizing* and obviously gets solely from our
experience—*a sense which philosophy can uncover but never alter* ..."
(177). One of the chief discoveries of the investigation which culminates
in the Fifth Meditation is, "The existence-sense [*Seinsinn*] of the world
and of Nature in particular, as Objective Nature, includes after all ...
'thereness-for-everyone'" (124). It would, however, be a misconstruc-

tion of the strategy of the Fifth Meditation to suppose that Husserl uses this discovery there to derive a refutation of solipsism. Husserl's aim there is not to refute solipsism nor indeed to generate an argument in support of its opposite. It is to establish that although transcendental phenomenology is transcendental idealism, it is not committed to solipsism. The "illusion" Husserl claims to have dissolved (176) is not that of solipsism. He is not saying that solipsism is an illusion. He is saying that it is an illusion that transcendental phenomenological idealism implies solipsism.

Yet it cannot be denied that there are places where it looks very much as though Husserl suspends suspension and adopts standpoints of the metaphysical sort he finds in Descartes and Leibniz. Many commentators cite passages where Husserl appears to be advocating metaphysical idealism. These are especially common in *Ideas*. The first volume of *Ideas* was published sixteen years before the *Cartesian Meditations*, but it remains relevant for the interpretation of the later work. J. N. Findlay also cites section 99 of the *Formal and Transcendental Logic* in support of the opinion that Husserl lapses into metaphysical idealism, and this book was published in 1929, the year in which the *Cartesian Meditations* appeared. The words from the *Formal and Transcendental Logic* to which Findlay refers represent what Husserl says immediately after the statement quoted above from *Ideen* 3 which, taken out of context, reads less like an affirmation of metaphysical idealism than an affirmation of metaphysical realism. But having said that the existence of the world is completely beyond doubt, Husserl goes on to say that its nonexistence is conceivable. It is conceivable, he writes, because we can think we are mistaken in presuming our future experience will tally with our past experience. Note that he does not say this is something we could think then when this radical disharmony occurred. And since Husserl thinks we can think this *now*, he would accept the statement Findlay makes, along the lines of Kant's Refutation of Idealism, that one "can make no sense of a conscious Life without permanent and independent objects in space with which consciousness can be busied."[11]

Although in the section mentioned in *Ideen* 3 and in the section of the *Formal and Transcendental Logic* to which Findlay refers Husserl says it is a presumption on our part that future experience will largely confirm our past experience, he also says this is a presumption we are right to make. We are justified in that "I could never summon up a doubt, where every new experience confirms existence."[12] Husserl's assertion that doubt is nevertheless thinkable is his way of saying that it is contingent whether or not a thing exists.[13] But from the contingency of the existence of a particular thing Husserl infers the contingency of the existence of everything, of the world.[14] Whether or not this inferred proposition is true, the inference is invalid. Yet Husserl's acceptance of the proposition that the nonexistence of the world is conceivable does not make him a metaphysical idealist. Acceptance of that proposition is indeed compatible with metaphysical idealism understood as the denial of things-in-themselves, but it is not obviously incompatible with metaphysical realism understood as the theory that there are things-in-themselves. What might seem to support the view shared by Findlay, Fink, Ingarden, and others that Husserl lapses into metaphysical idealism is his statement that we presume the existence of the world, in the sense that we take for granted what could be false. This alleged presumption is what in section 30 of *Ideas* 1 Husserl calls the general thesis of the natural standpoint, the implicit faith that

> "the" world is as actuality [*Wirklichkeit*] always there; it is at the most occasionally "other" than I supposed, this or that having as it were to be erased from it under some such description as "illusion" or "hallucination." But the world itself—in the sense of the general thesis—always continues in existence.

In the next section he emphasizes that while the natural standpoint is parenthesized by phenomenological reduction and the general thesis is not made use of, it is not abandoned and it is not transformed into a presumption (or suggestion, indecision or doubt). This concedes the invalidity of the inference from the conceivability of being mistaken about the existence of particular things in the world to the conceivability of being mistaken about the existence of the world. It also bars the phenomenologist from saying that the only things there are, are ideas. But it does not bar him from saying that a thing, by virture of the concept or *Seinsinn* of a thing, is infinitely explorable. That a thing is in this sense essentially an Ideal *telos* is something that Husserl, like Kant, does maintain.

Although this Ideal-ism does not lead to metaphysical subjective idealism, Husserl reaches this Ideal-ism from transcendental phenomenological idealism. Transcendental phenomenolgical idealism is a study of meanings—*Sinne*, in what Husserl himself describes as an extended sense of the term.[15] Meaning certainly presupposes mind, as reference does. No mind, no noesis; so no noema. It does not follow that an unthought-of thing is inconceivable. And I can think that there would have been things even if there had never been anyone to think anything. This observation is not tantamount to a statement that there are things in themselves. It is a claim that there could be things in themselves, things, in Thomas Hardy's phrase, "before the birth of consciousness." And that claim is grounded in a purely phenomenological analysis of the meaning of being, of what it is for a physical thing, like a rock, to be. It is quite consistent with Husserl's contention that the notion of a thing involves the notion of possible agreement among the judgments made by conscious beings. The truth of my thought now that there were things before there was thinking does not require, *per impossibile*, that there were thinking beings then.

Less dust might have been stirred up if, instead of calling himself a transcendental phenomenological idealist, and allowing for the fact that for Husserl concepts are eidetic essences, he had described himself as a conceptual analyst. This would have mirrored more faithfully the fact that his findings are neutral with respect to metaphysical idealism and metaphysical realism understood respectively as the doctrine that there are and the doctrine that there are not things-in-themselves. But Husserl warns in *Ideas* that the concepts he analyzes are not to be regarded as constructs, and constitution is not to be confused with construction.[16] The Husserlian concept is an Object. Are there then, in his view, Objects-in-themselves? What Husserl calls an Object, *Objekt*, in contrast to a thing, *Gegenstand*, is noematic, an intentional entity correlative with noesis. So the phrase "Object-in-itself" borders on absurdity. An Object is an Essence or Idea, and the phenomenological analysis of it is the description not of something invented by the imagination, but of something discovered by imaginative variation. For these reasons, therefore, we may fairly say that Husserl is an Objective or conceptual realist, so long as in saying this we do not imply a commitment one way or the other as to whether ideas and the mental are all there is or all that can be known.

Throughout this chapter I have been attempting to make clear what I take to be one Husserl's aims. I have not been arguing that he succeeds in achieving it. In the space available here I have thought it sufficient to bring out those aspects of Husserl's program that anticipate the program of the later philosophy of Wittgenstein. Both philosophers, it seems to me, are hoping to show that philosophy can be metaphysically neutral. I have argued in particular that Husserl's descriptions of how consciousness constitutes the way a thing is, its *Seinsinn*, must not be confused with the notion that the thing itself is created by consciousness. This suggests that it might also be relevant to see Husserl's program as an anticipation of Michael Dummett's explorations of the neutral ground between discovery and invention and between realism and antirealism. More relevant in the context of the present study, however, is comparison of the program I have attributed to Husserl with Heidegger's statement:

> The fact that Reality is ontologically grounded in the Being of Dasein does not signify that only when Dasein exists and as long as Dasein exists can the Real be as that which in itself it is.
>
> Of course only as long as Dasein *is* (that is, only as long as an understanding of Being is ontically possible), "is there" ["*gibt es*"] Being. When Dasein does not exist, "independence" "is" not either, nor "is" the "in-itself." In such a case this sort of thing can be neither understood nor not understood. In such a case even entities within-the-world can neither be discovered nor lie hidden. *In such a case* it cannot be said that entities are, nor can it be said that they are not. But *now*, as long as there is an understanding of Being and therefore an understanding of presence-at-hand, it can indeed be said that *in this case* entities will continue to be.
>
> As we have noted, Being (not entities) is dependent upon the understanding of Being; that is to say, Reality (not the Real) is dependent upon care.[17]

The distinction Heidegger is making here is the distinction that has been stressed throughout the interpretation this chapter has conducted into what Husserl calls *Seinsinn*. But although on that interpretation the controversy between metaphysical realists and metaphysical idealists as to what there is does not arise, it must now be granted that that controversy is not all there is to metaphysics. It must be granted that although Husserl sets aside from phenomenology all statements of fact about *Gegenstände*, the noematic senses that phenomenology does describe are Objects, albeit non-real, which bring with them much of the metaphysical luggage carried by the epistemology of the way of ideas as manifested in Plato, Aristotle, Descartes, Locke, and, Heidegger would say, even Hegel. Husserl, Heidegger would say, has not given Being its due. Since Husserl does not get beyond the notion of an accusative present to a subject, he does not get beyond metaphysics. Perhaps he would have had more success if he had anticipated the thoughts of the later Wittgenstein even more than I have claimed he did; if he had pressed his reflections on the lived world further in the direction of the de-objectification of concepts which Wittgenstein achieves in his descriptions of forms of life and which Heidegger approaches in his descriptions of being-in-the-world. The moves that Gadamer and Merleau–Ponty make in this direction are outlined in part two of this book. The outline of the teaching of Levinas given in part three reverts to Husserl's teaching regarding Others, which has been a topic of the present chapter and will continue to be relevant in the next.

CHAPTER THREE
SARTRE: EXISTENTIALIST
PHENOMENOLOGY AND
METAPHYSICAL COMMITMENT

Ere time and place were, time and place were not,
When Primitive Nothing *something strait begot ...*
                        —John Wilmot, Earl of Rochester

In this chapter and the next it is argued that there is a vicious circularity in the doctrines of Jean–Paul Sartre which prevents his reaching a
consistent account of the hermeneutic circularity to be treated in more
detail in later chapters of this book. The point could be put by saying
that Sartre both needs and rejects the possibility of co-respondence
among contemporaries that is provided for in a theory like that which
Husserl adumbrates in the *Cartesian Meditations*. As I indicated at the
end of chapter 2, however, we shall find theories of this sort challenged
once again in works to be expounded in part three. There, too, we shall
come back to the question What is metaphysics? Meanwhile, I suggest
that in spite of his declared intention to present a phenomenological
ontology, an intention he shares with Husserl and Heidegger, Sartre
forgets what the latter calls the ontological difference and resorts to a
theologically panoramic metaphysics grounding a theory of knowledge
vitiated by the circularity I shall now begin to describe.

1. *The circle of correlativity*

In the introduction to *Being and Nothingness* Sartre says that there is
a kind of being that is, is in-itself, and is what it is. He warns that these
statements are preliminary and gives notice that they will be elucidated
later in the book (xlii [34]).[1] There elucidations occur chiefly in the

chapters "Transcendence" and "Freedom." In a section of the former chapter headed "Determination as negation" Sartre notes, "The For-itself *is not* the world, spatiality, permanence, matter, in short the in-itself in general, but its manner of not-being-them is to have to not-be this table, this glass, this room on the total ground of negativity" (183 [232]). That is, from the two or three bleak Parmenidean predicates or unpredicates of the introduction Sartre proceeds in the immediately subsequent chapters to a discussion of what for Kant are forms of sensibility (space and time) or formal categorial concepts of the understanding (e.g., substance), to a discussion of individuality and the empirical properties of individual things. These discussions are logically interdependent, because the world is the totality of things and is related to them as everything is related to this thing and as the ground is to the figure. (We shall find Sartre arguing later that this totality is ultimately neither a totality of discrete things nor a totality of assertable facts but what Heidegger calls a totality of assignments.) Of course, the concepts of whole or ground and part or figure are internally related because reciprocally defined, but the relation between this thing and the whole is an external relation, according to Sartre.

To take another example, "Space is neither the ground nor the figure, but the ideality of the ground inasmuch as it can always disintegrate into figures; it is neither the continuous nor the discontinuous, but the passage from continuous to discontinuous" (184 [233]). In other words, spatial relationship presupposes the possibility of shift, shift from one figure-ground array to another. But shift presupposes temporality. Therefore the relations of external negation in which world and space consist presuppose the internal negation which stems from the for-itself's not being what it is and its being what it is not.

But, it must be asked, how can there be this internal negation without there already being the external negation; and how can there be the external negation without there already being the internal negation? There appears to be a dysfunction at the very heart of *Being and Nothingness*. According to this book, "There is *nothing* outside the in-itself except a reflection [*reflet*] of that nothing which is itself polarized and defined by the in-itself inasmuch as it is precisely the nothingness of *this* in-itself, the individualized nothing which is nothing only because it *is not* the in-itself" (176–77 [225]). The problem is to understand how on Sartre's analysis the nothing of the for-itself can be individualized if it is individualized in terms of the individual in-itself and how the in-itself can be individualized if it is individualized in terms of the for-itself. This looks like a circle. It is clearly not a virtuous hermeneutical one. It remains to be seen whether it is a virtuous dialectical one.

Sartre writes that "the term-of-origin of the internal negation is the in-itself, the thing which *is there*" (176 [225]). Being there is being real. But the real is realization, and realization in both the ontological sense of giving reality to something and in the gnosiological sense of apprehending the reality of something (179–80 [228]).

It must not be overlooked that although Sartre uses this duple notion of realization to explicate knowledge, already in the introduction to *Being and Nothingness* it is emphasized that the antinomies of rationalism will be avoided only if knowledge (*connaissance*) is not confused with consciousness (*conscience*). It might therefore be concluded that the apparent vicious circularity in Sartre's account would affect at most what he says about knowledge. But there are grounds for thinking the difficulty goes deeper than that. For realization is the key to an understanding of "the internal relation between knowing and being" (179 [228]) and knowledge is a mode of being (*un mode d'être*) (174 [222]). One of Sartre's principal aims is to establish that the epistemological relation is an ontological one, that "by a radical reversal of the idealist position, knowledge is reabsorbed in being" (216 [268]).

> Knowing is neither a relation established after the event between two beings, nor is it an activity of one of these two beings, nor is it a quality or a property or a virtue. It is the very being of the for-itself in so far as this is presence to ... ; that is, in so far as the for-itself has to be its being by making itself not to be a certain being to which it is present. (174 [222–23])

From this it is evident that the circle in Sartre's analysis has its source not in what distinguishes knowing from other modes of consciousness, but in what makes it a mode of consciousness. The weakness, if we are justified in suspecting one, is in Sartre's interpretation of the principle of intentionality, the principle that all consciousness is consciousness of something. It is in the heart of his book, not merely in one of its lungs. It spreads throughout the entire system. It is not cured by injecting the word "correlativity" into it, since the problem is precisely that of seeing how there can be correlativity. Nor does a vicious circularity become virtuous simply through being christened with the name of Paradox. It has to be shown that the viciousness is only apparent.

The chapter of *Being and Nothingness* entitled "Temporality" corresponds roughly to the Transcendental Aesthetic of the *Critique of Pure Reason*. The chapter entitled "Transcendence" corresponds roughly to Kant's Transcendental Analytic with the section of the former called "The time of the world" performing at least one of the roles fulfilled by Kant's section on Schematism. That there should be this structural similarity between the two books is not surprising. Although Sartre follows Kant in rejecting so-called Berkeleyan idealism, he also takes pains to reject what he regards as the relativism of Kantian idealism (217–28 [270]). One of Sartre's complaints against Husserl is that he is too Kantian in admitting laws and therefore opacity into consciousness. Yet one facet of the problem we have found in Sartre is that he himself may have to forfeit his principle that consciousness is translucid and can be limited only by itself (xxxi [22]). What is more, although this problem is first encountered in the chapter on Transcendence, it crops up again later in what might be called Sartre's Transcendental Dialectic of Freedom.

In Kant's Transcendental Analytic and in Sartre's chapter on Transcendence analyses of the conditions of scientific knowledge are developed. However, both analyses are intended to hold not only for scientific knowledge of generalities but also for everyday knowledge of particularities. To pass to comparison with a philosopher nowhere mentioned in *Being and Nothingness*—probably because the realism he stands for in Sartre's eyes is more sharply represented by Descartes—it will be recalled that Locke's examples of primary qualities are in some of his lists what might be described as, in a broad sense of the term, categorial or generic, for example, shape, solidity, extension, mobility, as opposed to this shape (e.g., rectangular), etc.[2] But for the primary qualities to explain the particularity of our ideas of secondary qualities, for instance the yellowness of this lemon peel, the primary qualities must also be particular; so Locke's lists sometimes include the particular shape, bulk, motion, etc.[3] The particular quality of a thing, of a *this* (*ceci*), is referred to by Sartre as "a new *this* on the ground of the thing." "It is the absolute determination of negativity, for it is not enough that the for-itself by an original negation should not *be* being nor that it should not be *this* being; in order for its determination as the nothingness of being to be complete, the for-itself must realize itself as a certain unique manner of not being *this* being" (188 [237]). It may be that in applying to this determination the adjective "complete" (*plénière*) Sartre has in mind the common phrase *liberté plénière*, "complete or absolute freedom," since he goes on to say at once that "this absolute determination, which is the determination of quality as a profile of the 'this,' belongs to the freedom of the For-itself." The natural scientist may occupy himself only with the disconnected thing and the technologist or social scientist only with means to ends. But things and externalized relations of means to ends are originally connected together in a hierarchy of instrumentalities, which is the objective in-itself correlate of an ordered series of possibilities constituted by the for-itself's free choice of a fundamental project. Sartre forestalls the objection made against Heidegger that he mistakes anthropological priority for logical priority.[4] He is careful to stress that "the thing is not first a thing in order to be subsequently an instrument; neither is it first an instrument in order to be revealed subsequently as a thing. It is an instrumental-thing" (200 [250]).

This gerundival characterization of the world is developed in Sartre's descriptions of the "situation." The descriptions given toward the end of his book in the chapter called "Being and Doing: Freedom" are amplifications of the doctrine of correlativity introduced in the chapter on Transcendence. They therefore pose once more the circularity puzzle that was stated in the third paragraph of the present section and that will be spelled out below. Sartre now gives a name to this puzzle. He calls it the paradox of freedom. Before going on to an investigation of this paradox, mention should be made of an argument that might be advanced against the contention that Sartre's correlativity involves a vicious circle. It might be proposed that the circle in Sartre's correlativity is of the same form as the perfectly virtuous circle linking parenthood with being an offspring. The trouble with this defense of Sartre is that it turns on a purely conceptual relationship. Sartre's correlativity is not a relationship of that sort.

2. *The paradox of freedom*

The paradox of freedom, according to Sartre, is that "there is freedom only in a *situation*, and there is a situation only through freedom. Human-reality everywhere encounters resistance and obstacles which it has not created, but these resistances and obstacles have meaning only in and through the free choice which human-reality *is*" (489 [569]).

The mention here of obstacles and resistances which human-reality has not created must be taken as a reference to independent things—an in-itself—whose resistance and interference are nevertheless in some manner dependent on human-reality. Otherwise it will be inconsistent with the statements "Our freedom itself creates the obstacles from which we suffer" (495 [576]), "There is no obstacle in an absolute sense, but the obstacle reveals its coefficient of adversity across freely invented and freely acquired techniques," and "The rock will not be an obstacle if I wish at any cost to arrive at the top of the mountain" (488 [569]). This last statement is judged by Professor Antony Flew to be not only reckless but false.[5] It is certainly provocative. But it is not without truth if the supposition is, for example, that the person concerned is out to break the record for the number of mountains of three thousand feet or more climbed in one day. In the context of that project, this mountain, if it is at least three thousand feet high, helps rather than hinders. Instead of having a coefficient of adversity it has a coeffecient of instrumentality or utility.[6] What Sartre, adapting the phrase from Bachelard, calls the coefficient of adversity is a function of four variables. Two of these, the ones that Flew considers, are the person's own freedom and, in the climbing example, the mountain. A third is the freedom of others. Sartre does not examine this factor until later, but he warns at the beginning of his detailed discussion of the structure of the situation that in any situation the variables he distinguishes are all operative and interconnected (489 [570]). The mountain, to which he ascribes brute being and which he describes as a brute existent, is only one of the kinds of data in the situation in question, a datum that my freedom *is not*. There is also a datum of another sort, a datum that my freedom *has to be* and that Sartre entitles the facticity of my freedom (ibid.), a term he also applies to my not being free not to be free (486 [566], 529 [612]). This second datum is a person's body and past.

Care should be taken to be clear about what Sartre is not saying here. Evidently, in the climbing situation my body will yield a different coefficient of adversity-instrumentality if I have been in the habit of indulging in strenuous sporting activities from what it will yield if my only physical exertion is to walk a few yards each day between the office and the car. The present state of my body is attributable in part to my past choices, hence it will be empirically difficult to apportion the degrees of responsibility among my choices and the other factors in the situation. This point about the causal consequences of exercising a choice is not the one that Sartre is making here. His point is that it is only if I choose to indulge in taxing physical pursuits that my body is weak or strong, the "is" being the "is" of appearances, the phenomenological "is to ..." or "is for ...". For the sedentary clerk his body is neither weak nor strong and rocks are neither difficult nor easy to climb.

Sartre goes as far as to say that "the *situation*, the common product of the contingency of the in-itself and of freedom, is an ambiguous phenomenon in which it is impossible for the for-itself to distinguish the contribution of freedom from that of the brute existent" (488 [568]). Flew's comment on this is that it is contradicted by Sartre's admission that "whether the rock 'to be scaled' will or will not lend itself to scaling ... is part of the brute being of the rock." The coefficient of adversity of Sartre's text is such that it would be rash to deny with any confidence that he is contradicting himself. Three ways of trying to defend him against this charge suggest themselves.

First, it may be suggested that Sartre is only repeating something he has already said, namely that I can never decipher the worldly image correlative with my possibilities since to do that I should have to be an object for myself and this reflective attitude would interfere with the lived situation I am attempting to analyze (200 [251]). This alone would not exclude someone else's doing the analysis. Hence it would not exclude a philosopher's saying of me in the situation in question that the rock's not lending itself to scaling is due to the brute being of the rock rather than to my free choice of a project. However, this way of saving Sartre from inconsistency where Flew sees it appears inconsistent with Sartre's doctrine that one cannot analyze a situation from outside (548 [633]).[7]

A second rescue attempt depends on how one reads Sartre's remark that it is impossible to decree a priori what derives from the brute existent and what from freedom (488 [569]). This could be taken to imply that the respective contributions could be assigned, whether by me or by someone else or by both of us, but only for each individual situation. On this reading the attempt fails. Sartre is not wanting to say that it is impossible to decree a priori, but that it is a priori impossible to decree. He states explicitly that "it is impossible to determine *in each particular case* what comes from freedom and what comes from the brute being of the in-itself."[8] And he adds that I can never know if the world is giving me information about it or about myself. This is conveyed by Heideggerian hyphenation in phrases like "being-in-the-world" and it is what Sartre is driving at when he says that the situation is an ambiguous phenomenon. "The situation is a relation of being," he writes. "The situation is the whole subject (he is *nothing but* his situation) and it is also the whole 'thing' (*there is* never anything more than things)."

The strongest defense against Flew's objection may be to note that it is open to Sartre to point out that whether the rock will lend itself to scaling can be part of the brute being of the rock *and* dependent on my freedom; this is a matter of formal logic, even if the nonformal logic of Sartre's exposition invites Flew's charge.

Flew alleges inconsistency also on the score that Sartre speaks of there being a situation in which a person finds himself and yet says that a person "is the one by whom it happens that there is a world" (553–54 [639]). The force of this objection is weakened by the fact that in our nontechnical talk of situations we allow ourselves to say such things as that someone found himself in an awkward situation but it was one entirely of his own making.

How brute is a brute existent according to Sartre? Some of his words give the impression that the brute existent is like the kernel of a walnut which is hidden in a shell of resistance which is covered by a skin of meaning. This analogy is prompted by the previously quoted formula for the paradox of freedom, which holds that "human-reality every-where encounters resistances and obstacles which it has not created, but these resistances and obstacles have meaning only in and through the free choice which human-reality *is*.' Other words, like the phrase *sens de contrainte* (551 [536]), imply that the resistance or adversity or in-strumentality are identical with the thing's meaning, or part of it.[9] This interpretation is supported by the statement "Freedom gives itself things as adverse (ie., it confers on them a meaning ...)" where Sartre adds that it is this meaning "which makes them things" (508 [590]). It is freedom's internal negating that, to put the same point in different ways, discovers the facticity without which freedom would not be possible (496 [576]), "constitutes in the in-itself its character as a *thing*" (506 [588]) and, while adding *nothing* to things, brings it about that there are things (509 [591]) and that there is a totality of things in a world.

Referring to this idea that the for-itself is "the one by whom it hap-pens that there is a world," Flew fails to see how it can be reconciled with Sartre's granting that the project of the for-itself which brings it about that there is a world can, in Flew's words, "embrace intransigent objective facts." Flew's difficulty derives in part from his giving the term objectivity a sense that allows there may be objectivity outside a situa-tion. He has not broken loose from the Lockean picture of reality which Sartre condemned and replaced by objectivity as early as the introduc-tion to *Being and Nothingness* (xxiii [13]), a notion Sartre has since ex-plicated in terms of the duple concept of realization. Flew is overlooking what is involved in Sartre's use of the phrase "there is," *il y a*. It is only within a situation, within the ambit of a project, within a hermeneutic circle, that there is a place for objectivity. "Consequently the situation can be called neither objective nor subjective although the partial structures of this situation (the cup which I use, the table on which I lean, etc.) can and must be strictly objective" (548 [633]). An object, *objectum*, is something on or in my way. Where there is no way, no hodological space, there is no object. The objective is correlative with the projective. Something falling within a teleological totality has to be referred to in an answer to the question What is there?, *Qu'est-ce qu'il y a?*, *Was gibt's?*, What gives? Only within a situation are there data. The independence of things, their substantiality and *Selbstständigkeit*, is dependent on the free choice of a project. That is at least part of what Sartre has to say about brute existents.

However, one suspects that there is more to his account of brute being than that. For he emphasizes that the resistance of the given is not an immediately experienced in-itself quality of the given, but is rather an "indication" of an inapprehensible (*insaisissable*), unnameable, and unthinkable residual *quid* (482 [562], 488 [569]). Is this the readmission of the Lockean something-I-know-not-what or Kantian *Ding-an-sich* in a "world behind the scenes" that was denounced in Sartre's introduction?

3. *The stillborn dialectic*

Sartre faces a dilemma. On the one hand, if the in-itself is originally such that all we can say about it is that it is, is itself, and is what it is, differentiation within the world and situations must originate in difference of character in the for-itself. For Sartre to follow this line of thought would be to follow what he regards as the Kantian and Husserlian error of allowing substantiality or opacity into consciousness. It would be to substitute essentialism for existentialism, to give priority to essence over existence. On the other hand, acceptance of Sartre's doctrine that the for-itself is translucid and even more featureless than a tabula rasa means that if one is to understand how the world can be other than a monotonous "total night of identity" (139 [184]) in which there are no cows at all, let alone only black cows, the original state of the in-itself which the for-itself negates cannot be characterless; and it seems that, contrary to Sartre's doctrine, it must have character *before* the for-itself's upsurge. "Upsurge" is the word used to translate Sartre's *surgissement* and that in turn is presumably his translation of Heidegger's *Ursprung* with its connotations of "source," "spring," and "leap."

But the original leap of the for-itself cannot be a leap in the dark, not if that primary project is free, which Sartre insists it is, and freedom, as Sartre also insists, presupposes the constraints of a concrete situation.

In the course of his discussion of freedom Sartre mentions the theory of random swerve, *clinamen*, which the Epicureans found wanting in Democritean atomism. Flew, though not without reservations, maintains that something like this concept of the capricious jerk plays a part in Sartre's theory of freedom. This can hardly be the case in view of the fact that Sartre refers to such a conception of freedom as a dangerous one and expressly rejects the idea that freedom is arbitrary or capricious. Free choice is not arbitrary or capricious, because the future of the for-itself is the assumption of a *tradition* (452–53 [529–30]). And the choice is free because it is the *assumption* of a tradition. To assume (*assumer, récupérer, recouvrer*) is to interiorize and carry forward. It is, however, the word surpass (*dépasser*) that is the best suited of Sartre's terms to convey the senses of Hegel's *aufheben* and to weld the link with the three temporal *ekstases*, in particular the past, *le passé*. "The importance of the past," Sartre writes, "cannot be exaggerated since for me 'Wesen ist was gewesen ist,'" essence is what has been ... I am in the past" (496 [577]). What is, he continues,

> takes on its meaning only when it is *surpassed* toward the future. Therefore what is is the past. We see how the past as "that which has to be changed" is indispensable to the choice of the future and how consequently no free surpassing can be effected except in terms of a past, but we can see too how the very *nature* of the past comes to the past from the original choice of a future. In particular the irremediable quality of the past comes from my actual choice of the future; if the past is that in terms of which I conceive and project a new state of things in the future, then the past itself is that which is *left in place*, that which consequently is itself outside all perspective of change. Thus in order for the future to be realizable, it is necessary that the past be irremediable. (497 [578])

This long quotation is not long enough to supply all the premises suppressed in Sartre's compact argument that "since freedom is choice, it is change." In particular, it does not explain why projects have to be for a new state of things in the future rather than for the preservation of the status quo, why the dialectic cannot mark time. More seriously, it does not explain how the dialectic can do anything but mark time, how it can ever get started. If my past is the residue left behind by my choice of a future, and if my future is a surpassing of my past, it seems that, in spite of the transition from talk of assumption to talk of surpassing, the circle of correlativity only appears to have been temporalized. There seemed to be a chance of earthing this circuit in an already given past. There was a risk that this given would have had the drawbacks Sartre discovers in the Kantian hinterland. Regress to it would therefore have been vicious, even if not infinite in the way that a regress of human traditions threatens to be. But Sartre escapes what from his point of view would be a vicious finite regress only at the price of getting stuck in a vicious circle.

Although temporality is proffered as the key to an understanding of Sartre's phenomenological ontology, it turns out to be an illusion. And the temporal dialectic is stillborn. Whether it fares any better in the *Critique of Dialectical Reason* is a question to be taken up in the next chapter. The present chapter concludes with the suggestion that dialectic is a nonstarter in *Being and Nothingness* because that book has no place for dialogue, another topic on which more will be said below.

In another passage where Sartre thinks what he declares to be unthinkable, he returns to the idea that

> there is an unchangeable element in the past, (e.g. I had whooping cough when I was five years old) and an element which is eminently variable (the meaning of the brute fact in relation to the totality of my being). But since, on the other hand, the meaning of the past fact penetrates it through and through (I cannot "recall" my childhood whooping cough outside of a precise project which defines its meaning), it is finally impossible for me to distinguish the unchangeable brute existence from the variable meaning which it bears. (497–98 [578–79])

In what follows the meaning is said to be dependent on the prevailing calendrical system and the terminology in general medical practice. But this, what is meant by whooping cough at five years of age, signification, import, *Bedeutung*, is not clearly distinguished from what my whooping cough means to me, its significance, importance, *Bedeutsamkeit*.[10] Whether or not the shell of what my whooping cough means to me can be detached from the skin of what is meant by whooping cough, the latter can certainly be peeled off the former. Sartre himself admits as much in his talk of collective techniques. But his way of admitting this is mistaken.

What Sartre expresses in his remarks about original projects Wittgenstein expresses in his remark that a person follows rules blindly.[11] Although my choice of an original project is not a voluntary, reflective choice, it is free. After all, reflective choices presuppose nonreflective ones. And although I may follow the prevailing calendrical system blindly, I follow it. I could opt out. But even if I do opt out, the alternative I opt for must be one that in theory, if not in practice, could become a general practice. It must be one that could become *ours*. It may only become an alternative functioning concurrently with the forsaken regime that for me is now *their* practice. But if in terms of their practice it was true that I had whooping cough when I was five years old, it remains trùe that I had whooping cough when I was five years old, notwithstanding that in my new system I had whooping cough when I was six years old. What I used to say one way is the same brute fact that I now say another way. And the same brute fact is thought and named when I say, "J'ai eu la coqueluche à cinq ans." Sartre will say that I can only name this unchangeable fact because I have left the first-personal situation with its shifting stratum of significance which prevents my grasping hold of the neat brute fact. If he does admit this much it is an advance on Roquentin's or Roquentin-Sartre's hankering after a grasp of the haecceity of things by referring to them without referring to them under any description, less even than a grunt.[12]

Yet the Sartre of *Being and Nothingness* trips himself up and falls short. "That brute fact *is*," he observes, "but apart from the witness of others, its date, the technical name of the illness ... what can it be?" Indeed, he might have gone on to out-Locke Locke by asserting not only that possibilities, potentialities, or "powers make a great part of our complex Ideas of Substance,"[13] but that the basic notions of all things are mixed modes. Merleau–Ponty claims as much when he writes, "Laplace's nebula is not behind us at our remote beginnings, but in front of us in the cultural world."[14] And Sartre caps this with his comment, "Even the concept of the non-human is a human concept" (533 [617]). But it is wrong for Sartre to call the testimony of others, the date of my illness and its technical name "an ensemble of meanings which depend on *my* projects."[15] This is not right even if he is using "my" here, as he often uses the expression "for-itself" (or "For-itself"), of me and you and you distributively rather than separatively just of me as opposed to you.

Sartre does not see that the first-person singular situation itself must find a place for the first-person plural. Granted, he has a section on Being-with and the "We," he discusses Heidegger on this subject, and he allows that the situation involves my neighbor and my fellow men so that "I find myself engaged in an *already meaningful* world which reflects to me meanings which I have not put into it" (510 [592]). But the world simply *reflects* these meanings. They are not ones I encounter. Like the past and unlike the future, they are unrealizable. Socio-cultural techniques and institutions originate with *das Man*, the third-personal Them. That there are these public utilities Sartre does not of course deny, but, whatever may be the case for human-reality, there could be cases of for-itself that managed without them, since, according to Sartre, the for-itself need not be for-others. "Being-for-others is not an ontological structure of the For-itself" (282 [342]). It is a merely meta-physical fact (297 [358]). As for being-with, for example with others as a member of a crew, Sartre treats this as no more than a psychological experience or feeling (414 [485], 424 [496], 427 [500]). It will be recalled that the wider context of Hume's reference to oarsmen is a theory of sympathy. Against Heidegger, who uses the same analogy, Sartre, following Hegel but not following him far enough, sees confrontation rather than participation as the basis of human relationships (246 [303]). The freedom of others is to be appropriated or else mine is to be surrendered. I can see you as an end and not just a means or I can see myself as an end and not just a means. Between the extremes of the sado-masochistic polarity there is no point at which I can see you and myself together as ends. In *Being and Nothingness* there is, so to speak, no way of making ends meet, no place for dialogue, whatever may be the position in the *Critique of Dialectical Reason* and the disowned *Existentialism and Humanism*.

A place for at least the possibility of dialogue must, however, be found in the system of *Being and Nothingness* if certain vital parts of it are to function. Consider the following passage:

> Thus this brute existence, *although necessarily existent and unchangeable*, stands as the ideal target [*le but idéal*]— beyond reach—of a systematic specification of all the meanings included in a memory. There is, of course, a "pure" matter of memory in the sense in which Bergson speaks of

> pure memory; but when it discloses itself, it is always in and
> through a project which introduces the appearance into the
> purity of this matter. (498 [579])

The first of these sentences sounds like the phenomenological phenomenalism welcomed in the opening pages of *Being and Nothingness*.
The second resumes the love-hate relationship with the Kantian *Ding-
an-sich* or Lockean *je ne sais quoi*. But it is noteworthy that Sartre wants
to say of this thing or unthing that *it is*. Hence one cannot help wondering by what right Sartre says that possibility and necessity originate with
the for-itself, whereas there is a sort of actuality and a sense of the verb
"to be" that does not. Supposing he were to dispense with the unworld
of reified unthings, he cannot dispense with what *is there* in the world of
teacups and tables, the *il y a*, the *es gibt*. Now even if we accept that I
with my project am responsible for this duple realization, the being
there of things, nevertheless their being there, their "strict objectivity"
(548 [633]), carries with it the idea that they are there also for others.
Whatever doubt or quasi doubt I may have about the existence of individual people, doubt itself presupposes the anonymous other. And this
anonymous other cannot be simply the unencountered source of the
Look before which I feel embarrassment, shame, or pride (252ff.
[310ff.]). The other must be a possible witness and co-witness, as the
following reflection will show.

Sartre contends that "the experience of the We-subject is based on
the original experience of the Other and can only be a secondary and
subordinate experience" (427 [500]). This is not so. Although Sartre
says "*being-for*-others precedes and founds *being-with*-others" (414
[486]), apparently because although the former is merely metaphysical,
not ontological, the latter is merely psychological, it must also be said
that the latter founds the former: They are equiprimordial. The very
notion of the Other calls for that of the We-subject to confer on the
Other his independence. I cannot do this alone. Or at least I can do it
alone only if I regard myself as a We-subject comprising a Tuesday self
in solidarity with a Thursday self who corroborate the experience of the
Wednesday self. "Even Dasein's Being-alone is Being-with in the
world," as Heidegger says.[16] And, of course, my experience of others
and of my alter ego is reciprocal with my experience of things. As Husserl demonstrates in the *Cartesian Meditations*, although you cannot
occupy my situation, every situation must include the for-us. If it does
not, the principle of intentionality cannot be maintained. There is no

something for consciousness to be consciousness of.

Furthermore, it will be remembered that although Sartre includes within a situation the tradition of meanings I don't myself originate (453 [530]), the independence of these meanings is dependent on me in the sense that I constitute their independence. Just as I constitute the residualness of things (217 [270]), so I constitute the being-left-behindness, the surpassedness, of the past, its already-being-there (183 [232]). But if I and I alone do that, there is no way out of the circle of correlativity. And if I and I alone constitute the temporality of my world, there is no world for me nor any temporality. I can be situated in a temporal world only if it is a world in intersubjective time, our time. Only in our time can there be an objective past on which, like the oyster on its fragment of grit, the for-itself can get to work.

CHAPTER FOUR
SARTRE'S MARXIST
EXISTENTIALISM

The components of social structure are persons.
—A. R. Radcliffe-Brown

1. *The negative legacy*

In chapter 3 two criticisms were made of the ontology of *Being and Nothingness*. It was argued, first, that Sartre's analysis of correlativity prevents his explaining how the temporal dialectic of surpassing can get started and, second, that his analysis of community is inadequate in that it does not succeed in providing for a public time and for a being with others in a public world.

These two criticisms are interrelated. The second is one that is sometimes directed at Kant. But he is less vulnerable than Sartre, for Kant's account of time is incomplete until the Transcendental Aesthetic is reread in the context of the theory of categories presented in the Transcendental Analytic. This theory is guided by the formal logic of judgment, which ensures for it and for the account of time associated with it access to objectivity. Such an access might have been available to Sartre through his use of the question, rather than the assertion, as a clue to the origin of negation and the existential "categories" of the for-itself. Sartre does sketch a sort of metaphysical deduction in which a rudimentary logic of the question is begun, but he makes it quite clear that he regards the question in dialogue to be a secondary kind, less basic than, for instance, the prejudicative attitude of interrogation with which a garage mechanic examines a faulty carburetor.[1]

In any case, Sartre refuses any analysis depending on the assumption that there is a given common human nature. In *Being and Nothingness* he refuses to rely on transcendental or other kinds of deduction that establish only concepts or logical relations between them. This refusal is maintained with regard not only to formal concepts or categories, but also with regard to empirical concepts. Obviously, inductive or hypothetico-deductive argument and synthetic a posteriori connections between empirical propositions cannot yield the ontological structures that Sartre seeks to expose. Conceptual and scientific knowledge cannot be the whole story about being-in-the-world. Epistemology, the theory of knowledge, according to *Being and Nothingness*, demands a foundation in ontology, a phenomenological description of being. That this is so is presumably something that Sartre claims to know; but this is not inconsistent with his holding that the study of the relations between knower and known presupposes a study of the relations between beings. In one sense this is a truism if the knower and the known are beings. But it is not a truism if ontology is, as it is for Sartre, a study of the meaning of being, of what it is to be. One does not have to read the phenomenological descriptions of *Being and Nothingness* in order to see how implausible it is to say that the only way of being-in-the-world is that of knowing subject to known object or of *percipere* to *perceptum*. Not even Berkeley maintains that *esse* is universally *percipi*. Nor does he hold that the *esse* of spirits is *percipere* only: It is also *agere*. And *agere* expresses the manner in which the Sartrian for-itself is in the world, provided the word is not confined to deliberately chosen acts but is allowed to cover the unreflective choice of projects and the carrying forward of a deposited past, what in the *Critique of Dialectical Reason* Sartre calls totalization and praxis. Other convergencies between the *Critique of Dialectical Reason* and *Being and Nothingness* will emerge in the course of the present chapter, where the main question being asked is whether there are divergencies that enable the *Critique of Dialectical Reason* to escape the two main criticisms made of *Being and Nothingness* in chapter 3.

2.   *Prolegomena to any future anthropology*

In *Being and Nothingness* metaphysics is said to be the study of individual processes that have given birth to *this* world as a concrete and particular totality.[2] Although there are some metaphysical speculations in *Being and Nothingness*, mainly toward the end of it, that book is not a work of metaphysics in Sartre's sense. It does not aim to answer questions about the existence of particular beings. It aims to describe the structures of being. It is a work of what Sartre calls ontology. Ontology for him is related to metaphysics as sociology is to history. Volume 1 of the *Critique of Dialectical Reason* contains quite a few illustrations from history, but the author's overriding aim in that volume is certainly not to write history. Nor was that to be the aim of the projected second volume announced as a "study of History in its development and Truth in its becoming," where the aim would be "to establish that there is *one* human history, with *one* truth and *one* intelligibility—not by considering the material content of this history, but by demonstrating that a practical multiplicity, whatever it may be, must unceasingly totalise itself through interiorising its multiplicity at all levels" (69 [156]).[3] Much of the middle chapters of volume 1, entitled "Theory of Practical Ensembles," would pass for sociology, but it is not the chief objective of volume 1 to produce a theory of sociology. It is rather to lay the foundation for a "prolegomena to any future anthropology."

This Kantian analogy is developed in the *Problem of Method*, which Sartre published along with the *Critique of Dialectical Reason*, and of course the latter title itself is an echo of Kant. Kant's first *Critique* attempted to justify the use of analytical reason in the natural sciences by fixing its limits. Sartre's *Critique* attempts to justify the use of synthetic dialectical reason by fixing its limits and its relation to analytical reason. Since Sartre continues to deny the idealist contention that to be is to know, to be known or to be knowable, he is bound to deny the legitimacy of Kant's method of justifying reason. He is bound to deny the legitimacy of the kind of reason Kant purported to justify in the *Critique of Pure Reason* if it is maintained that that kind of reason, analytic reason employing the principle of identity and the principle of universal causation, suffices to make intelligible the operations of human praxis. Kant himself made this latter denial. But the reason that Kant substituted was practical reason ruled by the moral law and the principle of noncontradiction. The moral law is a law of human, though not only human, nature and, as was shown in the examination of *Being and Nothingness* in chapter 3, Sartrian existentialism is critical of any doctrine that implies that human consciousness is endowed with a positive universal character. In the *Critique of Dialectical Reason* Sartre proposes to demonstrate that we cannot understand praxis in terms of the logic of identity or noncontradiction. The inadequacy of this logic for this purpose was already affirmed in *Being and Nothingness*. The principle of identity is limited there to being-in-itself. Only of what is in-itself does it hold that it is what it is. The for-itself is not what it is and is what it is not. The principle of identity and the principle of nonidentity are regionally circumscribed principles. The paradoxicality of this position would have been softened if Sartre had added that this position is consistent with the fact that the traditional principle of identity holds for the proposition that the for-itself is not what it is and is what it is not. A proposition is atemporally what it is. The for-itself, consciousness, *has* to be what it is; it is temporal surpassing.

The for-itself which was studied in *Being and Nothingness* remains the subject matter of the *Critique of Dialectical Reason*. Although such a study obviously cannot dispense with the propositional logic of identity, its concern with the making of the past and the carrying forward of it toward a future calls for a study of the dialectical logic of difference or nonidentity. Moreover, according to Sartre, this study must itself be dialectical. "Dialectic is necessary for dealing with dialectical problems" (823 [11]). The reasonableness of this statement must be conceded if Sartre's own investigation is acknowledged as a carrying forward of one project among others, namely, in the case of the *Critique of Dialectical Reason*, the application of the existentialist findings of *Being and Nothingness* to the social phenomena investigated by Marx. Sartre's own enquiry is *in situ* in the manner described in the section of *Being and Nothingness* called "Freedom and Facticity: The Situation." It will be recalled that in this section of *Being and Nothingness* one of the dimensions of the situation is what is due to "my fellowmen." It is this social coefficient of adversity or instrumentality—since one man's coefficient of instrumentality may be another man's coefficient of adversity (196 [260])—that becomes the main concern in the *Critique of Dialectical Reason*. The only other pages of *Being and Nothingness* where Sartre's attention is centered on this aspect is the section entitled "'Being-with' (*Mitsein*) and the 'We.'" This is part of a chapter entitled "Concrete Relations with Others." The relations discussed there are relations between individuals. The relations treated in the *Critique of Dialectical Reason* are those of the individual to human history and to ensembles and the structural and dialectical relations between varieties of ensemble. One similarity between the treatment in the two books deserves special notice. Among the interpersonal relations described in the earlier book are, first, love and masochism and, second, indifference, desire, hate, and sadism. These concrete relations exemplify my predicament of being a seen seer or, to employ a more Hobbesian metaphor, a hunted hunter. Each of them, like the strategems of bad faith illustrated earlier in the book, contains the seed of its own displacement by one of the others. Masochism, to give but one example, is doomed to failure, since it would be the endeavor to be fascinated by myself as object, that is to say, as I am apprehended by another. But such apprehension is in principle impossible. And any self-abasing postures I adopt are postures *I* adopt. "The more he (the masochist) tries to taste his objectivity, the more he will be submerged by the consciousness of his subjectivity—hence his anguish."[4] Sartre concedes that with each transition from one to the next of his typology of concrete relations there is an enrichment,[5] but he is not inclined to see the new relation as one in which the earlier is dialectically *aufgehoben*. That is, an individual's experience is not a dialectical passage from one kind of relation to another. The types of relation form a circle of positions on a (not very merry) merry-go-round. And perhaps another reason Sartre declines to say that the positions are related dialectically is that there is no one temporal order in which they must occur. Is this so, too, of the ensembles described in the *Critique of Dialectical Reason*?

The chapters in the middle of the *Critique of Dialectical Reason* deal in turn with collectives or aggregates like the series, for example people waiting, though not necessarily queuing, at a bus-stop; indirect gatherings, for example a radio audience; and classes, for example the French proletariat. Various types of group are then described, firstly the spontaneously emerging group in formation (*en fusion*), for example the mob storming the Bastille; then the more or less explicitly sworn statutory group, for example the deputies of the Third Estate who pledged themselves to solidarity at the Jeu de Paume; the organization, like a football team or an industrial firm, which comes together to achieve a more specific aim than the pledged group, the aim of which may be quite vague (solidarity, for instance, even though those who pledge themselves to solidarity may have in mind no precise purpose that solidarity is to serve). Finally, Sartre analyzes the institution, an example of which would be an army. With the institution we have reached the point at which men have moved from producing themselves to being produced by their products, as a tool or a machine dictates the operator's behavior.

In the chapters where these forms of assembly and their relations are examined, Sartre repeatedly issues a warning that he is not interested in presenting an account of historical genesis and evolution. Dialectic, he writes,

> as a formal law of movement—remains silent on questions of priority. There is actually no *a priori* ground for supposing

that seriality is an earlier statute than the group, although it is true that the group constitutes itself in and against it. Not only do we always find groups and gatherings (*rassemblements*) together, but also, *only* dialectical investigation and experience will enable us to determine whether the seriality in question is an *immediate* gathering or whether it is constituted by old groups which have been serialised. Indeed we have seen that sooner or later they return to the statute of inertia. (678 [643])

Elsewhere he observes that

regardless of their statute, groups can either arise from the practico-inert field or be re-absorbed into it; and there is no formal law to compel them to pass through the succession of different statutes described above. A group in formation may either dissolve instantaneously or be at the beginning of a long development which will lead to sovereignty; and in the complex world glimpsed here, the sovereign group itself may arise directly from the collective itself. (676 [641])

However, although Sartre says that an understanding of the structures of groups is dependent on an understanding of series, and vice versa, the ensembles described are patently introduced in an order of increasing complexity. That alone would not lead him to talk of dialectic. For there is that sort of order in the concrete relations between individuals dealt with in *Being and Nothingness*, and, as we have seen, Sartre holds that they are not linked together dialectically; he says they form a circle. In practice the ensembles of the *Critique of Dialectical Reason* also form a circle, for, as we have also seen now, nonserial ones continually run the risk of lapsing into seriality. It is not surprising that the risk of fall, which exists for the concrete relations between individuals, should threaten too the nonserial ensembles, for the suite of ensembles is rooted in relations between individuals. We know that according to *Being and Nothingness* the individual for-itself negates the inert in-itself and projects itself toward the inevitably unsuccessful consummation of being both for-itself and in-itself. The interpretation of my world by existential psychoanalysis will disclose the particular manner in which I represent my achievement of this unobtainable ideal.

It is to this existential psychoanalysis that Sartre is referring when he says that he wants to remedy a deficiency in Marxism by showing how psychoanalysis can be combined in dialectical materialism with a concrete social anthropology.[6] Just as Freudian psychoanalysis is in bad faith, so is Engelsian materialism and the vulgar official Marxism that Sartre had already derided in his article on "Materialism and Revolution," which appeared in *Les Temps Modernes* as early as 1946.[7] It is not determinism that Sartre objects to if by this is meant that, in the words of Engels, "men make their own history themselves, but in an environment which conditions them." However, Sartre interprets this as saying that over against the for-itself is the in-itself that it has to assume, and over against the individual praxis the exterior practico-inert that it has to interiorize. The practico-inert is what society has done or made, the product of being-for-itself, being-in-itself and being-for-others. The practico-inert is the human artifact available for the individual to employ toward the meeting of his needs. This "recuperation" of the practico-inert through my project is what Sartre calls totalization.

Totalization can be understood only by a totalizer and in terms of dialectical reason. It follows immediately from this, according to Sartre (and Kant would have agreed with him here), the mechanistic account Engels gives of the so-called struggle between the classes is incoherent. For that program sets out to explain all human activity, including itself, in terms of analytical reason, that is, from a desituated and hence unreal point of view. From this impossible vantage point class struggle and contradiction can be no more than metaphors for the collision of atomic particles. Thus, Engels "kills the dialectic twice over to make sure it is dead—the first time by claiming to have discovered it in Nature, and the second time by suppressing it within society." So, Sartre concludes, "If analytic Reason is to become economic Reason without losing its rationality, it must be within dialectical Reason, and as produced and supported by it" (712 [670]).

What Sartre calls analytical reason here is reductive reason, reason that tries to explain culture in terms of nature. It is therefore untrue to say that Sartre demonstrates the existence of dialectical reason by analytical reason.[8] This only seems to follow from Sartre's statements that his method is regressive-progressive and analytico-synthetic and that volume 1, where the demonstration of the existence of dialectical reason is undertaken, is regressive. From this it can be inferred that volume 1 is analytical, but not that it is analytical in the sense of reductive or positivistic reason. He tells us that his regressive-progressive or analytico-synthetic distinction derives from the model suggested by Henri

Lefebvre.[9] Sartre could have added that this model owes much to the distinction between analytic and synthetic methods made by Kant. The latter states, for instance, that the *Prolegomena to Any Future Metaphysics* and the first two chapters of the *Fundamental Principles of the Metaphysic of Morals* are analytic in method, proceeding from the known to its unknown presuppositions, whereas the *Critique of Pure Reason* and the third chapter of the *Fundamental Principles* adopt the synthetic method, aiming "to develop knowledge out of its original seeds."[10] There are more remote ancestors of the distinction in, for instance, Descartes and Plato. In all these places the analytic and the synthetic methods complement each other. And for Sartre their joint use is an application of dialectical reason. Admittedly, the regressive analytic procedure uncovers only the "traces of the dialectical movement" and to comprehend the movement itself the progressive-synthetic method must be used. Because to comprehend, *verstehen*, is in Sartre's view to grasp the way a situation is surpassed toward a future. A situation, as *Being and Nothingness* had already begun to show, includes a specific individual's past, and the world he inhabits is inseparable from how he sees it, and how he sees it is how he lives or "exists" it, his praxis. Accordingly, an attempt to understand Flaubert will be an analysis beginning with the things he has made, for example the book *Madame Bovary*, and therefore, since "Madame Bovary, c'est moi," what he has made of himself, then regressing upon his adolescence, his childhood, and his birth into a family of the intellectual petty bourgeoisie. That this regressive analysis retraces the path of a dialectic becomes apparent when it is appreciated that it consists in a to-and-fro movement between the actions of a unique individual and the social context he resumes.[11] But a deeper understanding of the relationship between the text and context calls for a progressive reconstruction or retotalizing of the totalizing project in which the individual—Flaubert or Robespierre or Valéry or Sade or Genet or Sartre—makes something new out of what has been made in a world in which "man is 'mediated' by things to the same extent as things are 'mediated' by man" (79 [165]).

This concrete existential dialectic of ambiguity is the alternative that Sartre would substitute for the abstract Hegelian idealist dialectic on the one hand and the abstract Engelsian or vulgar Marxist materialist dialectic on the other. This concrete dialectic is not simply a dialectic of individual biography. Even *Being and Nothingness* implies more than that. It is a dialectic that is also a heuristic for social history; "The study of the childhood of Flaubert, as universality lived in particularity, enriches the general study of the petty bourgeoisie of 1830."[12] Although in the *Critique of Dialectical Reason* attention is directed mainly on the social aspects, the constituted social dialectic, as we have seen, is rooted in the constituent dialectic of individual praxis. Hence, if, as we argued in chapter 3, the individual dialectic is stillborn, so is the social.

3. *Community*

What about the second of the two main difficulties we encountered in *Being and Nothingness*? Does the *Critique of Dialectical Reason* make good the earlier book's failure to meet the demand for community in a shared public time?

In seeking an answer to this question, it must be remembered that volume 2 of the *Critique of Dialectical Reason* never appeared. We cannot, therefore, say what should be made of the references in the final paragraphs of volume 1 to the possibility of "an intelligible totalization from which there is no appeal" where "we shall, for the first time, reach the problem of totalisation without a totaliser and of the very foundations of this totalisation, that is to say, of its motive-forces and of its non-circular direction" (817 [754]). Are we to look forward to a demonstration that, notwithstanding the "useless passion" stressed in *Being and Nothingness* and the continual threat of lapse into alienation through the practico-inert stressed in volume 1 of the *Critique of Dialectical Reason*, a properly understood Marxism offers a way out of these Sisyphean *éternels retours*? Until advances in technology and changes in social relations have freed man from scarcity, we have no means of conceiving what form such a way out might take and what philosophy would describe it. Until then there is no alternative to an existentialist Marxism.[13]

One might think, as Marjorie Grene does, that the *Critique of Dialectical Reason* is hinting at the possibility of a common time and a more than merely psychological we-subject in certain of its remarks about reciprocity. But the "immediate" reciprocity of page 735 [688] of the *Critique of Dialectical Reason* is none other than the concrete relations that in *Being and Nothingness* are predicated upon the "immediate structures of the for-itself": possibility, freedom, and lack. In other words, this immediate reciprocity is immediate only as opposed to social. It is nonetheless founded on the Other as object and occupies at the level of immediate individual relations a place analogous to that occupied by the unity of the practico-inert object at the level of sociality where two individuals are mediated by a third and series are transcended by the group, this formation and transformation being motivated by scarcity (193 [258]).

Scarcity, incidentally, cannot be identified with what in *Being and Nothingness* Sartre called lack, since lack is an ontologically necessary immediate structure of the for-itself, whereas scarcity is described in the *Critique of Dialectical Reason* as a contingent human fact (141, note 21 [214, note 1], 735 [688]). If scarcity were ontologically necessary, the future age of freedom Marx and Sartre talk of would be not only indescribable but also quite impossible. The scarcity of the *Critique of Dialectical Reason* is a social, not a totally brute, fact. Its explication requires what *Being and Nothingness* calls being-for-others of which Sartre says (in my view mistakenly) that it is not a structure deducible from being-for-itself, but, like scarcity, is a contingent fact of anthropology. "It would perhaps not be impossible to conceive of a For-itself which would be wholly free from all For-others and which would exist without even suspecting the possibility of being an object,"[14] and, we may add, without therefore experiencing the scarcity that presupposes competitive being-for-others. So long as the obvious qualifications are made, the analogy with Kant still holds. Just as the quest for the conditions of the possibility of man's sense of obligation leads Kant to an analysis of rationality in general, so Sartre's search for the conditions of the possibility of the anthropological fact of scarcity leads him to an analysis of the for-itself or *praxis überhaupt*. Furthermore, somewhat like Kant's conceiving of beings who, having no bodily senses, have no sense of a moral imperative, Sartre holds that morality is contingent on scarcity and is therefore Manicheistic, a mortal struggle between praxis and antipraxis, value and antivalue, not a conflict of blind instincts (736 [689]).

Sartre distinguishes positive and negative reciprocity, the latter being "struggle" (113 [192], 735 [688]). Should it be concluded that while the individual relations of *Being and Nothingness* are always conflictive, the *Critique of Dialectical Reason* allows for cooperation that may be a basis for mutuality in a Kantian kingdom of ends? This is explicitly rejected by Sartre on the grounds that it would imply an absolute idealism incompatible with his existential Marxist account of men as facticity-transcendence. "Only an idea amongst other ideas can posit itself as its own end" (112 [191]). Hegel too is chided, therefore, for ignoring matter as a mediation between individuals, and this criticism is extended to Hegel's account of negative reciprocity. Struggle is not, as the idealist puts it, one consciousness seeking the death of another. "The origin of struggle always lies, in fact, in some concrete antagonism whose material condition is scarcity, in a particular form, and the real aim is objective conquest or even creation, in relation to which the destruction of the adversary is only a means" (113 [192]). This is a key remark. It reveals that it is misleading to call Sartre a Hobbesian. If Sartrian anthropology shows man to be a creature of self-interest, the interpretation of self-interest that is appropriate is not that of Hobbes but that of Bishop Butler.

That this is so and that Sartrian authenticity is not to be identified with Hegelian, Bergsonian, or any other kind of self-fulfilment—how could it be, since the project of self-fulfilment is in bad faith?—is made clear by various texts. For example:

> Hegel's mistake was his belief that within everyone there is something to objectify and that work reflects the individuality of its author. In fact, however, objectification as such is not the goal, but the consequence attached to the goal. The aim is the production of a commodity, an object of consumption, or a tool, or the creation of a work of art. And it is through this production, this creation, that man creates himself, or in other words detaches himself gradually from things as he inscribes his work in them. (112 [192])

One of the striking features of this analysis is that it rules out not only the treatment of the Other but also of oneself as an end, that "in so far as my project is a transcendence of the present towards the future, and of myself towards the world, I always treat myself as a means and cannot treat the Other as an end." Signs of this doctrine were clearly visible in *The Transcendence of the Ego*, written twenty-four years earlier, where it is argued that my only self is what I have made and this is in the public world like any other instrumentality. The ideal Self of *Being and Nothingness* is a nonsense, like God. But what about freedom? Must I not treat that as an end? There are statements in *Existentialism and Humanism* implying that that is at least possible, for example: "I am obliged to will the freedom of others at the same time as mine. I cannot make my freedom my aim unless I make that of others equally my aim."[15] But there are statements in *The Transcendence of the Ego*, which antedates *Existentialism and Humanism* by ten years, that imply that freedom itself cannot be personalized as mine or thine, or his or hers. It is only reflective freedom-facticity that has the owner's mark stamped on it. Unreflective consciousness is impersonal;[16] so pure consciousness or freedom, if that is conceivable, would have to be impersonal too. According to Sartre, however, it is not conceivable. Consciousness is always consciousness of something, which it nihilates or negates. There is an "inextricable connection of freedom and facticity in the situation. Without facticity freedom would not exist—as a power of nihilation and of choice—and without freedom facticity would not be discovered and would have no meaning."[17] In so far, therefore, as Sartre's philosophy can accommodate respect and recognition, it cannot be respect for pure consciousness or freedom, whether or not this is equated with rationality. It can only be respect for embodied consciousness and freedom, respect for persons.

In *Existentialism and Humanism* Sartre's account of respect is very Kantian. That may be why he later expressed dissatisfaction with the piece. "Humanism" suggests there is a ready-made human nature. But "the quality of being a *man* does not exist as such," writes Sartre in the *Critique of Dialectical Reason*. There, when he speaks of the respect one person has for another, the respect tends to be of the kind a driver of a motor car has when he keeps his distance from the one in front; "They respect one another, there will always be two of them" (114 [193]). Respect is no more than another name for the standoffishness of every for-itself, their *Abstand*.

The *Critique of Dialectical Reason* frequently speaks, too, of recognition, as is to be anticipated in a book that, like *Being and Nothingness*, is so indebted via Kojève and Marx, to Hegel's discussion of the relation between master and slave. Typical of Sartre's approach to recognition is his statement "In order to *treat a man like a dog*, one must first recognise him as a man" (111 [190]). But mutual recognition or reciprocity is a "disunity within solidarity," the "unity of a dyad" which "can be *realised* only within a totalisation performed from outside by a third party" (115 [194]). This "realization," as we saw in chapter 3, consists not merely in the third party's becoming aware (103 [184]). When, as an intellectual on holiday, I look down from my hotel window and watch a gardener and a road mender working in ignorance of each other on opposite sides of a wall "we should not say that *for us* the two labourers are ignorant of each other. They are ignorant of each other *through me* to the extent that I become what I am *through them*." My perception of them leads to my experiencing myself as an intellectual through the feeling of being cut off from the worlds they inhabit. But when Sartre talks

of realization, he is not talking merely of a psychological or epistemological phenomenon. He is talking of being. Here, as in *Being and
Nothingness*, he is expressing a dissatisfaction with Kantian and Hegelian idealism.

> If the idealist dialectic misused the triad, this is primarily be-
> cause the *real* relation between men is necessarily ternary.
> But this trinity is not a meaning or ideal mark of the human
> relation: it is inscribed *in being*, that is to say, in the material-
> ity of individuals. (109 [189]).

These sentences are taken from a chapter entitled "Human relations
as a mediation between different sectors of materiality." In the same
chapter Sartre discusses language. One might suppose that it would be
in this discussion, if anywhere, that the basis of an account of reciprocity
and shared public time would be discovered.

Radical economism would handle language in the language of econom-
ics. Sartre himself makes the observation that use value is converted
into exchange value by the third party—the substitutable witness, *das
Man*, anyone and everyone—and he would doubtless be prepared to
apply this observation to language as readily as we refer to the coining
and currency of words. "Language might well be studied," he suggests,
"on the same lines as money: as a circulating, inert materiality, which
unifies dispersal" (98 [180]). But in the *Critique of Dialectical Reason*
Sartre is more interested in the converse operation, illuminating mone-
tary transactions by comparing them to linguistic behavior. The explanation for this is that he regards *all* human activity as linguistic. In
case this tempts one to draw an analogy here with Saussure and structuralism it should be noted immediately that when Sartre says "*praxis* is
always language" (99 [181]), his word is *langage*, by which he appears to
mean language in use, that is, performances of acts of *parole*, not the
object of scientific study which Saussure called *langue*. This is implied in
the qualification "truthful or deceptive" which Sartre puts in paren-
theses after the word *langage*. Sartre's "language" is the interiorizing,
that is, use of the exteriorized system that Saussure recommends as
the legitimate object of the science of linguistics, but not only of that
system, for articulated verbal discourse is only a secondary form of linguistic expression.[18] The *Critique's* thesis that praxis is always language is
foreshadowed in the affirmation in *Being and Nothingness*, "I *am* language. By the sole fact that whatever I may do, my acts freely conceived

and executed, my projects launched toward my possibilities have outside of them a meaning which escapes me."[19] However, in the paragraphs of the *Critique* where Sartre says that praxis is always language,
the word "language" is used in its narrower connotation to refer to verbal language.

Do these paragraphs of the *Critique* repair the omission from *Being
and Nothingness* of conditions for the possibility of a shared time? On
the face of it the existence of such conditions is implied in Sartre's comment on the idea that persons are substantive monads living in isolation
from one another, each speaking his own incommunicable private language. In so far as this privacy is possible, Sartre maintains, it

> can have meaning only in terms of a more fundamental com-
> munication, that is to say, when based on mutual recognition
> and on a permanent project to communicate; or rather, on
> the permanent, collective, institutional communication of,
> for example, all French people, through the constant media-
> tion of verbal materiality, even in silence; and on people's
> actual projects of particularising this general communication.
> (98 [181]).

This is promising. But the promise is not kept. For although it argues for
a medium of communication, for example the French language, when
we come to enquire how people plug into that system, how, as Sartre
puts it, people particularize it, they succeed not in communicating with
each other but in excommunicating each other. The position is not in
any fundamental way different from what it was in *Being and Nothingness*. There, referring to the speaker's production of a new sentence
against the background of a world already processed by the linguistic
and other techniques of others, Sartre remarks that "in the very act by
which he unfolds his time, he temporalizes himself in a world whose
temporal meaning (*sens*) is already defined by other temporalizations:
this is the fact of simultaneity."[20] This simultaneity turns out not to be a
projective simultaneity of action, however, but a retrospective simultaneity of the traces of action, of, in Bergsonian parlance, the space
traversed rather than the transition. This is because, as Sartre goes on to
say in *Being and Nothingness*, "the for-itself is compelled to make the
Other's existence manifest to himself in the form of a choice." The
choice is between regarding the other as subject and regarding him as
object. If the speaker takes the first alternative, the other is the look and

has mastery over the institution of language. If I, the speaker, take the second alternative and regard the Other as object, the Other is fixed by my look and, along with the foreign meanings deposited in institutions, is transcended by my temporal project. In neither case do he and I live in the same time. One of us dies in the time of the other.

The *Critique of Dialectical Reason* makes little advance beyond this position. "If," Sartre says there, "the *praxis* of the individual is dialectical, his relation to the other must be dialectical too" (99 [181]). That is, just as the speaker transcends material practico-inert words toward the completion of a speech act, so he transcends the hearer, uses him in the furthering of his own project. Notwithstanding Sartre's assertion that reciprocity implies "that I recognise the Other as *praxis*, that is to say, as a developing totalisation, *at the same time as* integrating him as an object into my totalising project" (what more could one look for?), the only dialectic of reciprocity to be extracted from the *Critique of Dialectical Reason* is an oscillation between dominance and servitude. It is the old story of "he flees me when I seek him and possesses me when I flee him" (112–13 [192]).[21] According to *Being and Nothingness*, "We shall never place ourselves concretely on a plane of equality; that is, on the plane where the recognition of the Other's freedom would involve the Other's recognition of our freedom."[22] The most that one might look for and fail to find in the *Critique of Dialectical Reason* is a recognition of equality, if not before the moral law, at least before the law of language.

In practice, for Sartre, the scales of linguistic justice tilt this way or the other. That this is so is borne out by his endorsement of Paulhan's idea that the laws of language exist not for the speaker but for the listener. This is a mistaken idea. The listener normally needs to reflect on the syntactico-semantic rules only when the speaker is suspected of committing a solecism or when the subject matter is heavy going. But in the latter circumstances the speaker too may need to invoke these rules. In the normal course of events the conversation proceeds with as little call for "interpretation" or deciphering as there is when we understand someone's feelings from his gestures or looks. Indeed, looks, like tone of voice, are commonly integral to the reciprocal understanding of those taking part in a conversation. It is as little a phenomenological necessity that all looks be hostile as it is that the Other "captures" or steals the meaning of my words.

It merits repetition that Sartre's phenomenology entails there being a circularity in the situation and hence in the linguistic situation. Language presupposes itself (99 [181]). The speech act presupposes instituted linguistic schemata, but the latter "exist always only incarnated and sustained in their very incarnation by a freedom."[23] Again it is the speaker and his freedom on which Sartre puts the emphasis. So much so that he fails to work out a dialectic of dialogue that would serve as a foundation for an intersubjective, as against a depopulated interobjective, time. God is dead, so a preestablished temporal harmony grounded in Him is out of the question. Contemporaneity bought by a dialectic of dematerialization leading to absolute knowledge would be contemporaneity bought at too high a price, the price of the sacrifice of temporality and therefore of contemporaneity. Since there is never to be a second volume of the *Critique of Dialectical Reason* we will never know whether Sartre could provide for contemporaneity through an adaptation of dialectical materialism. I suspect that if he had been able to achieve this result in this way, that is, if he had been able to meet the second of the two objections mentioned in the opening paragraph of this chapter, it could have been only by becoming more obviously vulnerable to the first of the objections mentioned there and developed in chapter 3—or by discarding altogether his negativist phenomenology.

The *Critique of Dialectical Reason*, I have argued, does not solve the problems we met in *Being and Nothingness*, because it is raised on the same foundations. My criticism can be viewed as a complaint that Sartre pays too little heed to what Husserl is trying to do in the Fifth Cartesian Meditation. But it is nearer the truth to say that I have been complaining that Sartre needs something like Heidegger's analysis of *Mitsein*. He refuses this analysis because he wrongly supposes that it is an analysis of fellowship such as Hume called sympathy and illustrated by referring to the togetherness of members of a rowing team. Sartre might have avoided this mistake if he had taken due note of Heidegger's statement, made with Scheler and Husserl in mind, that "only on the basis of Being-with does 'empathy' [*Einfühlung*] become possible." Being-with is a precondition of such states: of sympathy, friendship, and love; of indifference; of antipathy, hate, and the menacing look; of all concrete relations with other individuals and society. Heidegger, by implication, warns his readers against confusing his analysis with Husserl's because the latter's analyses, even of practical and axiological attitudes, are always modeled on visual perception. This goes for a person's relations with others. And Sartre carries on this Husserlian and Cartesian tradition by making his analyses of concrete relations with others pivot on The Look. According to him, the axis of interpersonal relationship is object-for-subject, how I see the other, how he sees me, and how I see myself. The relationships are ones of consciousness and self-consciousness, not of preepistemological being. Like Sartre's interpretation of the relation between the for-itself and the in-itself, his interpretation of being-for-others fails to give being its due. His phenomenological and ontological program recognizes no less clearly than Heidegger's that the circle of knowledge is inscribed within the circle of being, but that program and its Marxist appendage, like the program initiated by Husserl, are still fed by the optical metaphysics that Descartes inherited from Plato.

CHAPTER FIVE
BACHELARD: COUNTER-
PHENOMENOLOGICAL
DIALECTIC OF SCIENCE

*Il s'agit de savoir, par exemple, comment un concept—
chargé encore de métaphores ou de contenus imaginaires—
s'est purifié et a pu prendre statut et fonction de concept
scientifique.*

—Michel Foucault

Sartre's ontology rejects the ontology of Bergsonism in which the
negative and the possible are at most epiphenomena of the positive and
the full. It is the phenomenological equivalent of those classical physical
and metaphysical theories that maintained the reality of the vacuum.
Although Gaston Bachelard does not see himself as a Friend of phenomenology, whether it be essentialist or existentialist, he agrees with the
author of *Being and Nothingness* that Bergson is wrong to give nothingness and negation second place relative to plenitude and affirmation.

1. *Bachelardian negativism and Bergsonian positivism*

In chapter 4 of *Creative Evolution* Bergson argues that emptiness and
nothingness are secondary to and parasitic on fullness. Emptiness is the
no longer or not yet being there of something. Bachelard argues that as
a matter of logic emptiness and fullness are interdependent, and that
although Bergson is right in saying that the notion of emptiness presupposes that of fullness, he is mistaken in denying that the notions are
correlative.

But Bachelard's disagreement with Bergson goes deeper than this. In
Bergson's account, the affirmative judgment is more basic than the
negative judgment. Ironically, this is plausible only if one takes a narrow view of what Bergson calls spiritual energy and limits judgment to

the repetition of already acquired beliefs. If one considers instead a judgment announcing a discovery, for instance the discovery of a blue dahlia, one sees that it may be the exclamatory rejection of the prior belief or supposition that there is no such thing as a blue dahlia.

In the light of Bachelard's stress on the interdependence of the concepts of emptiness and fullness, it might be expected that he would hold that just as the affirmation "There is a blue dahlia" is a rejection of "There is no blue dahlia," so the announcement "There is no blue dahlia" is a rejection of the judgment "There is a blue dahlia." His failure to do this can be explained by his insistence that he is concerned with what can be proved. The uncircumscribed existential denial "There is no blue dahlia (anywhere)" cannot be proved. This insistence does not, however, explain why Bachelard does not say of a circumscribed existential denial, for example "There is no blue dahlia in this herbaceous border," that it is the rejection of the corresponding positive proposition. He could have said this. But there is no need for him to. His argument is not aimed at showing the priority of negative over positive propositions. It is not about propositions at all, if by this is meant propositions in logical thin air. It is about sentences in use, judgments. His claim is that whether these are positive or negative in their surface grammatological form, they are always denials in their rhetorological form. All claims are counterclaims, whether a No against a Yes or a Yes against a No.[1] He is occupied with the interrelations of speech acts, even if, following Bergson and a French tradition going back to Maine de Biran and earlier, he believes himself to be doing psychology, what he himself calls effective or probative psychology. Bachelard reasonably assumes that this is the sort of psychology Bergson also must do if any philosophical conclusions are to be grounded on it, and he would be abandoning this scientific psychology in Bachelard's opinion if he tried to establish the primacy of the positive on the basis that knowledge must start with the recording of first impressions. "Scientific psychology can no more invoke a first impression than astronomy can be founded on Genesis." Wherever there is positing or affirmation there is exclusion and denial of an alleged or imagined opposite. "In so far as affirmation has any psychological significance [*sens*], it is a reaction against antecedent negation or ignorance. Its force [*tonus*] is a function of the number and importance of the negations it challenges."[2]

It is tempting to regard this as an endorsement of the doctrine of propositional bipolarity espoused by the early Wittgenstein which implies that the content of a concept is a function of the opposites it excludes, and, when conjoined with the verificationism he adopted in the 1930s, that the meaning of a proposition is the method of the falsification of the propositions it excludes.[3] Bachelard does support a version of this doctrine, but he puts more stress than Wittgenstein does in the 1930s on the temporal and polemical aspects of dialectic. Bachelard is mainly interested in the polemics and practice of science. This practice is most scientific, according to him, when science is changing. "It is at the moment when a concept changes its meaning that it has most meaning."[4] A concept is sharpest at the point of concept formation since it is there that it manifests most evidently the traces of everything the scientist purports to exclude from it.[5] Hence Bachelard's declares, "The first clear thought is the thought of what is not the case."[6] Although this is a riposte against Bergson, it is also an extension to all concepts of Bergson's own analysis of the concept of nothingness.

2. *Science and pre-science*

Bachelard adheres to the principle that a concept has no identity in isolation from a judgment. He adds that a sharp concept is inseparable from its conceptualization. By this he means that it must bear the imprint of everything we have refused to embody in it. A concept is a historical phenomenon. It conveys the history of our refusals. It is not surprising, therefore, that Bachelard's theory of science is a theory of the history of science. That history he holds to be misrepresented by the Bergsonian model of a biological system whose growth is impeded and whose needs are frustrated only by obstacles impinging upon it from the outside. With a wealth of documentation cited in a dozen or so of his books, Bachelard tries to demonstrate that science sets up stumbling blocks for itself. It proceeds by rectification. This process is not one of development but of envelopment. And although the process is dialectical, it is not a process of contradiction in the sense that that term has in the square of opposition of traditional formal logic. A new theory, in Bachelard's account, is not incompatible with the theory it replaces. It transcends it but complements it. His account implies "an ontology of complementarity which is less severely dialectical than the metaphysics of contradiction."[7] By the metaphysics of contradiction he means Hegelianism, though he never discusses Hegel in sufficient detail to dispel the suspicion that he exaggerates the difference between his own and the Hegelian dialectic. Non-Euclidian geometries, non-Archimedean mensuration, non-Newtonian mechanics, non-Maxwellian physics, non-Lavoisian chemistry, noncommutative arithmetics, and non-Aristotelian logics, Bachelard argues, improve on their predecessors by demonstrating that these predecessors are more limited in their field of application than was assumed.

Is not this an overoptimistic idea of science? Is not it overoptimistic even if it is applied to only the last century or two of the history of science on which, as indicated by the titles of many of his works, Bachelard's interest tends to be focused? Have there been no theories in science—alchemical, astrological, phrenological, or theories of the circulation of the blood—where things have been got so wrong that it has been impossible to salvage anything from them? Perhaps Bachelard could reply that there is no knowing whether an apparently barren theory might not bear fruit. He asserts on the one hand dogmatically that alchemical theories will never achieve scientific respectability and on the other generously that a superseded scientific theory always survives as part of a new one. He goes so far as to state that we can rest assured that some notions, for example that of specific heat, will never lose their scientific respectability.[8] Is it because phlogiston theory is pre-scientific or because it is a mistaken scientific theory that it is counted among the rejects of the history of science, *l'histoire périmée*, while the theory of specific heat is retained as part of *l'histoire sanctionnée*?[9] A satisfactory resolution of these problems demands recognition that in some places, for example in *La Formation de l'esprit scientifique*, Bachelard is talking about how the scientific has superseded the pre-scientific, whereas in other places, for example *Le Nouvel esprit scientifique*, he is talking about how a new scientific theory supersedes an old scientific theory, and in yet other places, for example *La Philosophie du non* (pp. 144 and 147), he is talking about how scientists ought to proceed. The confusion is further confounded by the ease with which the word science accepts an evaluative connotation.

One of the kinds of a-priorism Bachelard objects to is that of philosophers who pretend to be able to work out a philosophy of science without a detailed knowledge of scientific practice. Bachelard's attitude to such a-priorism is not, however, inconsistent with acknowledgment that the scientist and the philosopher of science bring philosophical prejudices to their research, a fact summed up in his remark that applied rationalism or surrationalism, as he calls the modern scientific outlook, does not start from scratch but rather carries something forward.[10] The philosophy of origins implicit in this comment will be examined later. It is relevant first to draw attention to two further kinds of a-priorism that sometimes emerge in the way Bachelard treats on the one hand recent and on the other hand superseded scientific theories.

Quantum theory is for him the subject of pious reverence.

> That the notions of force and energy are reciprocal becomes more and more obvious. What will the basic notion be in the last analysis? It is of course too early to answer this question. The appearance on the scene of quantum theory may in any case put an end to the debate in an unexpected way by introducing entirely new principles for defining experimental notions in mathematical terms.[11]

True, Bachelard is here only suggesting that the dialectic *may* reach its culmination with quantum theory. And he immediately moves on to emphasize that the scientist is or should be receptive and open-minded.[12] He is as firmly against closed systems in science as is Bergson in morals and religion, and he does not share the faith in the unity of science manifested by many members of the Vienna Circle.[13] Room must be allowed for a plurality of methods, presumably also for a non-Bachelardian philosophy of science, a *polyphilosophisme*.[14] The problem of the unity of science has been badly formulated.[15] Its unity—the unity of, for example, organic chemistry and inorganic chemistry—is the discontinuous unity of complementarity. Bachelard never abandons this pluralism, notwithstanding his prediction that the language of modern physical science will be increasingly that of mathematical probability and that *homo faber* is to make way for *homo mathematicus*.[16]

Less readily unraveled are the reasons for Bachelard's seeming confidence that discarded theories will never be reinstated. How can one know that a discredited theory—for instance the heliocentric theory of Aristarchus or Heraclides—will not later regain the esteem of scientists? Does not the denial that this may happen betray a too naively unidirectional idea of the history of science? And does not it deny the hermeneutic situation of all scientific explanation? Might there not be kinks, loops, or zigzags in the dialectic? Might it not err from the path of truth and later return to it?

Bachelard would say that these questions are prompted by a simplistic picture of meaning, error, and truth. The first step toward correcting this picture is taken when one grants that if one changes a concept's environment one changes the concept.[17] This alone would not imply that no theoretical system could be revived. It is, however, implied by Bachelard's account of the historicity of a theory. According to this account, a scientific theory is historical not in the sense that it has grown out of a previous theory like a dragonfly from its nymph. Nor is it historical in the sense that it may have been influenced by earlier theories. Biologistic influentialism, whether of a causal or Bergsonian noncausal kind, is ruled out. Of course the *pastness* of a theory calls for a more or less worked out current theory in the light of which it stands condemned, *dépassée*, even if still conceded a partial truth within the more specific new theory. But one commentator contends that Bachelard must and does maintain also that the present *state* of science is independent of its past.[18] It seems to me that notwithstanding Bachelard's denial of the continuity of the history of science he can and should be taken to be offering an "applied," "surrationalist," and more voluntarist version of Bergson's doctrine that the phases of duration are interpenetrative and interdependent.[19] This reading seems indeed to be required by Bachelard's interactionist theory of scientific sense. It is only a contingent fact if there are no rearguard advocates of an outdated scientific theory around to defend it against the advocates of a theory by which it has been displaced. And if the identity of the new is partly dependent on the identity of the old, may not the converse also be the cast? Whether we say in these circumstances that the rearguard is supporting a theory that is past, over and done with, obsolete, or that their theory is only obsolescent will turn on where we draw the bounds of what is to count as the scientific community and whether that community has to be monolithic. We have noted already that Bachelard is for pluralism. In any case, if he were to take the view that the *cité scientifique* must be agreed on principles and in its language at least, the identity of the theories that prevail within it would still depend on how its citizens *would* react to threats from without, whether or not such threats were made.[20]

3. Science and Surrealism

Bachelard gears concepts to judgments, judgments to prior judgments, and theories to prior theories, the relationships being comparable in some respects to those of the teeth of a cogwheel to the wheel, and of one wheel to others with which it is or could be engaged to perform the tasks the assembly was designed for. Meaning and claims to truth arise in a dialectic of noncontradictory opposition. This dialectic is corrective and retrospective. Since the content of a contemporary scientific theory is a function of the theory it displaces, the present theory is dependent upon the contemporary theory of the earlier theory and therefore, presumably, that earlier theory can be expected in some way to influence the present theory, however strongly one may resist, as Bachelard does, the idea that its influence is that of an efficient cause. It would indeed be strained to describe a theory as an efficient cause. And, according to Bachelard, what is given, as far as the scientist is concerned, is never a *donnée immédiate*; it is always mediated, always a theory. "The moment something is given it is already understood."[21] The given is therefore not a thing-in-itself. For science, modern science at least, the real is the realized. He calls this a noumenon, meaning by this that reason is a prerequisite for its existence, not that it is something behind the phenomena.

So the real is the realized and the realized is the rational. Moreover, the rational is the relational, though Bachelard makes a somewhat hazardous departure from traditional philosophical usage in saying that because all scientific qualities are relational they are *secondary*. Although in its early stages science may picture its data as substantial individuals, in science since Dirac a substance is a family of cases, a coherent plurality whose coherence is plotted in mathematical equations. He coins the word ex-stance to convey this relational character of scientific qualities, which Locke acknowledged in saying that "powers make a great part of our complex ideas of substance."[22]

It is not so much his coining of terms as it is his reckless adaptation of old ones that makes it difficult to say that Bachelard belongs to this or that school. He labels himself with such dadaist abandon that it is impossible to deny he is making a joke at the expense of academic philosophy. He sketches out a case for this dadaism in a chapter of *La Philosophie du non* where epistemological profiles are traced out and a program for an archaeology of philosophical knowledge is presented that is reminiscent of the theories of epochal stratification found in Vico, Saint-Simon, Comte, and Marx. The closest family resemblances, however, are with Hegel and Wittgenstein, particularly in those pages of *Le Rationalisme appliqué* where an epistemological spectrograph is displayed in which pairs of philosophical standpoints are viewed in the light of Bachelard's own scientific epistemology in such a way as to make it look as though each member of the pair collapses into its apparent opposite, so that it has to be concluded, for instance, that realism and idealism are one.[23] No wonder Bachelard can call himself an idealist as well as a realist. But his realism is a second-order realism.[24] First-order, positivist, phenomenalist, or Baconian empirical realism moves from putative observations to general laws. It could never admit concepts like Dirac's negative mass and negative energy. Second-order, idealist, or surrationalist realism begins with "noumenal" rational constructions which are either disconfirmed or confirmed, as happened when Blackett and Occhialini discovered the positive electron. First-order realism is prone to subscribe to the fallacy of simple location and the myth of absolute simplicity. Second-order realism denies that we have a right to speak of the position of an electron unless we can construct a method by which we can actually fix its location.[25] It will also allow us to say that an atom that possesses several electrons is in certain respects simpler than an atom that possesses only one, if the former is a more systematically organized whole than the latter.[26]

Like the comprehensive, critical rationalism of Karl Popper, the surrationalist realism supported by Bachelard exposes itself to the risks of refutation by experience and is most successful when these risks are greatest.[27] It is an applied rationalism the foundation of which is not simply the subject nor simply the object but the project or transaction through time between the object, the subject, that is, the scientist, and the instruments employed by the subject. "Every definition is an experiment; every definition of a concept is a functional one.[28] In so far as the language of modern science is mathematics, this holds also for mathematical definitions. "Parallel lines exist *after*, not *before*, Euclid's postulate."[29] Even so-called pure mathematics cannot be divorced from application;[30] nor a fortiori can the concepts of mathematical physics.[31] Although Bachelard objects vehemently to positivist empiricism, he is no happier with formalism. His objections to the latter, however, are usually cast in such a way as to suggest that the question at issue is the psychological one of whether the mathematician and the scientist will find it difficult to develop their theories in isolation from an application or illustration of them. His objection sometimes seems to be merely that the mathematician needs the help of diagrams or similar intuitive aids and that when a mathematical theory is applied to the physical world it is as though a blood transfusion were being administered to what could already stand on its own feet. This appears to be the burden of his remark that "the mathematics of the new physics is nourished by its application to experience. There is no denying that the psychological persuasiveness of the ideas of Riemannian geometry has been augmented by their employment in the theory of relativity."[32] In these sentences it is the physical application that is said to come to the aid of the mathematical theory. But a few sentences earlier it is the other way about.

> Tensor analysis is the very framework of relativist thought. It is a mathematical instrument which creates contemporary physical science just as the microscope creates microbiology. No new knowledge is possible without the mastery of this new mathematical instrument.

However, whereas the previously quoted sentences seem to be speaking of a contingent empirical connection, here the reverse connection is described as though it were a conceptually necessary one. And there is no reason why Bachelard should not say both, that the application is a psychological and pedagogical aid to the understanding of the theory and that there cannot in principle be a scientific theory that could not be applied. That Bachelard would want to say both of these things is borne out by the following statements. "The extended form of the microphysical object exists after, not before, the method of geometrical discovery."[33] "Tell me how you are to be found and I'll tell you who you are."[34] More explicitly, "What something *is* is defined by method,"[35] "The conditions for applying a concept must be built into its very meaning,"[36] and "A concept becomes scientific in proportion as it becomes technical, ie. acquires a technique for its realisation."[37]

This last quotation demonstrates that Bachelard's stress on the breaks as opposed to the continuities in scientific thinking does not prevent his holding that a concept becomes more scientific as its range of application and testability becomes more articulated. Perhaps, like Wittgenstein, he would let the balance of advantage and disadvantage in each particular case determine whether under these circumstances we should say we have the same concept or a different one. Notwithstanding the words just quoted, it is fairly clear that Bachelard's own penchant would be toward choosing to say that we have a new concept when the technicality of a concept is increased. For him science proper is revolutionary science.[38]

But even revolutionary science must be normal in parts. The dialectic of polemical provocation must, for the time being at least, leave unchallenged the concepts in terms of which it issues its challenge. These are the concepts that define the scientific community, that make testability possible, and that save science from subjectivity. The following passage explains what goes on when the old pictures are challenged and replaced by articulated concepts:

It seems to me in fact that we cannot understand the atom of
modern physics without bearing in mind its pictorial history,
going back to its realist and rationalist prototypes to construct its epistemological profile. A description of the history
of its various schemata is here a pedagogical necessity. Whatever is excised from the picture must find a counterpart in the
corrected concept. I should be happy to say that the atom is
the sum of the criticisms to which its pictorial prototype has
been subjected. Coherent knowledge is a product not of
architectonic reason but of polemical reason. Thanks to its
dialectic and criticisms surrationalism somehow defines a *superobject*. The superobject is the outcome of a critical objectivation, of an objectivity that retains from the object only
what it has criticised. The atom of contemporary microphysics is the superobject par excellence. As against its pictures
the superobject is quite precisely a non-picture. Intuitions
are very useful; they are useful when they are eliminated. In
eliminating primitive pictures scientific thinking discovers its
organic laws. The noumenon is revealed when, one by one,
the principles of the phenomenon are exposed to the dialectic. The schema of the atom proposed by Bohr a quarter of a
century ago proved to be a good picture: nothing whatsoever
of it survives. But it suggested a large enough number of
nons to enable it to continue to play an indispensable role in
introductory classes on contemporary science. Fortunately
these *nons* are coordinated and in fact constitute contemporary microphysics.[39]

The word surrationalism which Bachelard employs in this passage is
obviously a word he has selected with an eye on the word surrealism.
His surrationalism is a surrealism. As was noted earlier, he is willing to
call himself a second-order realist, a realist, that is, for whom, as Sartre
too says with a different sense, the real is realization. But in volume
after volume he criticizes the first-order realist's belief in passively in-
tuitable immediate data, a belief subscribed to by defenders of common
sense like Emile Meyerson.[40] *La Formation de l'esprit scientifique*, subti-
tled *A Contribution to a Psychoanalysis of Our Knowledge of Objects*, is
a sustained examination of this realist mentality and of the pictures that
in the author's opinion have delayed the onset of the new scientific attitude. The generally derisory tone with which in this book Bachelard

conducts his studies in pre-scientific palaeontology[41] raises the question as to how it squares with his view that the history of science is one of envelopment and with the studies undertaken in his series of books on poetry and dreams in which the positively valuable and productive aspects of archetypal images are brought out. Compare, for instance, the reference in *La Formation de l'esprit scientifique* to the regrets over epistemological obstacles created by alchemy with the psalms he sings in praise of alchemy in, say, *L'Air et les songes* with its injunction "Adressons-nous aux alchimistes."[42]

One way of answering these questions would be to recall the distinction made above between the shift from one scientific theory to another and the shift from pre-science to science. Pre-science might be a sort of poetry, and its images would not be open to criticism simply because of their being images. They would be open to criticism if it were pretended that they had scientific validity. But this answer is inadequate. The long passage quoted from *La Philosophie du non* makes it plain that Bachelard is ready to grant that pictures and intuitive schemata have a contribution to make at the beginning of a science. The point is made also in *Le Nouvel esprit scientifique* on behalf of the naive imagery associated with the primitive notion of gravity.[43] Here, too, the picture cedes ground to the idea, an order of succession, incidentally, that is seemingly reversed in a comment on Sartre Bachelard makes in *L'Activité rationaliste de la physique contemporaine.*[44] Sartre had written,

> And we grasp here at its origin and with all its ontological import the antinomy of the continuous and the discontinuous, the feminine and masculine poles of the world, whose dialectic we then see developing right up to quantum theory and wave mechanics.[45]

This elicits the following comment from Bachelard:

> Sometimes when ideas make way for images scientific language acquires a certain facility. Thus quantum chemistry speaks of unmarried electrons and the pairing of electrons of opposite spin. But these images are effective only *after* the ideas are there. Existentialist philosophers on the contrary are inclined to introduce the images *before* the ideas. The minute they talk about matter they sound like belated alchemists.

This is only apparently inconsistent with the passage cited from *La Phil-osophie du non*, since there he says that images precede ideas only at the beginning of modern science, not in it. In both passages he decries the tendency for thinking to become dominated by images taken to be rep-resentations or copies of the way things are. This danger can be miti-gated by varying one's diet of images. He recommends a pedagogy of ambiguity[46] in which the imagery of solid corpuscles, fluids, pastes, and agglomerates are run in harness. This is another regard in which his philosophy of science is surrealist and another link between his works in epistemology and his studies of surrealist poets like Lautréamont.[47]

Bachelard's pedagogy of ambiguity is not merely a discourse on method. It is a salutary exercise to make oneself aware of the limits of an analogy by thinking, for example, of particles in terms of waves and waves in terms of particles.[48] To anyone who protested that, this side of dreaming, these two pictures are incompatible, Bachelard would prob-ably reply that that is one reason why this exercise is valuable. It forces the scientist to "realize" the complementarity, to produce it,[49] in the language of mathematics. This does not mean that the scientist has cut himself off from reality. He has cut himself off only from a pre-scientific prejudice. In doing so he has placed himself in a position from which he can see that, as also Merleau–Ponty tries to show, ambiguity is ontolo-gical. In *Le Nouvel esprit scientifique* he writes of an ontology of complementarity[50] and asserts that "it is not knowledge but reality which bears the mark of ambiguity."[51] Thus, it is not unfair to say that the mathematics emerging in the 1920s and 1930s plays a part in Bache-lard's philosophy of scientific concepts that corresponds to the part play-ed by oneirology in his psychoanalysis of poetic imagery. The latter is a subject that cannot, however, be examined here where our concern is simply to draw attention to one connection between Bachelard's theory of imagery and his theory of knowledge.

When the scientist does use images he must not forget that they are not copies but metaphors to be mixed. (We shall find that this Nietz-schean clashing of metaphors is encouraged too by Derrida, but we shall also find that he is not a friend of the Bachelardian *rupture*.)

"Intuition," Bachelard proclaims, with Bergsonism in view, "should never be a datum. It should always be an illustration."[52] Scientific con-cepts are internally related to application, he says, as Wittgenstein im-plies when he maintains that "what we call 'measuring' is partly deter-mined by a certain constancy in results of measurement."[53] Science must be demythologized. It must ultimately be purged of all imagery, leaving only concepts.

Bergson, who holds that conceptual thinking is spatial thinking and whose philosophical writings exploit imagery, would object that concepts are more likely than images to make scientific thinking rigid. Bachelard's reply to this objection would no doubt be that it should not be supposed that scientific concepts mark time, and anyone who supposes they do is probably confusing concepts with images. To this reply it must be objected that it does not show that there are not nonscientific concepts that lead to spatial thinking. This reply and, more generally, the arguments and illustrations reviewed in this chapter show that Bachelard's criteria of teachability[54] and applicability are criteria not for a concept's being a concept but for its being a scientific one. He is making a contribution to the philosophy of science, what the French call *épistémologie*, which is only a part of the study English-speaking philosophers call epistemology or theory of knowledge. This brings out another respect in which Bachelard's work is closer to Karl Popper's interest in demarcating what is scientific than to the logical positivists' preoccupation with demarcating what is meaningful.

Another claim that the arguments and illustrations reviewed in this chapter have not been able to show is that scientific concepts can be severed from pre-science as cleanly as Bachelard often implies. If, as he says, a scientific concept is the sum of the criticisms to which its pre-scientific pictorial prototype has been subjected, the pre-scientific prototype survives as the ghostly presence that is exorcised by the scientific concept and remains part of its content. Why should we distinguish in this respect the transition from one scientific theory to another and the transition to science from nonscience, even if what counts as science or *episteme* will differ from one epoch or community to another?

This brings us back again to the notion of hermeneutic circularity. We investigate and illustrate this in part two. There the topic of application will be resumed. Also resumed there will be the question of the relation between the scientific and what may be called the poietic. This question regarding the connection between the poetry and the prose of the world leads into part three, where the idea of the clean break we have been considering in this chapter is exposed to further tests.

PART TWO
THE HERMENEUTIC CIRCLE

CHAPTER SIX
GADAMER: PHILOSOPHICAL HERMENEUTICS

*Um sich zu verstehen, muss man sich in einem andren Sinn
sich verstanden haben.*

—Wilhelm von Humboldt

1. *Understanding, interpretation, and application*

At the end of chapter 5 it was asserted that Bachelard does not justify
the claim that scientific superconcepts and superobjects can be cut off
cleanly from what is pre-scientific. The later work of Husserl, the work
of Hegel, and, above all, the work of Heidegger lie behind the objection
to this claim implied in the philosophical hermeneutics of Hans-Georg
Gadamer. It has to be said that this objection is usually only implied in
his writings, since, unlike Bachelard, who is primarily concerned with
the natural sciences, Gadamer is primarily concerned with the human
sciences, the *Geisteswissenschaften*. Nevertheless, as we shall note in the
final section of this chapter, Gadamer maintains that his principal theses
hold of any form of understanding. What he has to say will hold therefore for the natural sciences if it can be shown that the understanding
presupposed by the human sciences is presupposed by the natural sciences too. One attempt to show this is made by Heidegger. Gadamer's
philosophical hermeneutics is avowedly inspired by Heidegger, in particular by Heidegger's doctrines regarding language, his doctrine that all
understanding comes into its own in interpretation,[1] and his doctrine
that interpretation is based on fore-having or pre-possession, fore-sight
and pre-conception. Gadamer directs his attention toward showing that
however this infrastructure may be articulated, understanding is
achieved because of it, not in spite of it. A convenient way of bringing
out why Gadamer says this is to examine his response to the highly

critical discussions of his hermeneutic theory published by E. D. Hirsch and Emilio Betti.[2]

Hirsch and Betti take Gadamer to task for refusing to go along with the separation of understanding, interpretation, and application made for centuries by Protestant practitioners of exegetic hermeneutics. For Gadamer this trinity is a tri-unity. His grounds for affirming this internal relatedness begin to come clear as soon as it is realized that he is not proposing an alternative methodology for practitioners of textual or any other kind of hermeneutic science. His aim is not to provide a method but to describe the structure of understanding, whatever method is used for reaching it. It is to make as plain as possible the nature of truth. The truth about truth is that it is inseparable from beings that have understanding, and the truth about understanding is that it is inseparable from interpretation and application. "All understanding [*Verstehen*] is interpretation [*Auslegen*]" (350 [366]).[3] "Understanding includes always an element of application [*Applikation*]" (364 [381]).

To take first the case of application, it seems obviously false to say that there cannot be understanding without it. It seems so to Betti. For is there not a world of difference between the historiographer's interest in establishing what happened in history and the interest of, for example, the statesman in applying its lessons? And is there not a clear distinction to be drawn between the theoretical discipline of the legal historian and the practical purpose of judges whose task is to decide whether and how a law that may be of long standing is to be applied in the courts today? Gadamer admits this difference between the aims of the judge and the aims of the historian. But he contends that if the latter is to understand the law he is studying, he "will have to understand the development from the original application [*Anwendung*] to the present application of the law" (290 [308]). It is plausible to say that in applying a law the judge had better take into account transformations it has undergone since it was first promulgated. But is it plausible to say that the legal historian studying the origins of that law should not ignore the application of its descendent to circumstances now? Gadamer believes it is, since the legal historian will not understand the original meaning of the legal text unless he is conscious of the way it differs from "the legal meaning which he automatically accepts now in the present" ("demjenigen Rechtsgehalt ..., in dessen Vorverständnis er als Gegenwärtiger lebt," 292 [310]).

Suppose we could agree that this holds for a historian investigating an ancestor of a law that obtains in his own society. Does Gadamer believe it holds also for a citizen of the German Federal Republic examining any law of any more or less exotic society like Sumer or Judea? He does. In both kinds of circumstances understanding is possible, he claims, only if the historian is conscious of the difference between his point of view and that of the society whose law he is studying. The need for this self-consciousness is not, however, in order that the historian may detach himself from his own preconceptions so that he can identify more objectively the intentions of the original legislator or identify himself with the persons to whom the original law was addressed. Savigny's faith in the possibility of this identification, maintains Gadamer, is as misconceived as Schleiermacher's faith that an interpreter can identify himself with an original reader or with the author. Schleiermacher sees the identification with the original reader as a means to the identification with the author. The interpreter must "put himself on the same level" as the reader by, for example, deepening his knowledge of the language and customs of the reader's time. This will give the interpreter a base from which to reach an understanding of the author. This hermeneutic access to the author will be facilitated by sympathy made possible by the fact that, as Schleiermacher expresses it in words that Gadamer quotes (166 [177]), "everyone carries a tiny bit of everyone else within himself, so that divination is stimulated by comparison with oneself." The art of hermeneutics is thus comparative, but it must also be divinatory if the interpreter is to understand those bits that he does not share with the author, bits that may be very large and very strange if the author is Sophocles or Shakespeare.

Among the difficulties Gadamer has with Schleiermacher's theory of the art of hermeneutics is that of identifying the addressed reader with whom the interpreter is to try to identify himself. Does that reader have to be an exact contemporary of the author? Can it be someone reading the book a year after it is written? Ten years after? If Schleiermacher's answer is that the original readership is the one the author intended, will it be possible to understand anonymous works or works by authors who had no thoughts about who might be reading them? Only, says Gadamer, if identification with an original readership is not made a necessary condition for understanding. But in any case to fall back on the intentions of the author either as a necessary condition for understanding or as a means to identifying the original readership is to expose oneself to at least some of the objections that are made by Gadamer and others against the idea that to understand a work is to understand what the author intended, an idea that Hirsch shares with Schleiermacher. The objection most commonly made to this idea is that the author often does not understand what he is doing, or he may have conflicting views about what he is driving at. Frequently he will be at a loss for words when asked to explain what he is aiming to do. But this last fact is not enough to show that the author's intentions cannot be the key to understanding the text. A capacity to create does not necessarily carry with it a capacity to put into words how the work created is to be understood. This is obviously so with nonliterary works. The best an author or other artist may be able to do when asked to explain what he intends is to tell us to read, look at, or listen to it again. This is especially so where the product is such that it is odd to ask how it is to be understood. Witness the puzzlement of Wittgenstein's readers upon coming across his remarks about understanding a theme in music, for instance in *Philosophical Investigations* 527[4]—though I am assured that *verstehen eines Themas in der Musik* does not sound too intellectual or otherwise odd to a German ear. And it evidently does not sound odd to Gadamer's German ear, unless the quotation marks betray discomfort when, referring specifically to music, he insists that "All reproduction is primarily interpretation and seeks, as such, to be correct. In this sense it, too, is 'understanding'" (xix [XIX]). But where we have no qualms about speaking of understanding a work of art, a legal text, sacred Scripture, or other historical document, discovering the author's intentions will not ensure that we have understood what he has produced; for, as with any action, intentions are frequently not fulfilled. This does not, however, show that discovery of the author's intention is not a necessary but insufficient condition for understanding the product. Nor are any of the other arguments mentioned so far conclusive against this view. Schleiermacher himself would agree not only with Paul Valéry that the author has no privilege as an interpreter of his own work; he would agree with Gadamer that in a sense (to be distinguished below) the author is in a worse position than others.

Schleiermacher and Gadamer also agree that the process of interpretation is a circular one calling for a movement from part to whole and back to the part. The paradigm for this hermeneutical circle or, better, helix is the understanding of a sentence. This requires an understanding of individual words which requires an understanding of the sentence which requires an understanding of the paragraph which requires an understanding of individual sentences which requires an understanding of the language and social practices with which it is interwoven.

Before going on to mention a third aspect of agreement between

Schleiermacher and Gadamer it deserves to be noted that Gadamer's doctrine of the inseparability of understanding and application implies this connectedness of language and praxis. Hence his approving references to Wittgenstein. Hence also Habermas's approving references to Gadamer, in spite of the disapproving references to be considered later in this chapter. But Habermas is mistaken when he says (discussing Dilthey) that it is this connectedness of language and the practical social context of life that saves the hermeneutic circle from being a vicious one.[5] For even if we could isolate language from that practical context, the understanding of a bit of it would be dependent on the understanding of other bits of it, and vice versa, without this circularity within the putatively pure extruded language being vicious. This is because coming to understand a text is a process of temporally progressive feedback. I understand the first word in a sentence in the light of an expectation regarding what kind of word will follow, and likewise for the words that do follow. But my expectations are not always fulfilled, and they are usually fairly general. By the time I have reached the full stop or the end of the paragraph, hitherto possible meanings of preceding words have been excluded. Yet later sentences or paragraphs may have surprises in store for me that will call for a revision in my understanding of the text so far. This is why the so-called hermeneutical circle is really a spiral or zigzag.

A third side of Schleiermacher's hermeneutics that Gadamer welcomes is its intolerance of the assumption made by hermeneutic theorists of the Enlightenment that understanding is the norm, hermeneutic skills being called for only when there is some special impediment to understanding. Schleiermacher holds that the norm is misunderstanding occasioned by common linguistic and other cultural variations.

It is important to be clear about the limitation upon the range that Gadamer allows to the principle that the interpreter has greater authority than the author. He is simply saying that mastery of a technique does not presuppose or imply mastery of the technique of describing that technique. I can be good at doing something but bad at telling others how it is done. He is not maintaining that the interpreter has in comparison with the author a privileged access to the meaning or significance of the text or work of art itself. This would not only be paradoxical in the sense that it would suggest a critic would be a greater genius than the genius whose work he was interpreting; it might also suggest something Gadamer takes pains to deny, namely, that there is a definite meaning contained in a work, as an ingot of gold is hidden at the bottom of a

lake. From this picture it would be natural to infer that just as the con-
tours of the ingot would be discerned best by someone who actually
touched it and thus escaped the distorting influence of the water through
which it was seen, so direct access to the real meaning of the work could
be had only by canceling out the bias arising from the interpreter's preconceptions. This is precisely the Enlightenment realism that Gadamer
rejects. But he wants to reject it without swinging to the extreme of
Romantic relativism represented by Herder and von Humboldt or the
permissiveness of the belief that the meaning of a work of art is whatever the interpreter attributes to it. His attempt to achieve this middle
way hinges on the thesis that the interpreter's preconceptions cannot be
excluded from the hermeneutic circle and should be regarded not as
barriers but as springboards to understanding.

2. *Operatively historical consciousness*

It is a little shocking to say that a person acquires understanding by
way of his preconceptions rather than in spite of them. And it is more
shocking if, instead of "preconceptions," the word prejudices is used to
translate Gadamer's *Vorurteile*. The shock is diminished when one recognizes that, like Burke when he speaks of "just prejudices,"[6] Gadamer
is speaking of prejudgments. Is he saying no more then than that if you
are to understand a text or a work of art you must set out from where
you are? There is more to Gadamer's thesis than that, as is appreciated
once it is seen as a response to the notions that understanding demands
the dropping of all presuppositions and the adoption of a neutral point
of view from which the work is contemplated *sub specie aeternitatis*, or
of a nonneutral point of view from which the work is contemplated *sub
specie auctoris*. Our prejudgments are not prejudicial to our understanding, according to Gadamer. Not only is it impossible to discount them,
since we are inevitably finite, children though not prisoners of our place
and time, our prejudgments have a positive part to play in facilitating
our understanding.

The positive aid that our prejudgments furnish toward the understanding of a work produced even in a remote time or place is explained
partly by the fact that it is through them that we are agents in history and
inheritors of a tradition. Gadamer's concept of operative history, *Wirkungsgeschichte*, is related to objective historiography somewhat as
Aristotle's concept of practical wisdom is related to his concept of con-
templative wisdom and as Heidegger's readiness to hand is related to

presence at hand.[7] Practical wisdom is not a capacity to apply rules mechanically. It connotes sensitivity to nuances, imagination, discrimination, judgment. So, too, with what Gadamer calls prejudgments. They are our links with a tradition. But a tradition is not something that ties us down. It is something we carry forward in a modified form. Hence, although Gadamer describes his project in *Truth and Method* as an attempt to improve the image of traditionalism, this attempt does not take the shape of a defense of antiquarianism. He is not a slavish preservationist but, to employ an ugly word for a beautiful idea, a rehabilitationist. This way of describing him has its dangers, however, since it makes it look as though he is prescribing a methodology, as were most hermeneutic theorists until Heidegger. In fact, following Heidegger, he holds that he is engaged in descriptive ontology. According to this description, understanding is the advent (*Geschehen*) of a new horizon through a fusion of the horizons of a historically (*geschichtlich*) situated interpreter and a historically situated text. So, Gadamer infers, "Not only occasionally, but always, the meaning of a text goes beyond its author. That is why the occurrence of understanding is productive, not merely reproductive ... we understand *differently if we understand at all*" (264–280).

Some of Gadamer's readers have been alarmed by these claims. Hirsch considers them vulnerable to the charge Gadamer himself levels at the theory that the meaning of a work of art is whatever the interpreter attributes to it (85 [90]). How can Gadamer escape a hermeneutic free-for-all unless he can admit a standard against which proferred interpretations can be checked? What standard can he admit? He has excluded the idea of a fixed meaning in itself, whether that be a fixed meaning intended by the author, a fixed meaning imposed by an independently authorized interpreter, or a fixed meaning somehow demanded by the text itself. There are no fixed meanings, because anything that means anything means it for someone, and everyone is a child of his time, that is, his horizon of prejudices is different from that of his predecessors; he is, as Heidegger puts it, *geschicklich*, party to a historical dispensation.

Would not Gadamer have been more consistent therefore if he had said that there is no room for truth—or untruth—in interpretation? His belief that there is requires him to allow that although prejudices are a necessary foundation for understanding, some prejudices are conducive to misunderstanding. And he does allow this. He not only allows but stresses that the fusion of horizons, like travel, changes my horizons and that some of my prejudices fall by the wayside. However, that they do, it may be said, does not suffice to show that those that do not survive are less valid and less suited to serve as a foundation for valid interpretations. Rather, as when we say of biological evolution that the fittest survive we say no more than that those that survive are most fit to survive, "fittest" having normative force only if it is introduced by way of a goal, so when Gadamer sorts out interpretations and their grounding prejudices into valid and invalid he can be making a normative distinction only if the classification is made in the light of a *telos*. Surely, failing such an independent *telos*, his remarks about validity of interpretation can be construed only as references to the fact that some interpretations survive and others do not. We cannot even say of the survivors that their mettle has been tested, since the notion of testing is empty unless associated with that of a standard in comparison with which some may pass and some may fail. So far no such standard or *telos* has emerged from our examination of Gadamer's theory of hermeneutics apart from the standards implicit in the particular prejudices of particular interpreters. But they, Gadamer himself says, offer no exit from hermeneutical relativism or nihilism.

Is this entirely true? Can there not be at least a grading of alternative interpretations within the horizon of each individual interpreter? Unless there can it is difficult to understand what can be meant by saying he has prejudices or preconceptions, for to talk of these is to talk of what determines in part a person's beliefs about what is true or false and good or bad. It will be objected that this intrapersonal criticism permits only a subjectively objective validation and that relativism is avoided only if interpersonally objective criticism and validation is possible. One way of trying to ensure the latter would be to invoke an unsituated perspectiveless or omniperspectived neutral observer, a step Gadamer cannot take without denying the principle of the finitude and historicity of man, which is as central in his hermeneutics as it is in Heidegger's.

Habermas has difficulty in seeing how hermeneutics can avoid arbitrariness unless it is embraced within something like a Hegelian theory of the absolute movement of reflection.[8] Wolfhart Pannenberg is ready to accept Gadamer's objection to a Hegelian teleology of infinite spirit, but suggests that Gadamer overlooks a teleology that is not vulnerable to this objection. Instead of the Hegelian eschatology, which according to Gadamer and Pannenberg denies man's irreducible finitude, there is an eschatology revealed by the message of Jesus in terms of which "the end of history can ... be understood as something which is itself only *provisionally* known" and the finitude of human experience is pre-served.[9] Should Gadamer reply that this suggestion of Pannenberg's begs the hermeneutic question in that it assumes we have already established the authority of the message of Jesus? Toward the end of this chapter a passage will be cited in which Gadamer himself makes this suggestion. Although he is not in my opinion therefore guilty of arguing in a vicious circle, his position is made more vulnerable by this move. So it is fortunate for our present purposes that, instead of relying on agreement with Pannenberg, Gadamer can rely on his agreement with Heidegger in finding a role for *Mitsein*, public conventions including those of everyday language. Do not these embody standards that enable interpersonal criticism? They obviously do, so whatever difficulty there may be in explaining how such criticism can be possible between subscribers to different traditions, Gadamer should apparently have no special difficulty in explaining how such criticism can take place between subscribers to the same tradition. Hirsch maintains that Gadamer should have a difficulty here. Hirsch's argument is that the solidarity of a tradition is never so dense as to require that there be no difference of outlook between adherents to it. This difference among contemporaries is in principle the same kind of difference that holds between adherents to historically separated traditions. Hence, Hirsch argues, since Gadamer rules out understanding between the latter, he should rule it out between the former; but he does not. Against this argument it must be pointed out that Gadamer does not exclude understanding between people of historically separated traditions. What he does is offer an account of this understanding as a corrective to the account that leads either to the extreme of naive realistic repetitionism (the copy theory of historical knowledge) or to the extreme of Romantic radical historicism. Against the latter Gadamer contends that we can understand texts, events, artifacts, and people of distant times and places, but this understanding is always self-understanding, therefore never mere replication such as Schleiermacher and Dilthey envisaged.

Hirsch's impression that Gadamer is advocating historicism may be explained by his overlooking Gadamer's assertions that traditions are porous and that

> there is no more an isolated horizon of the present than there are historical horizons to which access has to be won. Rather, understanding is always the fusion of those allegedly independent horizons. . . . Under the sway of tradition such fusion

is continually going on. For there old and new continually grow together to make something of living value, without either being explicitly distinguished from the other. (273 [289])

Hirsch thinks there must first be an explicit distinguishing of one horizon from another if they are to be combined to make interpretation possible. He asks,

How can an interpreter fuse two perspectives—his own and that of the text—unless he has somehow appropriated the original perspective and amalgamated it with his own? How can a fusion take place unless the things to be fused are made actual, which is to say, unless the original sense of the text has been understood? (254)

Gadamer's reply to this is implicit in his statement that in conversation with someone

the thing that has to be grasped is the objective rightness or otherwise of his opinion, so that they can agree with each other on the subject. Thus one does not relate the other's opinion to him, but to one's own views. Where a person is concerned with the other as a case, e.g., in a therapeutical conversation or the examination of a man accused of a crime, this is not really a situation in which two people are trying to understand each other. (347 [363])

And, Gadamer adds, the relation of an interpreter to a text is very similar to the relation between participants in a conversation. Hence Gadamer's reply to the move Habermas makes to reduce the scope of the former's hermeneutic theory. Habermas argues that there are limits to hermeneutic understanding because this occurs within ordinary language and there are forms of life prior to and inexpressible in ordinary language, for example the self-deceptive strategems exposed by psychoanalysis and the false ideological consciousness from which we can be emancipated, he maintains, only by special critical techniques. Gadamer goes some way toward forestalling this objection when he observes that a therapeutical situation is commonly not one in which patient and therapist are primarily concerned to understand each other.

In claiming universality for his hermeneutic theory Gadamer is claiming that it applies to all human understanding, not that it applies to all human experience. His position vis à vis Habermas would have been made clearer if he had distinguished understanding as the name for a state of epistemic success from epistemically neutral understanding and arriving at such an understanding. It may well be that the special scientific techniques Habermas invokes are a prerequisite for correct understanding. But even the mystified consciousness has an understanding of itself and its situation. And to understanding in that nonepistemic sense Gadamer's hermeneutic theory may well still apply without this entailing the unacceptability of what Habermas gives as an account of the preconditions of demystified understanding in the epistemic sense. And because Habermasian demystified understanding will presuppose the conventions of the particular sciences thanks to which it is achieved, Gadamer's description will apply to it.

Gadamer's belief that the original sense cannot be replicated arises, Hirsch further suggests, from a failure to take seriously enough the difference between the significance or meaning of a text for us today, which changes, and the meaning of the text, which does not change but "being reproducible, . . . is the same whenever and wherever it is understood by another" (255). David E. Linge does not see how this distinction can explain the fact that there has been so much disagreement throughout the history of biblical interpretation. In his introduction to a collection of essays by Gadamer he writes: "Interpreters of Paul, for instance, have not been arguing all these centuries only over what Paul "means" *pro nobis*, but also over the claim Paul makes regarding the subject matter."[10] This misses what I take Hirsch to intend by "meaning for us today." Professor X is not going to disagree, *qua* biblical exegete, with Professor Y about what a Pauline text means for him, Professor X. But there is no reason why they should not disagree in that capacity about what the text means for the recipients of Paul's Epistles, about what the text meant *pro eis*. Moreover, Hirsch would obviously reply to Linge that the multiplicity of interpretations is explained by the complexity of the linguistic and empirical questions that have to be answered before a correct interpretation can be given. But this notion of correctness, and the notion of correspondence or adequacy associated with it, is as anathema to Linge as it is to Gadamer, Heidegger, and Hegel in contexts of this kind: "It denies the role of our own hermeneutical situation and thus exhibits a neglect of the reflexive dimension of understanding that Gadamer has shown to be operative in understanding."[11]

Although this simply begs the question against Hirsch, it suggests a way of resolving the disagreement between him and Gadamer. For it may be that what Gadamer says fits "inspired" texts like the Epistles of Paul and maybe at least some of the dialogues of Plato, but does it fit Aristotle? And would it do as an account of the interpretation of "The cat sat on the mat"? Perhaps we understand this sentence without interpretation. Gadamer could not grant this, however, without abandoning his doctrine of the triunity of understanding, interpretation, and application. On the face of it he does abandon that doctrine when he writes, "Interpretation is necessary when the meaning of a text cannot be immediately understood" (301 [319]), since this remark implies that with some texts understanding is possible without interpretation. Would not "The cat sat on the mat" be a good example of such a text, and would not Hirsch's analysis of understanding fit this better than Gadamer's? Has not Gadamer been led to exaggerate the extent to which understanding tolerates the analysis that may well be appropriate in the context of theology? This context is the cradle of modern hermeneutics, and many of Gadamer's illustrations are drawn from it. Not all inspired texts are as gnomic and enigmatic as pronouncements of the Delphic oracle, nor are they necessarily parabolic, but the understanding of them typically cries out for interpretation, and, since they are often taken to be relevant for all time, the issue of their applicability to a particular time and place is as relevant as is the issue of the applicability of a law to a particular time and case. But Gadamer sees it as his task to use theological and legal hermeneutics as the key to hermeneutics in human studies in general. Thus, when he maintains that hermeneutic understanding is inseparable from application, he is saying, to return to our recent example, that the biblical exegete interpreting a text must ask himself not only what the cognitive content of the text was for Paul's Roman *destinataires* and/or what its cognitive content is for the exegete himself; it requires also that the exegete ask what the normative force of the message is for himself. The so-called cognitive meaning of any subject matter is for the hermeneutic sciences a function of its normative significance (274–78 [290–95]). It is not possible to separate, as Betti thinks it is, cognitive, normative, and merely reproductive interpretation. If, with outlandish historical and anthropological cases in mind, it were objected that there seems sometimes to be no normative significance for us in the text or myth under investigation, Gadamer might reply either that in that case we shall fail to reach an understanding or that we shall have to exercise our imaginations further until we can envisage a normative correlative that speaks to our own situation. This would not be capitulation to the doctrine of empathy advocated by earlier hermeneutic theories, for we should not be exercising our imagination in order to achieve a replacement of our horizon of experience by the horizon of the originators of the text or other artifact we are trying to understand.

A caveat must be entered. In saying that Gadamer's paradigm of interpretation is the interpretation of sacred writ, it is not implied that a valid interpretation can be given only by a believer. Gadamer himself observes, "Only the person who allows himself to be addressed— whether he believes or whether he doubts—understands. Hence the primary thing is application" (297 [315]). And he does not regard this as a feature peculiar to theological hermeneutics.

> We can, then, bring out as what is truly common to all forms of hermeneutics the fact that the sense to be understood finds its concrete and perfect form only in interpretation, but that this interpretative work is wholly committed to the meaning of the text. Neither jurist nor theologian regards the work of application as making free with the text.

Gadamer here reaffirms the triunity of understanding, interpretation, and application. But is he saying anything more than that a good interpreter must be a good listener? That would be a disappointingly trite conclusion to draw after three hundred pages. However, the remaining one hundred fifty aim to show that what has to be listened to is language. This doctrine will be considered in the next section. The present section concludes by considering and offering a reply to one further objection that might be made to Gadamer's doctrine of hermeneutic triunity.

In a passage that is important for the light it casts on the relation between interpretation and operatively historical consciousness Gadamer writes:

> The intimate unity of the processes of understanding and interpretation is confirmed by the fact that the interpretation that reveals the implications of a text's meaning and expresses it in language seems, when compared with the given text, to be a new creation, but yet does not maintain any proper existence apart from the understanding process ... the inter-

pretative concepts are cancelled out in the fullness of understanding because they are meant to disappear. This means
that they are not just tools that we take up and then throw
aside after using them, but that they belong to the inner
structure of the thing (which is meaning). What is true of
every word in which thought is expressed is also true of the
interpreting word, namely that it is not, as such, objective.
As the realisation of the act of understanding it is the actuality of operatively historical consciousness, and as such it is
truly speculative: having no tangible being of its own and yet
throwing back the image that is presented to it. (430–31
[449])

The interpretation is sacrificed and resurrected, *aufgehoben*, in a new
understanding. Interpretation is mediatory intercession. As Gadamer
goes on to say: "Compared with the immediacy of communication between people or the word of a poet, the language of the interpreter is
undoubtedly a secondary phenomenon." Interpretation, *hermeneusis*,
like Hermes, is a mediator. And that, as I have more than once observed, is what we ordinarily take interpretation to be. Although a verbal interpretation of a story or painting gets absorbed into our understanding of the story or the painting as soon as it is accepted or tried for
fit, it begins by having an existence of its own. This is especially so where
there are competing and incompatible interpretations, as frequently
happens with what we may call professional interpretation. But if we
think of interpretation in that sense, it becomes difficult to see how
Gadamer's doctrine of triunity can be valid for commonplace remarks
and truisms that we seem to understand without any interpretative
mediation. It also becomes difficult to see how it can be valid for our
own pre-understanding, our understanding of our own preconceptions
or prejudgments. We could understand them only if we had first become
reflectively conscious of them so that we could see them in terms of a
proposed interpretation. It might be argued that we should escape this
implication by accepting the paradox that we do not understand our
pre-understanding. This argument might be strengthened by noting how
difficult it is to become aware of one's own preconceptions, let alone to
understand them. But even if we accept this argument, we are still faced
with the task of explaining how we can understand an interpretation on
Gadamer's view if all understanding calls for an interpretation. For the
understanding of a particular interpretation will have to be mediated by

another interpretation, and that by another, and so on.

If Gadamer's view that understanding is inseparable from interpretation is valid, he cannot mean that an interpretation always begins by being apart from the text to be interpreted, even if it then gets absorbed into the understanding of the text. He must allow that interpretation sometimes begins by being integral with our understanding. It is very easy to suppose that he does not allow this, because so much of the time he is writing about what I have called professional interpretation, as were all those previous hermeneutic theorists who were preoccupied with understanding in such fields as biblical exegesis, historiography, law, anthropology, and the arts. For interpretation in this sense Heidegger's German word is *Interpretation*. For this the translators of *Being and Time* give "Interpretation" with an upper-case initial. When they write this word with a lower-case initial it usually translates *Auslegung*, which can also mean "explanation." Professional interpretation is, to use Heidegger's term, apophantic or explicitly assertoric. But the apophantic "as" of assertion, Heidegger maintains, is founded ontologically on the existential-hermeneutical "as" of circumspective concern.[12] Just as we understand the use of a hammer without first understanding a rule for its use, so we can speak before we understand how to. The forestructures of the understanding and interpretation of explicit discourse (*Rede*) are founded on the forestructures of the understanding, interpretation, and discourse implicit in our circumspectively concernful modes of operating in the world. What Gadamer says about operatively historical consciousness is an endorsement of this teaching of Heidegger's on the hermeneutic circle of understanding. And the unclarity there is in it and in what Gadamer says about the linguisticality of understanding may well derive from unclarities in Heidegger, for example in what Heidegger says about discourse.

Discourse, Heidegger says at one point, is the articulation of intelligibility.[13] This could lead one to suppose that discourse is related to understanding as clenching or unclenching one's fist is related to the bone structure of one's hand. But Heidegger says that because discourse is the articulation of intelligibility it underlies both interpretation and assertion. So discourse must be, or must also be, the equivalent of the hand's structure. Just as we can articulate the hand because of its articulations, so we can make assertions because of the implicit structure of the understanding with which it is equiprimordial. Discourse is articulation according to significations, but significations need not be expressed in words. Words are added unto them. "Den Bedeutungen wachsen

Worte zu." *Rede* in *Being and Time* is *logos*, which can be either spelled out or implicit. Implicit *Rede* is the structure of circumspective concern and of operatively historical consciousness.

3. *Language and validity*

Language has to be listened to because language is the house of being.[14] In returning to this doctrine we are returning to the problem of validation raised in section 2. There that problem was shown to be acute for Gadamer since he seemed to be rejecting the standard favored by Schleiermacher, Dilthey, and Hirsch without offering an alternative to it. This rejected standard is one that calls for a correspondence between an interpretation and the intentions of the author of the text or other work that is being interpreted. In terms of this account of interpretation, interpretation is retrospective. With the rejection of this account it becomes natural to ask whether Gadamer wishes to substitute one according to which interpretation is prospective.

One possible alternative that comes to mind is that proposed by Hegel. Whereas the standard by which the validity of interpretation is judged on the retrospective theory is centered on the intention or achievement of a particular person, the standard on the Hegelian account transcends any individual person and resides, in the last analysis, in supraindividual absolute spirit where all otherness is overcome; or, rather, resides in the last synthesis, for the progress to that ultimate culmination is through a conceptual dialectic of cancellation and reintegration. Until the journey is completed, or unless the journey is in some way already completed, it is difficult to see how this teleology could be employed to test the validity of interpretations. This is Hegel's problem. Is it a problem also for Gadamer?

Notwithstanding his assent to many things that Hegel says, Gadamer's path finally takes him closer to Heidegger. Neither Gadamer nor Heidegger can accept the Hegelian absolute. And neither sees how hermeneutics can be confined within the limits of a dialectic of concepts.

It is Heidegger who goes more deeply into the grounds for challenging the tenability of Hegel's optimistic faith in the sublation of man's finitude. But it is wrong to say, as Hirsch does, that Gadamer simply accepts the thesis of man's finitude on Heidegger's authority. For what is Gadamer's own exploration of prejudice and situation if not confirmation of the thesis of finitude and a demonstration that in principle there is no truth that is free of untruth, no light that casts no shadow? Not that

Gadamer's version of this Augustinianism should be described as pessimistic in contrast with Hegelianism:

> The fact that the text to be understood speaks into a situation that is determined by previous opinions ... is not a regrettable distortion that affects the purity of understanding, but the condition of its possibility, which we have characterised as the hermeneutical situation.... The apparently thetic beginning of interpretation is, in fact, a response and, like every response, the sense of an interpretation is determined by the question asked. Thus, the dialectic of question and answer always precedes the dialectic of interpretation. (429 [447])[15]

Interpretation is a response to questions put not solely by the interpreting subject to an object, the text, as the Baconian inquisitional theory of interpretation assumes. It is a response to questions raised by the subject matter of the text.

This brings us to the second of the two issues mentioned on which Gadamer and Heidegger diverge from Hegel. Hegel's dialectic is reflective and presents "the truth" of what he calls the speculative. But this distinction between the speculative and the dialectical disappears at the level of absolute knowledge (425 [443]). That Gadamer must reject this doctrine of absolute knowledge follows from his acceptance of the principle of human finitude. Hegel is too "Greek" for Heidegger. Likewise for Gadamer. He sees in Hegel's dialectic too great a willingness to adopt Plato's treatment of *apophansis*, "assertion," as the key to the workings of language. It is not surprising that he welcomes the corrective embodied in the work of John Austin and his German counterpart Hans Lipps.[16]

It is surprising that the retrospective hermeneutics of Schleiermacher should be not so widely different in some respects from the prospective hermeneutics implicit in Hegel. As Gadamer observes, "Because of his doctrine of the divinatory perfection of the understanding Schleiermacher came close to Hegel." Against both of these types of hermeneutic theory Gadamer holds that:

> if we start from the linguistic nature of understanding, we are emphasising, on the contrary, the finiteness of the linguistic event, in which understanding is constantly concretised. The

language that things have—of whatever kind the things may be—is not the *logos ousias*, and it does not attain its perfect form in the self-contemplation of an infinite intellect, but it is the language that our finite, historical nature apprehends. This is true of the language of the texts that are handed down to us in tradition, and that is why it was necessary to have a truly historical hermeneutics. It is as true of the experience of art as of the experience of history. (433 [451])

As he puts it at the end of his paper on "The Idea of Hegel's Logic," in sentences that reveal how strongly opposed Gadamer's theory of hermeneutics is to Bachelard's theory of the hermetic isolation of the scientific from the pre-scientific,

The linguisticality of all thought continues to demand that thought, moving in the opposite direction, convert the concept back into the communicative [*verbindende*] word. The more radically objectifying thought reflects upon itself and unfolds the experience of dialectic, the more clearly it points to what it is not. Dialectic must retrieve itself in hermeneutics.[17]

But, to return to the problem raised earlier, what standard of validity does Gadamer's theory of hermeneutics propose to replace those of the retrospective and the prospective theories he condemns? Some light can be cast on this problem if we make a distinction between hermeneutic standards, hermeneutic criteria, and hermeneutic canons. Let the term "criterion" be used of a characteristic that serves as a mark by which an interpreter can recognize the good from the bad or the true from the untrue. The retrospective account of interpretation might claim to provide a criterion, but the decision whether or not the criterion is present will often call for the use of various methodological canons of the sort familiar from the arts and sciences of exegesis and establishment of texts. The more or less scientific canons may need supplementing by empathetic projection and cultivated guesswork. To give what we are calling a standard is to give only a general description (e.g., "adequacy," "correspondence," "coherence") of the circumstances under which truth or understanding would be reached whether or not there is a test by which to discover if the circumstances hold. Retrospective hermeneutics of the kinds referred to above and dominated by the ideals of

Ranke presume to furnish criteria as well as standards. Hegelian prospective hermeneutics furnishes a finite understanding with a standard only. Gadamer's hermeneutics appears to give neither. What about hermeneutic canons?

The title of Gadamer's book could not have been *Against Method*. For the contents of it make it clear that the author is not wishing to recommend discarding all the canons of methodological hermeneutics. He is merely wanting to put them in their place within the context of a descriptive philosophy of universal hermeneutics. They are provided for. But, deprived of standards and criteria, are they not deprived of an architectonic, like a bag of tools in search of a job specification, a purposefulness without purpose? It must be borne in mind that when Kant employed this last phrase of the work of art, his paradigm of understanding was the conceptual understanding represented by natural science. This is the paradigm that still held sway among the neo-Kantians whom Heidegger, Bultmann, and Gadamer were conspiring to depose in the Marburg of the 1920s. As we have seen, Gadamer finds even the Hegelian alternative unsatisfactory. As we have also seen, however, he does not reject its pretensions altogether. He rejects the Hegelian dialectical teleology. But he does not reject every sort of teleology or every sort of dialectic, for "where there is no question of the setting of goals and the choosing of means, as in all living relationships, they can be conceived only within the concept of finality, as the mutual harmony of all the parts with one another" (417 [437]). The finality and dialectic that one can legitimately claim to characterize understanding is that which is exemplified in the hermeneutic circle of dialogue. A conversational dialogue has an unfinal finality. It is an open-ended process in which understanding is built up by a reciprocity between parts and a continually widening whole which takes in more and more of the questions and prejudgments that compose each participant's starting point— or, rather, standpoint, for not only does this dialectic have no logical conclusion; it has no absolute start; it is not touched by the problem of where one should begin that arises for the Hegelian dialectic.[18]

Conversation suits Gadamer's account of foundational dialectic because it is *dia*-logical, *inter*-play. Conversation and the game also exemplify a purposefulness without purpose which makes them an apt illustration for the experience of the work of art. In fact, Gadamer uses the work of art to illustrate the nature of all understanding. Understanding is *poiesis*, "production." Stock or technical terms and prose formulas like "The cat sat on the mat" have dictionary or sentence meanings, but (and here Gadamer and Bachelard agree) even scientific concepts are more scientific when their use involves conceptualization, that is when they are being used creatively, than when they figure only in subsumption and syllogism.[19] According to Gadamer, creativity is a feature of all language in use. His reason for saying this seems to be the previously mentioned open texture of language which has the consequence that there is no recognition and no application of a word that does not exercise the imagination. This is reminiscent of Kant's theory of judgment, but it is Aristotle whose authority Gadamer invokes in support of this assertion of "the fundamental metaphorical nature" of linguistic consciousness. "Just as speech implies the use of pre-established words which have their universal meaning, there is at the same time a constant process of concept formation by means of which the life of a language develops" (388 [405]).

Why, it may be asked, does Gadamer believe that language must develop? Is it not an empirical accident that it does? Gadamer obviously does not think so. His reason is the same as his reason for denying that an interpreter might happen to share precisely the same point of view as the author and hence have no difficulty in identifying what the author meant to say. Gadamer is right to hold that no two people share the same point of view. A's view of B does not coincide with B's view of A, however close their imaginative sympathy. Nevertheless, it is a big step from this to the inference that "the universal concept that is intended through the meaning of the word is enriched by the particular view of an object, so that what emerges is a new, more specific word formation which does more justice to the particular features of the object." In spite of the inevitability of perspectivism, might not the porosity of language insisted on by Gadamer itself facilitate the crystallization of universal concepts and protect them from being deformed by the particularity of each person's point of view? Gadamer's reply to this also bears against Bachelard's assumption that scientific concepts can be insulated from pre-scientific ones—though it must not be forgotten that on Bachelard's account scientific concepts deserving so to be called are always in a state of flux. What Gadamer adds is that even the relatively rigid concepts of formalized natural languages float in the ambient fluid of prereflective, unformalized natural language. Although he makes exception for "the pure sign language of logic," "the use of technical terminology (even if often in the guise of a foreign word) passes into the spoken language. There is no such thing as purely technical speech, but the technical term, created artificially and against the spirit of language, returns into its stream" (375–76 [392]).

Gadamer says all interpretation is linguistic (359 [375]), and this holds too for understanding if we accept his doctrine that understanding and interpretation are indissolubly bound up with each other (360 [376]). By this he seems to mean that all interpretation and understanding, including interpretation and understanding in music and the plastic arts, is achieved through verbal language. The interpretation of nonliterary artifacts requires that they be put "on the scales of words." He acknowledges that our experience of works of art not uncommonly appears to be inexpressible in words. This, he maintains, is no more than a reflection of the inadequacy of the conventions for coping with the experience. But he denies this implies that words cannot be found (362 [379]): "It says nothing against the essential connection between understanding and language. In fact it confirms this connection. For all such criticism which tries to reach an undertstanding by going beyond the conventionality [*Schematismus*] of our statements finds its expression in the form of language." Does this not beg the question? Gadamer may not be arguing that it must be possible to give a literal prose translation of, for example, an abstract sculpture or dance, but as far as I can see, he gives no reason for believing it must be possible to express what they "say" by means of a poem. No doubt we try to find words to help ourselves and others understand the sculpture or the dance, but we may just be trying to do something we should not try to do. And there remains the likelihood mentioned above that it will be unnatural to speak of understanding in connection with some kinds of works of art.

It would be a mistake to think that this narrowly verbal concept of interpretation is narrowed still further by Gadamer's assertion that written texts present the real hermeneutic task (352 [368]). He is not denying there could be hermeneutic tasks in a world where we all had auditive memories like high fidelity tape recorders. His point is that, the way things are, written language calls for more interpretative labor than does spoken language because the author is not usually at our shoulder to answer questions by reading the text himself with the right intonation, cadences, etc. The alienation of a text from its author and original addressee underlines Gadamer's proposition that the present reader is the arbiter of the text's claim to truth (356 [372]). The written text presents a hermeneutic and dialectical problem in that "all writing is ... a kind of alienated speech and its signs need to be transformed back into speech and meaning" (354 [371]). The literary transmission of tradition is no different in principle from oral transmission, but only "makes the task of real hearing more difficult" (420 [438]).

What does Gadamer mean by "real hearing"? This is the notion that was invoked in the enigmatic remark about listening to language made at the beginning of this section. When Gadamer praises Aristotle for recognizing that hermeneutics must give primacy to hearing, *hören*, and when he speaks of listening, *zuhören*, these words are being used with Heideggerian overtones of *zugehören*, "to belong." Both sets of harmonics resonate in the jingle that language does not belong to us, but we belong to language. This in turn is echoed by the idea that history does not belong to man, but man belongs to history. These two formulas are connected through the doctrine that language is an event, a *Geschehen*; and *Wirkungsgeschichte*, "effective or operative history," is crucial in Gadamer's philosophical theory of hermeneutics.

As that theory is expounded in *Truth and Method*, it undergoes a transition analogous to the one from Hegel to Heidegger that he himself remarks on, a transition from stress on *Geschichte*, "history," to stress on *Geschick*, "destiny" or "dispensation".[20] This step from *Geschichte* to *Geschick* will be regarded as a step backward by some of his readers. By Hirsch, for instance. But there is a simple fallacy behind what Hirsch says on this question. He contends that Gadamer appears to hold that "textual meaning can somehow exist independently of individual consciousness" (248). He cites Gadamer's statement that "the condition of being written down is central to the hermeneutic phenomenon because the detachment of a written text from the writer or author as well as from any particular addressee gives it an existence of its own." Hirsch's paraphrase of this is, "The text, being independent of any particular human consciousness, takes on the autonomous being of language itself." This is indeed what Gadamer says, but it is very different from saying that textual meaning can exist independently of *any* consciousness. That Gadamer does not want to say this is borne out by the answer he gives in the paper "Man and Language" to the question How then is language present? "Certainly not without the individual consciousness, but also not in a mere summation of the many who are each a particular consciousness for itself."[21] Hirsch also overlooks the fact that Gadamer insists that written signs depend for their meaning on backtranslation into speech. When referring to "the autonomous being of language" Hirsch apparently forgets that although Gadamer grants language can be an object of scientific study, he denies it can be only that. Even Saussure's science of *langue* employs chess as a model, thereby acknowledging its relationship to historical acts of *parole*, moves in the language game. Likewise Gadamer's talk of listening to language is not a falling away from his earlier comparison of language to the playing of a game.

In his analysis of the structure of games quite early in his book he argues that the players are more played on than playing; "alles Spielen ist ein Gespieltwerden" (93–95 [99–102]). "Thus it is literally more correct to say that language speaks us, rather than we speak it" (421 [439]). As Lichtenberg might have put it, it plays in me, *es spielt in mir*.[22] For language is not originally a being, an entity, a *Seiendes*. It is, in Heidegger's words, the house of being, *Sein*. *Sein* is a verbal noun, and this advent of being is not independent of those who belong to language and listen to being. It is *Ereignis*, mutually appropriative disclosure or mutually disclosive appropriation. *Sein* enters into *Dasein*, so that in listening and belonging to being we are also belonging to ourselves and our forward-looking tradition. Understanding is self-understanding.

We have considered Gadamer's case for affirming the priority of operatively historical consciousness over objectivizing historiographical consciousness, and, more generally, his case for describing understanding as fundamentally not a state of correspondence but of co-respondence. That case, I believe, is well made in so far as his doctrine of the linguisticality of all understanding is an assertion of the co-respondent or dialogical character of understanding. But although we may be able to accept that understanding is linguistic in the sense that it has the character of dialogue or conversation, *Gespräch*, Gadamer's doctrine of the *Sprachlichkeit* of all understanding is sometimes expressed in a fashion that suggests that having ruled out explicitly or implicitly accounts of understanding that depend on adequation in the classical realist sense, absolute spirit in the Hegelian idealist sense, or Holy Spirit in the sense of Christian theology, he nevertheless reverts to a view of understanding that depends not only on the hypostatization of a universal spirit of language, but also on the optimistic faith "that the false paths of human self-understanding only reach their true end through divine grace ... only thereby do we reach the insight that all paths lead to our own salvation."[23] With this affirmation, as I indicated in commenting on Pannenberg, Gadamer's description of the hermeneutic circle may appear to become viciously circular. For in the course of giving a general philosophical description of hermeneutic understanding he makes use of a finding in one specific field of understanding. This procedure is not, however, viciously circular. It is not viciously circular to support a conceptual analysis of understanding by appealing to specific kinds of understanding, so long as it is remembered that such support is only exemplary and that it may fail us when we turn to consider other kinds of understanding. But although Gadamer's procedure does not beg the

seems itself to be an intelligent adaptation of the Cartesian rules. This does not mean, however, that it is no more than a methodological instrument like Mill's canons of induction. Although we can tell ourselves to question what a person in authority may have said and to avoid haste in coming to a conclusion, the discipline we achieve through following these rules is a disposition. Gadamer himself compares it to tact and practical wisdom. We can lay the foundations for these by following rules, but the person who possesses these qualities is one who can and sometimes must make the right decision where no rule is available to make it for him.

Do Mill's scientific rules of inference, for example, leave such a margin for the exercise of the scientist's discretion, or do they constitute, in the words of Helmholtz cited by Gadamer, an "iron procedure of self-conscious reasoning"? If it is argued that in the human sciences at least they do leave a margin of indeterminacy, the question arises whether this can be closed by other methods, for example the method of psychological empathy advocated by Schleiermacher and Dilthey. Gadamer's view is that no methodological rule or set of rules can take the interpreter all the way and that the so-called method of empathy is based on the misconception, confirmed by a questionable reading of Husserl's method of phenomenological reduction, that the interpreter's presuppositions must be neutralized. The misconception assumes that interpretation is the grasping of a meaning in itself, whereas it is rather a new creation prompted by cues given in one's heritage. That is to say, interpretation is a historically different assimilation of tradition (430 [448]). The interpreter's standard is therefore both retrospective and prospective without being a datum to which one was, is, or will be present. The standard or measure is not an object to which one appeals as one applies a rule or ruler. One's consciousness of it is operatively historical. It is not something of which one has an experience, an *Erlebnis*. It is a fallible wisdom one acquires through experience, *Erfahrung*, that is to say, through trial, error, and the travail of negation.

To reach this concept of understanding we have traveled a long way, it must seem, from the concept of understanding appropriate for the understanding of a proposition like "The cat sat on the mat." The stages of the journey are not clearly signposted by Gadamer. At the end of the second section of this chapter we found it necessary to distinguish on his behalf between correct understanding, which we called epistemic understanding, and an understanding that may be a misunderstanding and is therefore epistemically neutral. We argued that Gadamer's analysis applied to the former only because it applied to the latter less specific concept of understanding. We have now discovered that Gadamer's concept of understanding is generically different from epistemically neutral understanding. For it is not a purely epistemic or epistemically neutral concept if the epistemic is taken to be a matter of theoretical knowledge. His concept encompasses a kind of wisdom, and this is not neutral with regard to truth and falsehood if by these terms we mean something different from theoretically cognitive correctness and incorrectness. This is why, although Gadamer is not concerned to affirm or deny standards of propositional ontic truth, he finds himself having to admit a standard of prepropositional ontological truth.

4. *Prescience*

In the foreword to the second edition of *Truth and Method* Gadamer writes, "Heidegger's temporal analytics of human existence (*Dasein*) has, I think, shown convincingly that understanding is not just one of the various possible ways in which the subject may behave, but the mode of being of There-being itself. This is the sense in which 'hermeneutics' has been used here. It asks (to put it in Kantian terms): How is understanding possible?"

Although *Truth and Method* is largely taken up with the discussion of the relation between truth and method in the human sciences, Gadamer observes that we speak also of a language of nature. "For man's relation to the world is absolutely and fundamentally linguistic in nature, and hence intelligible. Thus hermeneutics is ... a universal aspect of philosophy, and not just the methodological basis of the so-called human sciences" (432–33 [450–51]). Thus the natural scientist's understanding of a theory is earthed in the open-ended dialogue with his subject matter, with other natural scientists, and with himself. We tend, as Heidegger and Wittgenstein show, to forget the participatory practices from which the concepts of the natural sciences arise. We forget that understanding is, as Gadamer argues, inseparable from application. We posit an independent totality of present at hand entities with present at hand qualities and relations that may be affirmed or denied of these entities in present at hand propositions. Neither Heidegger nor Gadamer nor Wittgenstein wishes to put an embargo on what is called pure science. They wish simply to remind us, especially the philosophers among us, that objectivizing science and the technological domination of nature is possible only within the context of nonobjectivizing forms of life whose character is linguistic—*sprachlich* and *gesprächlich*— not because it is limited to the propounding of propositions that purport to correspond to reality, but because its mode of life is wondering and response, co-respondence, *Ent-sprechung.*[24]

The reference just made to technological domination points up a kinship between what Gadamer says about methodological hermeneutics regarded as mastery of a text and what Heidegger says about technology regarded as a device by which man controls nature. It must seem to some of their readers that in arguing that presence at hand is secondary to readiness to hand Heidegger and Gadamer are inconsistent in giving priority to man's technological conduct while implying that there is something inauthentic with the way man forces nature to submit to his needs. This paradox arises if it is wrongly assumed that in Heidegger's view technology can only be inauthentically self-assertive and that readiness to hand, because it is prior to presence at hand, is therefore the essence of authenticity. However, in "The Question of Technology" Heidegger maintains that although modern technology is masterful, technology can be a way to an *Ereignis* by which truth discloses itself. And in "The Origin of the Work of Art" Heidegger takes a product of technology, a pair of boots, as an illustration of his claim that equipmentality does not exclude *poiesis*. Through the eyes and hands of van Gogh the old boots are allowed to disclose their nature. If allowed to, nature, Heidegger contends, appealing to an etymological connection between *phusis* and *phos*, brings itself into the light, into the clearing provided for it by language. It is by nature linguistic, *logos*. It is not an in-itself over against there-being. Heidegger, Gadamer, and Bachelard are agreed in wishing to destroy that Meyersonian image of nature.[25] But that image, whether it is the image of a world as a totality of things or the image of a world as a totality of facts, is still the image of something present at hand. And the scientific world that supersedes this world in Bachelard's philosophy is a world of present at hand relations. Heidegger and Gadamer would not deny that mathematical formulas and propositions affirming the presence of so-called primary qualities and relations may be correct or incorrect scientific descriptions of what is in the natural world. (It will be remembered that Bachelard calls all scientific qualities secondary, because they are, according to him, relational.) Assertions like "The cat sat on the mat" may be correct or incorrect descriptions of the everyday world. Statements like "The word let in the third line means 'obstruct,' not 'allow'" may be correct or incorrect interpretations of the meaning of a text. But the ontic correctness or incorrectness of such statements about entities in a world presupposes ontological truth, the coming to light of the worldhood of a world whose contents those statements purport to describe. This emergence of there-being (*es gibt*) is not a natural cosmogony as opposed to the creation of a logico-linguistic universe of discourse. Its *phusis* is also a *logos*. Its emergence is a *poiesis*. Therefore, behind the saying that describes and demonstrates, there is a monstrative saying that mediates what shows and conceals itself. Behind conceptual dialectic, for example that of Hegel or of Bachelard's philosophy of science, and beyond metaphysics, is the speculative hermeneutics of Heidegger and Gadamer. There is a hermeneutic circle which returns science to the origin it shares with art.

CHAPTER SEVEN
MERLEAU–PONTY AND
SAUSSURE: HERMENEUTIC
SEMIOLOGY

Douceur d'être et de n'être pas

—Paul Valéry

In reading the works of Maurice Merleau–Ponty it is common to have a feeling of *déjà lu*. They seem to have been written in the margins of the works he himself was reading. But it would be as unjust to say of him as it was for him to say of Hegel that he is "the museum," if the implication is that other people's thoughts are embalmed in his books.[1] The "hyperdialectic" he has with their thoughts is not a retrospective mapping of ground covered but a prospective opening up of new paths.[2] How one can think something new is a question that perplexes Merleau–Ponty as much as it perplexed Meno. In this chapter we consider the way he uses some of the ideas of classical Saussurian structuralism to try to shed light on this question and to indicate a way between idealisms and realisms that avoids the pitfall into which Sartre's attempt stumbled.

1. *Signs*

Fundamental in the theory advanced in Ferdinand de Saussure's *Course in General Linguistics* are the distinctions between the signifier and the signified, between language and speech, and between synchrony and diachrony.

The signifier (*signifiant*) and the signified (*signifié*) are abstract aspects of the sign. The signifier is the relatively material aspect, the acoustic (or visual) image, as Saussure describes it. The signified is what some would call the concept or idea. Saussure prefers to call this the signified because it brings out the interdependence of the two aspects of the sign and enables him to indicate an important respect in which he parts company with those who suppose that concepts can exist ready-made independently of sounds (or marks) and that words or signs can exist independently of concepts.

One can see immediately how appealing this analysis of the sign would be to a philosopher like Merleau–Ponty, who in the *Structure of Behaviour* and the *Phenomenology of Perception*, neither of which works mentions Saussure, had been trying to use Gestalt notions like that of the body schema to show how a proper understanding of the role of the lived body (*corps propre*) would make it possible to supersede the alternatives of idealism, realism, and dualism—to pass, as Merleau–Ponty himself puts it, from the antinomies of Descartes's Second Meditation to a solution of them. The solution follows a clue furnished in Descartes's letter of June 28, 1643, to Princess Elizabeth of Bohemia. In that letter Descartes writes that whereas thought is understood by pure intellect, and body (i.e., extension, shape, and movement) is understood by intellect and the imagination, the union in one person of body and thought is best understood by turning back from metaphysical meditation and the exercise of the imagination in mathematics or kinematics toward ordinary conversation and the sensory perceptions of daily life. It was, writes Descartes, because Her Highness was endeavoring to understand that union by philosophical reflection that she had become caught up in the difficulties from which she had asked him to extricate her.

Merleau–Ponty's endeavor is to practice a kind of philosophical reflection which will enable him to succeed where the princess failed. He would not be content, obviously, with the "thus" refutations of those antiphilosophers who believe they can, for example, answer Zeno simply by observing that arrows reach their target or defeat Berkeley by kicking a stone. He does not consider that such reminders are entirely out of place,[3] but he does consider that he is called upon to explain why we are led into difficulties like those in which Princess Elizabeth found herself. His explanation cannot take the form of Descartes's, since that is given in terms Merleau–Ponty cannot accept. Pure thought and the matter and motion of the Cartesian scientific imagination are inconceivable and unimaginable in their own right. They are abstractions from the sense perception of ordinary life—as meaning and the material of expression are inseparable.

If meaning and thought are not conveyed by their vehicles like the pilot by his ship, what similes suit? Saussure tries out several. Comparison with the molecule is rejected because atoms, for instance those of hydrogen and oxygen which make up the molecule of water, can exist outside any combination. A comparison of the signifier-signified complex with that of the mind and body begs too many metaphysical questions and would be of no avail to Merleau–Ponty since it simply reverts to the problem that recourse to Saussure's theory of the sign is meant to illuminate. More attractive to Saussure are the analogy of the recto and verso of a sheet of paper and the analogy of the surface of a sheet of water whose contour is a function of atmospheric pressure. It is easy to spot defects in these comparisons too. The second of them leads Saussure astray by suggesting that without language there can be thought, if only vague thought, thought without thoughts. This comes perilously close to the doctrine against which the comparison is meant to be used. And it gives less help than Saussure imagines as an illustration of his principle of the arbitrariness of the sign.

The principle of the arbitrariness of the sign affirms that there is no natural tie between the sound (or sight) of a sign and what the sign signifies, at least not with the signs that are the subject matter of the Saussurian science of linguistics, which is the paradigm to which Saussure believes other disciplines of semiology should aspire.[4] Apparent exceptions to this principle are icons, symbols, onomatopoeia, and interjections. Onomatopoeic words are a small proportion, Saussure points out, and are on or beyond the fringe of the genuinely linguistic system. Anyway, like interjections, they have a conventional element which accounts for the fact that one rarely finds the same onomatopoeic words and interjections used by native speakers of different languages, contrary to what would be expected if the tie with what they mean were entirely natural. To the degree that gestural pantomime and pictures or symbols, for instance the scales of justice, rely on a natural connection, Saussure relegates them to nonlinguistic departments of semiology. This procedure does not render his principle of the arbitrariness of the sign arbitrary if as a consequence of following the procedure we obtain a theory that is an improvement on alternatives. But it does raise the question whether Saussure is right to treat linguistics merely as a paradigm with respect to which other kinds of semiology are nonlinguistic declensions, or whether Roland Barthes is justified in diverging from Saussure by proposing that once we go beyond rudimentary codes like the Highway Code we realize that apparently nonlinguistic systems like those connected with advertising, sartorial fashion, the cinema, and food are in fact dependent upon interpretation in language in a narrow sense of the term. Gadamer, it will be recalled, takes a view similar to this when he argues that for there to be any question of understanding of the nonliterary arts, they must first be interpreted in words.[5]

It is not quite clear whether Barthes's intention is to allow that the Highway Code is autonomous in relation to language or to affirm that as soon as we move from systems like the Highway Code to ones "where the sociological significance is more than superficial"[6] we appreciate that all semiological systems, including the Highway Code, are dependent on language. The unclarity is due in part to the ambiguity of the phrase semiological system. A system in which the units are kinds of dress is a system of nonlinguistic signs, according to both Saussure and Barthes. But a science of that system, no less than a science of a system of verbal language, will not be possible without language. Barthes's further claim is that not only the practitioner of linguistics but also the practitioner of those parts of semiology whose basic subject matter is not in the ordinary sense linguistic cannot avoid talking about language. He concedes, however, that whereas the units the linguist talks about are phonemes (or, in the more psychologistic terminology which Saussure also employs, acoustic images),[7] the units Barthesian translinguistics deals with will be

> larger fragments of discourse referring to objects or episodes whose meaning underlies language, but can never exist independently of it ... myth, narrative journalism, or on the other hand objects of our civilization, in so far as they are *spoken* (through the press, the prospectus, interview, conversation and perhaps even the inner language which is ruled by the laws of imagination).[8]

The word spoken is italicized by Barthes himself in this passage. The implications of his doing so will be considered in the next section of the present chapter in the context of Merleau–Ponty's interpretation of Saussure. The remainder of the present section spells out further implications of Saussure's theory of the sign on which Barthes, Merleau–Ponty, and Saussure himself are in general agreement.

In saying that the relation between the signifier and the signified is arbitrary, Saussure does not mean that it is determined by the fiat of an individual. The arbitrariness or unmotivatedness to which he refers is consistent with constraint, but the constraint derives not from any natural resemblance between signifier and signified; it derives rather from a social convention. Saussure is as concerned as the later Wittgenstein to exorcise theories that construe language as nomenclature, an aggregate of words that name what they signify, what they signify being regarded as a self-subsisting idea or entity of some other ontological status.

Like Wittgenstein and Husserl, Saussure is struck by the analogies between language and the game of chess. Like Ryle, he is impressed by the analogies between language and money.[9] He makes a distinction between value and signification. The value of a coin is its purchasing power, but there is no intrinsic reason why a coin of less purchasing power than another should be smaller than it or why it should be made of a baser metal, unless of course its baseness is determined directly by what you would have to pay for a given quantity of it. Nor, so far as the game to be played with them is concerned, does it matter whether the pieces in chess are made of ivory, wood or plastic. Similarly, although the fact that the word sheep rather than shupe is used to name a certain kind of animal has a historical and etymological explanation, the linguistic transactions we perform with "sheep" could be performed just as well with "shupe." The latter could have had precisely the same exchange value. That is, there could have been the same oppositive differences between the signifying component of "shupe" and other signifiers and the same set of oppositive differences between the signified component of the putative sign and the signified components of all other signs. We should then have had what, from the point of view of linguistics, would have been the very same sign, since the sign is constituted by the combination of the series of auditory or visual differences and the series of differences of concepts, the latter being inseparable from the former. The sound that is the raw material of the signifier is the subject matter of the science of acoustics. For linguistics this positive substance is of no relevance or of less relevance than the negative differential or diacritical form—Saussure expresses both views.[10]

What corresponds on the side of the signified to the material substance informed by the signifier? Apparently, the nebulous thought mentioned previously or a particular idea regarded as subject matter for psychology.[11] It is far from plain how Saussure sees the relation between an idea regarded as a psychological entity and what he calls the significance of a word. Nor is it obvious that what he calls the signified includes both signification and value. I take him to locate the signified, signification, and value in the logico-linguistic space generated by social convention. The value of a sign is the product of the differences of the signifier and the differences of the signified. Thus the value of the French word *mouton* is different from that of the English word sheep, because in English the word mutton is used over an area where French continues to use the same word.

Value is a category of *langue* and, at both the level of the signified and the level of the signifier, has two subcategories, syntagmatic and paradigmatic. Syntagmatic relations define the combinatorial possibilities of units. For example, the phonological scope of "sh" is defined in terms of its capacity to combine with "-eep," "-op," "fi-," etc.; the morphological scope of "sheep" is defined in part by the illegitimacy of "sheeply"; and the syntactico-semantic scope of "sheep" is fixed by the fact, among others, that we can say, "The farmer shears the sheep," but not "Sheep the farmer shears the." The paradigmatic relations are the substitution possibilities. For example, the phonological powers of "sh" derive in part from the contrast between "sheep," "keep," "deep"; the morphology of "sheep" is constituted by contrasts like that between "sheepish" and "piggish"; and its syntactico-semantic structure derives in part from the fact that as well as "The farmer shears the sheep" we may say, "The farmer shears the goat."

It should be noted that the syntagmatic analysis of, for instance, the morpheme "undo" would be impossible if there were no other words such as untie, unlock, or unleash in paradigmatic relation with it. If these disappeared from the language, "undo" would lose a kind of complexity, and its value would change, unless the gaps were filled by neologisms. Conversely, one of the principles according to which the class of paradigms gets constituted is precisely this syntagmatic complexity.

Furthermore, what I have called syntactico-semantic structure presupposes the morphological, and the latter presupposes the phonological and vice versa. This is a way of affirming the interdependence of the signifier (not to be confused with the subject matter of acoustics or phonics) and the signified (not to be confused with the subject matter of psychology). This second kind of interdependence leads Saussure to suggest that the traditional grammatical distinctions between syntactical, morphological, and lexicological identity would, in the science of linguistics he envisages, give way to the more basic distinction between syntagmatic and paradigmatic difference.

Merleau–Ponty employs Saussure's theory of difference to uncover an alternative to theories of mind, body, and meaning cast in terms of substantive identity. We should therefore expect Merleau–Ponty's theory to be capable of accommodating phonology, morphology, and syntax even if he usually talks about the semantics of words.[12] For in talking about words he would by implication be talking about syntax, morphology, and phonology. Now and then he talks explicitly about these, for instance where, following Saussure, he compares the French and English ways of saying "the man I love," arguing that the English syntactical structure is no less adequate than that of the French "l'homme que j'aime" although the second seems to provide more positive marks to distinguish its structure than does the first.[13]

However, it might be said that Merleau–Ponty misinterprets Saussure.[14] It will help to understand the reason for saying that they differ at least in what they emphasize if we first understand how what Saussure calls value is related to what he calls signification.

Having said that value at the level of the signified is an element in signification and that the value of the modern French word *mouton* is not the same as that of the English word sheep, Saussure says that the former "can have the same signification" as the latter.[15] They might have the same signification when a Frenchman says, "Le fermier a tondu le mouton," and an Englishman says, "The farmer has shorn the sheep." That is, whereas value, according to Saussure, is a category of language, *langue*, signification is a category of speaking, *parole*.

2. *Language and speech*

Halfway through the *Course* Saussure takes stock of his position: "Linguistics here comes to its second bifurcation. We had first to choose between language and speaking ...; here we are again at the intersection of two roads, one leading to diachrony and the other to synchrony."[16] From a very cursory reading of these words the impression might be formed that Saussure superimposes the second pair of alternatives on the first, meaning that language is diachronic and speaking is synchronic. Whether or not it is by such a hasty reading of these words that Merleau–Ponty comes by it, he does somehow gather the impression that Saussure "made a distinction between a synchronic linguistics of speech and a diachronic linguistics of language."[17] It is evident from the paragraphs immediately following these words of Saussure's, and from the whole chapter these paragraphs conclude, that his distinction between the diachronic and the synchronic is applied only to language. Certainly, his remark that "speaking operates only on a language-state"[18] might appear to support the inference that speaking is synchronic, but it is plain from the discussion of the chess analogy in which it is made that this is not what Saussure intends. His point is that the performance of speech acts is carried out against the background of a linguistic status quo. The status quo is the synchronic cross section or epoch of a language. The language no doubt evolved into that state through epochal states in which the system of values was different. There can be a linguistics that studies this evolution from one state to another. This diachronic kind of linguistics is the one most favored during the nineteenth century by the neogrammarians. Saussure conceives his own task as that of laying the foundations for a nonhistorical synchronic linguistics. He allows only grudgingly that there could be a linguistics of *parole*, warning that this must not be confused with "linguistics proper," linguistics of *langue*, even if the latter draws illustrations from acts of speech (as on p. 130 [179] of the *Course*).

Saussure compares originative speech acts and speech accidents to phenomena that impinge from without on a celestial system causing it to shift from one state of equilibrium to another. While what interests Saussure is the language in a given state of equilibrium, Merleau–Ponty is more interested in examining the process of transition from one state to another and, in particular, how, when linguistic forms fall into disuse and lose their expressiveness, "the gaps or zones of weakness thus created elicit from speaking subjects who want to communicate a recovery and a utilisation, in terms of a new principle, of linguistic debris left by the system in process of regression."[19] Merleau–Ponty is taking up, though at a level of greater particularity, the question of the relation of decadence to *poiesis* which Heidegger took up from Hölderlin, Schelling, Nietzsche, and others. It is not surprising, therefore, that Heideggerian themes should recur so insistently in *The Visible and the Invisible*, the book on which Merleau–Ponty was working at the end of his life. But it is to Husserl and H.-J. Pos that he refers in the article "On the Phenomenology of Language"; and it is his reading of the article by Pos on "Phenomenology and Linguistics"[20] that leads him to say such things as, "According to Saussure, language is a system of signs *in the process* of differentiating one from the other,"[21] an assertion that would be more fittingly made of Jakobson, whose theories Merleau–Ponty is paraphrasing when he makes this reference to Saussure. Pos discusses the distinction between the objective scientific knowledge of language and the phenomenological experience of speaking. He says, echoing Bergson, that the attitude of the linguist is reflective and retrospective. "The scientist, the observer, sees language in the past," as Merleau–Ponty puts it in reporting Pos. That Merleau–Ponty is here reporting Pos is not made clear in Ricoeur's criticism of Merleau–Ponty in *Le Conflit des interprétations*,[22] but this does not nullify his criticism, since Merleau–Ponty agrees with Pos that linguistics studies the relations among the historical states of a language. Linguistics, as both Pos and Merleau–Ponty describe it, is of the diachronic kind from which Saussure turns away. However, the past of a language studied by diachronic linguistics is, says Pos—using what was to become a key word in the work of Merleau–Ponty—"invisible" to the originary consciousness, which is involved in speaking and is absorbed in the present.[23] With Pos's distinction between the scientific and the phenomenological attitudes in mind, Merleau–Ponty takes the terms diachrony and synchrony, which Pos himself does not use, to mean respectively past and present, a usage that cuts across the Saussurian usage according to which synchronic linguistics can study either a past or a present state of language. Pos of course would say, in the manner of Bergson, that Saussure's linguist is *regarding* even the present state of language as past. And it is indeed clear that the present Pos and Merleau–Ponty want to investigate is the *living* present, the Husserlian *lebendige Gegenwart*, of speaking. Unfortunately, Merleau–Ponty makes this less clear than one would like when he writes,

> At first the "subjective" point of view envelopes the "objective" point of view; synchrony envelopes diachrony. The past of language began by being present,[24]

adding, with the implication that neither Pos nor Saussure goes far enough:

> Far from our being able to juxtapose a psychology of language and a science of language by reserving language in the present for the first and language in the past for the second, we must recognise that the present diffuses into the past to the extent that the past has been present.[25]

So Merleau–Ponty believes that their accounts need filling out with an account of an inner "incarnate logic" along lines suggested by Gustave Guillaume's theory of sublinguistic schemata. This is unobjectionable if this logic is the dialectic by which what has become disorderly is taken up into a new order. What is objectionable, if taken as a comment on Saussure, is Merleau–Ponty's argument on the page immediately preceding that on which the sentence just quoted occurs:

> The series of fortuitous linguistic facts brought out by the
> objective perspective has been incorporated in a language
> which was at every moment a system endowed with an inner
> logic. Thus, if language is a system when it is considered
> according to a cross-section, it must be in its development
> too.

This reference to an alleged system in the process of development invokes system in a sense very remote from the sense Saussure gives to the
word when he uses it of a totality of signs constituted by differences. It
may well be possible to explain why one state of language is superseded
by another, but Merleau–Ponty's argument does not show that the explanation may not be in terms of accident; indeed, this is conceded by
his allusions to what from an external point of view is random and for-
tuitous. And survival or revival in the new state of a language may be
explicable in terms of utility. It would need more than this, however, to
justify talk of an inner incarnate logic, as Merleau–Ponty realizes. What
more he wants can be elicited with the aid of some remarks of Saussure's
on the analogy of language and chess.

Saussure says that a person who has watched a game of chess from the
start is not therefore in a better position to describe the state of play
than someone who has arrived late in the game. That makes the point
about the claimed irrelevance of the history of a language for someone
wishing to describe its current state. However, it suggests also that the
state of a language is altered when someone uses it to say something, for
saying something in it is presumably the analogue of making a move in
chess. But making a move in chess is not making any difference in the
powers of the pieces or the rules of the game. Nor normally does the
performance or act of speech make or contribute to making a change in
the language spoken. A change in the language game is effected only
when one does something analogous to dispensing with the queen or
picking up the spherical ball and running with it in one's hands. Of
course the new type of move has to catch on. Otherwise we are simply
infringing a rule. And it need not be one's intention to initiate a new
practice. It may result from a slip. It is unintended modification, change
brought about by what Saussure calls "blind force,"[26] which he sees in,
for instance, the substitution of the modern German plural form *Gäste*
for the Old High German form *gasti*. Merleau–Ponty however stresses

the part played in linguistic change by intentionality. But this stress on the role of significative intention does not require him to hold that a change that comes about in language, *langue*, as a consequence of the significative intentions expressed in acts of speech, *parole*, is in fact intended by any speaker. It may be an unintended consequence.

What does Merleau–Ponty mean by *intention significative*?

3. *Significative intention and creative expression*

Crucial but difficult to answer is the question whether Merleau–Ponty would allow that a significative intention is expressed, for example, when a child, in order to assure his father that the money received from him is safe, says, "The money you gave me is in my pocket." If this is a sentence the child has uttered before, its utterance would perhaps be an instance of what Merleau–Ponty calls empirical or secondary, as opposed to creative, speech. If it is a sentence the child has not used before, Chomsky would say that in uttering it the child might be performing creatively, notwithstanding the prosaic form and content. For the child might never before have tried out a sentence incorporating a relative clause. We should be still more willing to credit the child with originality if we accept that he is capable of coming out with more and more complex sentences with subordinate clauses embedded in subordinate clauses to such a degree of complexity that it would become less and less plausible to say he was only repeating something he had heard. It is true, as we shall see, that Merleau–Ponty does not share with Chomsky, Lévi-Strauss, and others the doctrine of a priori universals. He contests this Cartesianism. The universal, according to him, is not a given point of departure but a point at which we arrive by way of what Gadamer calls a fusion of horizons. Nevertheless, Merleau–Ponty can and should agree with Chomsky that on unprecedented occasions like the ones we have been postulating the child does manifest a kind of creativity.

But what if it is only the nonlinguistic context that is new, as when the child receives his pocket money again the following week and comes out with the same sentence he had spoken the week before? And what if this time it is his mother who gives him the money? What if he is wearing a different jacket or puts the coins in the pocket of his trousers instead of the pocket of his coat? There is certainly something new about these situations, but if we think that this novelty is enough to credit the child with *linguistic* creativity, we should not allow this to conceal how different these cases are from those considered in the preceding paragraphs.

An intermediate case would be that in which the child uses the same words as he had previously used but now, for the first time, not to assure the donor that the money is safe but to deny that he has already spent it.

We need to distinguish between syntactic, performative, and referential originality. It is clear that referential originality would not be enough to exclude an utterance from what Merleau–Ponty calls secondary or empirical speech as opposed to originary or authentic speech like "that of the child uttering its first words, of the lover revealing his feelings, of the 'first man who spoke', or of the writer and philosopher who reawaken primordial experience anterior to all traditions."[27] Here the creative use of language is contrasted with empirical or secondary uses of language, Merleau–Ponty's idea being, if I am not mistaken, that the latter presuppose that we have learned a language and that learning is creative. There is no difference in principle here between literary invention and the child's acquisition of his first words. But there are more distinctions to be made than Merleau–Ponty makes, and some of those he makes need making more carefully. It is odd, for instance, to *equate* empirical language with speaking about speaking (*une parole sur des paroles*), particularly if by this is meant metalinguistic or, as the English translation of the *Phenomenology of Perception* has it, a second-order act of speech.[28] What Merleau–Ponty means by *expression seconde*, however, is what he elsewhere calls the opportune recall (*rappel*) of preestablished signs.[29] He is talking about acquired language, where the meanings of words are already sedimented in universal concepts. Where what we want to say can be said with the meanings already laid down in our words we are using spoken words, *la parole parlée*. This is contrasted with the speaking word, *la parole parlante*. Only this *oratio naturans*, as we might call it, is really speech that signifies.

This may appear to set too severe a constraint on signification. For even if we can isolate utterances where what is said is said solely through the common terms of the instituted language, Merleau–Ponty agrees with Saussure that the meanings of all terms are differential, that is, they lie between the terms. This is certainly not sufficient to demonstrate that language is open-textured in a way that implies that it is never coincident with but always ahead of itself. If Merleau–Ponty thinks, as he sometimes seems to, that this is sufficient, it is difficult to see how there can be such a thing as *parole parlante* in contrast to *parole parlée*. These can at best differ only in degree. And it is the burden of his chapter on "The Cogito" that the doctrine of fixed essences cannot be sustained.

The way out of this apparent impasse is to accept an account of concepts in terms of open texture and family resemblance which holds that concepts that seem to have a closed texture owing, say, to stipulative definition depend ultimately on definitions that are either ostensively indeterminate or expressed in terms whose texture is not hermetically closed.

However, taking this way out does not take away the difficulty in understanding why Merleau–Ponty should say that when a speech-act is performed solely with concepts having the porosity we have ascribed them, it does not follow that the statement signifies (*signifie*).[30] The quickest exit from this difficulty would be effected by saying he means only that such a statement would not be important, that it would be insignificant in comparison with one that went creatively beyond usage, not that it would be nonsignificant or nonsense. This reading may be thought to put some strain on the French *la parole vraie, celle qui signifie*; and when he uses the word *signification* elsewhere in the same and adjacent paragraphs he is clearly not intending it, even if the French language allowed him to, in the sense of importance. An alternative, though it may be thought to put too much strain on our credulity, is to suppose that Merleau–Ponty takes the meaning of the terms of common usage to stand in no need of any significative intention on the part of the speaker, at least when they are not being used by him to say something creative in a still unclarified sense of the word. This second reading takes "significative" to mean sign-making. Merleau–Ponty is doubtless translating Husserl's word *significativ*, but when Husserl mentions significative intentions he is ready to call them also *Bedeutungsintentionen* and meaning-acts.[31] There is no implication in Husserl that these acts are baptismal, and no neology is implied. He is simply wishing to distinguish the use of a word with meaning from its use, for example to teach someone how it should be pronounced or to serve as a pattern on wallpaper. When Husserl describes these acts as sense-giving, *sinngebend*, he no more implies that a new meaning is made than Kant does when Kant says the moral agent must be able to regard himself as *gesetzgebend*, implying that the moral agent must be able to regard himself as a law-*maker*.[32] I am not comparing what Paton's translation does to Kant's theory of morality with what Merleau–Ponty's translation does to Husserl's theory of meaning. Merleau–Ponty, though mindful of that theory, is not concerned here with reproducing it. He is more concerned than Husserl with specifically creative expression.

Merleau–Ponty sometimes uses the word *expression* narrowly for the

creative use of a medium,[33] and the word *parole* is sometimes used as
equivalent to poietic *parole parlante* when contrasted with *langue*.[34]
Creative expression is a reaching out into a void. It is not unnatural,
therefore, to think of it as the making of a sign. Not, however, a making
ex nihilo. Poietic expression relies on the institutional prose of the
world. So whereas the system of acquired linguistic values is secondary
relative to the originary expressive acts from which they arise, further
creative expression is possible that is secondary in relation to the tradition on which it depends in order to transcend it dialectically. Hence
Merleau–Ponty's confusing but not confused statement that in empirical
language, which he elsewhere equates with secondary language or
speech possessing only a secondary power (*pouvoir second*),[35] lies hidden "a language raised to the second power [*à la seconde puissance*] in
which signs once again lead the vague life of colours."[36] The vagueness
here referred to is not vagueness of the sort exemplified by words like
mountain, hill, longevity, and bald. Nor can Merleau–Ponty be referring only to the oppositive relations that constitute words and their
meaning according to the theory of Saussure, since this account of words
and their meaning is applied by Saussure to words of what Merleau–
Ponty calls the sedimented empirical language and can therefore supply
no feature that distinguishes poietic language from it. Merleau–Ponty
nevertheless sees himself to be groping toward that feature with the aid
of Saussure's account. This is borne out by his explicit acknowledgment
of Saussure in the pages preceding the phrase about the vague life of
colors and by the implicit acknowledgment embodied in the words following this phrase in which poietic language is described as one "in
which significations never free themselves completely from the inter-
course [*commerce*] of signs." But this commerce of signs must be more
than the exchange value of which Saussure talks. As well as this diacritical relationship which defines the most determinate signs there is also
an indeterminacy, a gap (*lacune*). Is the expressive speech that fills this
gap controlled by the originator's significative intention? To say that his
intention controls his choice of words must be false if the control dictates every word. For expressive speech on that view would be a sort of
translation. Any originality would belong to the intention, and we
should now want to know in what way original intentions differ from
unoriginal ones. We should also want to know in what medium these
intentions are formed. For Merleau–Ponty to say that they are pure
thoughts would be to cancel his endorsement of the thesis of signifier-
signified interdependence.

Endorsement of this thesis is, however, compatible with recognition of the fact that a speaker (and a listener) can, as Mallarmé required of the poet, *céder l'initiative aux mots*.[37] This handing over of the initiative to the words could go as far as a confinement of attention to the sound. To this "phonetic isolationism" Jakobson prefers Valéry's description of the poem as "a prolonged hesitation between sound and sense."[38] This relaxation of the controls of acquired language under the guidance of a schematic idea of what one wants to say might satisfy Merleau–Ponty's description of poetic speech in particular; but whether it would satisfy his description of poietic speech in general, for example innovative philosophy, is something the reader of the following sentences will judge for himself.

> Expressive speech ... gropes around a significative intention which is not guided by any text, and which is precisely in the process of writing the text.... In already acquired expressions there is a direct meaning which corresponds point for point to turns of phrase, forms and established words. Apparently there are no gaps or expressive silences here. But the meaning of expressions which are in the process of being accomplished cannot be of this sort; it is a lateral or oblique meaning which comes about by interpenetration between the words [*qui fuse entre les mots*]. It is another way of shaking the linguistic or narrative apparatus in order to tear a new sound from it. If we want to understand language as an originating operation we must pretend to have never spoken, submit language to a reduction without which it would once more escape us by referring us to what it signifies for us, *look* at it as deaf people look at those who are speaking, compare the art of language to other arts of expression, and try to see it as one of these mute arts. It is possible that the meaning of language has a decisive privilege, but it is in trying out the parallel that we will perceive what may in the end make that parallel impossible.[39]

Whether Merleau–Ponty does come to think that parallel impossible is a question we shall answer in the next section. Before coming to that we must ask how the verbal alchemy mentioned in the sentences just quoted relates to what we referred to as the author's schematic idea of what he wants to say. For, on pain of implicating Merleau–Ponty in a

tort we claimed Saussure commits, we must show that he does not con-
travene the principle of signifier-signified interdependence by permit-
ting at least relatively unstructured intentions to breathe the rarified air
of a world of pure thought.

In so far as a significative intention has some structure, it is embodied
in the acquired language I already inhabit. My inhabiting of the language is my possessing or, rather, being possessed by its structure. I
know my way around it without needing to consult a map as, when I
trip, I know how to save myself from falling without having to appeal to
my knowledge of anatomy and physiology. But what about that part of
my significative intention that goes beyond the lexical, syntactical, stylis-
tic, and other resources deposited in my language? What is its embodi-
ment? According to Merleau–Ponty, "The significative intention gives
itself a body and knows itself by looking for an equivalent in the system
of significations represented by the language I speak and the whole of
the writings and culture I inherit."[40] Does not this generate a dilemma
like Meno's? If there is an equivalent already in the language, what
room is there for a significative intention to express something new? If,
by contrast, we say, as Merleau–Ponty does, that it is only when he has
expressed what he wants to say that the speaker becomes aware of what
he wants to say, how can what he wants to say guide him at all to what
he says? In the first case we know too early, in the second we know too
late.

The dissolution of this dilemma, as to some extent of Meno's, consists
in distinguishing the interrogative pronoun "what" from the relative
pronoun meaning "that which." If the speaker were to put into words
what he wanted to say before he said it he would do so by giving some of
the specifications it would have to satisfy. What, that is, that which,
would satisfy these specifications would still remain to be discovered. It
would still not have been expressed. It would still be no more than a lack
that he had a silent wish (*un voeu muet*) to fill. But the gap to be filled
would, as Merleau–Ponty says, have a determinate shape, since the
speaker could in principle state some of the features the filler would
have or would manifest his awareness of these features by rejecting
candidates that did not have them. A person's knowing what he does
not want to say is a limiting case of his knowing what he wants to say.

4.   *Rationalism, empiricism and phenomenological motivation*

Let us now answer the question raised by the last sentence of the
passage under discussion. Does Merleau–Ponty find reason to put lan-

guage in a special category which distinguishes it fundamentally from other modes of expression like music and painting? He agrees we do ordinarily suppose it has a privileged status. He agrees that some of our reasons for doing so are valid. But some of our reasons, he argues, are invalid and confused. We are right to reserve a special notion of truth for the universe of linguistic expression. And we rightly regard statements,whether they be those of scientific discourse or of literature, as purporting to be directly or indirectly about different regions and aspects of one and the same world. Furthermore, they can also be about other statements. He does not mention the "quotations" one composer or painter may make from the works of another, but it would be odd to describe, for instance, Berg's quotation from Wagner as a metamusical comment about it. That would be in order only if, along the lines of Gadamer and Barthes, we first interpreted the music in words: "Here he's expressing impatience with the sweetness of the harmony," or suchlike. A similar recourse to verbal interpretation would be called for if we were able to regard different musical traditions, Indian, Western classical, and atonal, for example, as being really one tradition or as perspectives of one auditory or nonauditory world. A Pythagoras might have that thought, but it would not be a musical thought. In addition, even if the project of a perfect language makes prima facie sense, does the project of a universal ideal music? It might be said that the project of a universal music already exists (musak). It might also be said that there already exists a universal musical grammer underlying the various surface musical languages. Merleau–Ponty is nevertheless justified in saying that whereas philosophers have dreamed of an ideal language that would be an improvement on existing languages, painters and composers do not envisage a painterly or musical *Begriffschrift* that would say everything and say it better than it was ever said before.

For these three reasons, Merleau–Ponty concludes, a privileged position is given to language. But, he adds, if on these grounds we accord a privileged position to reason, we must take care not to misconceive that position. As we have been led to expect by our analysis of the use he makes of Saussure, Merleau–Ponty regards the assumption of thoughts subsisting independently of the sensible world as no more than a myth fostered by a forgetting of our forgetting of the historical acts of expression that have yielded the tradition without which nothing new could be said.

> Thus there is no fundamental difference between the various
> modes of expression, and no privileged position can be

accorded to any of them on the alleged ground that it expresses a truth in itself. Speech is as dumb as music, music as
eloquent as speech.[41]

That dispatches realism of truth, ideas, and sense. And when he says,

The clearness of language stands out from an obscure background, and if we carry our investigation far enough we shall
eventually find that language is ... uncommunicative of anything other than itself [*ne dit rien que lui-même*], that its
meaning [*sens*] is inseparable from it,[42]

he is by implication dispatching a naive realism of the referent. Both
rationalist realism of truths in themselves and materialist or empiricist
realism of things in themselves are deemed absurdities.

In the rationalist theories of Plato, Augustine, and Descartes, real
thinking is re-thinking. Hence there is no real innovation. So-called innovation is a nonoriginative return to the wellspring of pure thought
from which truths are translated into words like water into a bucket.
However, Merleau–Ponty argues, in order to explain why a particular
thought is conveyed by a particular set of words and not another, this
intellectualist theory has to fall back on the associationist theory of
empiricism. But this empiricist theory has to be rejected. I shall not
attempt to assess here those of Merleau–Ponty's reasons for rejecting it
that are based on the findings of experimental and clinical psychology
and physiology. They rely chiefly on the teaching of the Gestalt school
that atomistic stimulus-response explanations ignore the extent to which
competences are transferable, as demonstrated by a person's ability to
write on a blackboard although he learned to write on paper and
although in the two activities different muscles are employed. Of the
many cases of compensatory reorganization that Merleau–Ponty cites I
reproduce but one. I take a biological case since if what he says shows
the limitedness of stimulus-response analyses in the biological realm, it
will show a fortiori that they are limited in the realm of linguistic behavior.

It has long been known that the dung beetle, after the
amputation of one or several phalanges, is capable of con-
tinuing its walk immediately. But the movements of the
stump which remains and those of the whole body are not a

simple perseveration of those of normal walking; they represent a new mode of locomotion, a solution of the unexpected problem posed by the amputation. Moreover, this reorganisation of the functioning of an organ (*Umstellung*) is not produced unless it is rendered necessary by the nature of the surface: on a rough surface where the member, even though shortened, can find points of application, the normal process of walking is conserved; it is abandoned when the animal comes upon a smooth surface. Thus, the reorganisation of the functioning is not released automatically by the removal of one or several phalanges as would happen if a pre-established emergency device were involved; it is accomplished only through the pressure of external conditions, and we are led to believe that it is improvised.[43]

The organism is selective, and Merleau–Ponty questions whether this selectivity can be provided for in a theory according to which behavior is a mechanical response to stimuli. He criticizes the Gestalt psychologists themselves for trying to get by with causal explanation instead of rejecting the alternatives of cause and reason in favor of motivation understood in a way suggested by Husserl. But they give a better account than the behaviorists of the systematic structure of experience, for instance of the hermeneutical dependence of the meaning or "effect" of a "stimulus" word not only on the words that precede it, but also on those that follow it in the sentence and its wider context. The behaviorist would contend that this dependence can be explained by the theory of feedback. I shall not enter into this debate. Nor shall I comment on endeavors like, most notably, that made by Jonathan Bennett in *Linguistic Behaviour*, to combine behaviorist theories of meaning inspired by Quine with a theory of speaker's intention inspired by Grice.[44] These theories, as explanations of my behavior from someone else's point of view, may well be compatible with phenomenological descriptions of my experience from my own point of view. But the behaviorist theories of association and reinforcement have the wrong vocabulary to describe the world as I experience it. At best they can describe my world as I see myself experiencing it. Left out of the empiricist explanation is an explanation of how the psychologist himself identifies the stimuli and responses alleged to be constantly conjoined. The very terms of the stimulus-response theory, the items related externally in associative chains, are not there to be related to each other externally unless they are first related internally as figures to a ground. Our experience, and the "our" includes the scientist's, is structured physiognomically. The first things we see are such things as faces, not surfaces or discrete and absolutely simple sense-data. Experiences of the latter are come by with difficulty or under the influence of drugs or when it is induced in the psychologist's laboratory. Merleau–Ponty, like the later Wittgenstein, would say that the assumption of an absolute in-itself simplicity is an assumption—and a confused one—derived from a realist prejudice in favor of a world-in-itself. The "things themselves," when looked at in the face without metaphysical bias, never reveal themselves without "bias," or, in Gadamer's sense of the word, prejudice. A stimulus-response account of them must leave room, therefore, for a question-response account.

Now just as the empiricist account has the problem of identifying the stimulus, so Merleau–Ponty's account has the problem of identifying the question. The latter's problem is in one respect more difficult. For whereas the empiricist believes the regressive analysis of experience and language eventually reaches a full stop or, rather, a full start (compare Sartre's regress which, in spite of himself, goes back to an absolutely empty start),[45] there seems to be no nonarbitrary way of halting the regress on the account offered by the phenomenologist. There might be if the phenomenological account could make room for a theory of innate ideas, innate categories, or innate principles. But would not that be a form of the rationalism that Merleau–Ponty rejects? If only he could accept it he would be able to halt the regress at least where the question at issue was one of formal necessity or, on a Chomskian theory, deep linguistic structure. But we should still be in need of an explanation of how the necessary truths and the deep syntactic structures are connected in linguistic performances with the phonic or graphic medium in which they are expressed. To attempt an explanation of a hypothetico-deductive kind would be to quit the field of phenomenology. We should be abandoning phenomenology, too, if our attempt to explain why a person raises one particular question as opposed to another were cast in terms of the facts of his physiological or psychological makeup or factors of his environment. Such explanations are not ruled out by the phenomenologist. But they are not ones that he, as phenomenologist, will be concerned to give. He is more concerned to show that such explanations cannot stand on their own feet, since the concept of cause these empirical explanations employ, no less than the notion of reason employed by the rationalist, is abstracted from and incomprehensible without the explainer's own experience of phenomenological motivation.

Phenomenological motivation is what in *The Structure of Behaviour* was called circular causation. Husserl introduced the term motivation to distinguish since-then relations of the noetic-noematic field from the causal relations of the psychological and other empirical fields.[46] It is used in a sense extended from that of its ordinary use where we say an action was motivated by a desire to bring about something to which it was seen as a means. Whereas a cause and an effect have to be conceptually separate, there is an internal relation of one kind or another between the motive and what is motivated. The relation may be conceptual but not a relation of entailment such as holds between logical ground and consequent. Thus, running away, cringing, or standing stock still may be motivated by fear although no one of these patterns of behavior in particular and, *per impossibile*, not all of them together need be followed. I am not motivated by fear unless, other things being equal, I manifest one or more of these and other recognized patterns of behavior. The internal relation may be perceptual, like that between areas of a painting or notes of a tune. It may also be phonological, morphological, or syntactic, like the various paradigmatic and syntagmatic oppositions illustrated in section 1 or this chapter. Phenomenological motivation, as Merleau–Ponty's first name for it implied, exhibits one or another sort of hermeneutic circularity.

Does this extended concept of motivation help Merleau–Ponty clarify the structure, assuming it has one, of creative expression? On the rationalist theory innovation, we saw, is an illusion. It is no more than the making explicit of what is already there. Theoretical invention at least, as etymology might seem to confirm, is discovery, and discovery is anamnetic recovery. We also saw that although in the rationalist story there is room for a thinker, if the thinker's thoughts are to be put into words or some other medium, that story must be expanded. Assuming the rationalist does not wish to go so far as to posit a theologically preestablished harmony, his rationalist theory would need fleshing out with an empiricist one. But it is doubtful whether on this latter theory there would be room for a speaker. There would be a string of "words" connected according to contingent laws of association, but they would not be words spoken by the thinker, for the thoughts of the thinker on this dualist theory would be their own medium and would be related to the tokens of the phonic or graphic medium at best in the naturally indicative way that fire is betokened by charred timber. There would be no room on this theory, therefore, for convention or for speaker's intention. Nor again would there be room for innovation. The new would be no more than a combination and recombination of old data according to psychophysical laws of cause and effect.

5. *The productive imagination*

Merleau–Ponty articulates motivation not in terms of reputedly immaculate conception nor in terms of allegedly raw data of sensation, but in terms of schemata of what he himself describes as the productive imagination.[47] In going back to the things themselves he is going back to Husserl. He is also going back to Kant, to those parts of Kant's theory of the imagination that he believes he can wed to Husserl's theory of preconceptual open-textured types, typics, or typicalities (*Typik*).[48] With a faculty now on hand called the productive imagination we may feel entitled to expect a better account than we obtained from rationalism and empiricism of the structure of creative expression and how such expression is possible. The problem, to put a finer point on it, is to understand how someone can do something that is originative and for which he is responsible. The difficulty we met in section 3 was to show how one can be responsible for what is original, how one can *make* something new. If the *poiesis* is an action, does not that mean one is following a rule? Or is one following it only so far, then departing from it? In that case, is not the bit of the deed that matters not a deed at all, but a happening, a gift?

These problems cannot be seen, let alone solved, unless we define more clearly than Merleau–Ponty does what is to count as creativity. Is what is created to be new, for instance? Or can the idea or other artifact be a reproduction provided that the person has worked it out or up for himself, so long as there has been what Husserl in the *Crisis* (e.g., sec. 15) calls reestablishment, *Nachstiftung*? If these and other distinctions are made, some of our problems will solve themselves. Others, for example some of those discussed in section 3 of this chapter, would be solved if we dispensed with talk of significative intention. This is a locution that may well be in place where we are explicating expression in a sense not implying the special creativity of the artist or inventor. Husserl uses the words in discussing expression which we should not ordinarily dignify with the epithet creative. Where in the course of his treatment of expression in the *Logical Investigations* he does use this epithet, he concedes he is not using it literally.[49] Where in perfectly prosaic contexts as opposed to *la grande prose*[50] we say what we mean (*voulons dire*) or what we want to say (*voulons dire*), we are normally conscious of what we mean. What we mean is an intentional object of our consciousness. So there is some justification for talking here of significative intention. This is also justified where we say something in a strong sense creative, assuming we have some understanding of what we say. But in this case it is by no means clear that we understand the creative or new bit of what we say. We may be hesitating between sense and sound with most or all of our weight resting on the sound. It would therefore be safer to say that in these necessarily uncommon cases we understand what we say, not what we want to say, not what we mean. What we say may well be what we mean to say, what we intend to say. But if we are saying something creative relative to *our* past performances, not just creative relative to some other norm, it is doubtful whether we intend to say no more than what we understand. Hence it is dangerous to talk in these special cases of significative intention. Even if we remember that the intentionality intended in Merleau–Ponty's phrase is not that of an intention *to* signify but the intentionality *of* signifying, it would be preferable, in these special cases at least, to speak of significative motivation.

A phenomenological description of the productive imagination, then, does not promise to be rich. We are prepared for this disappointment as soon as Merleau–Ponty begins talking in these Kantian terms. For had not Kant called this faculty "an art concealed in the depths of the human soul"?[51] And now of his version of Kant's faculty and its descendent in the third *Critique* Merleau–Ponty agrees that "it is impossible to draw up an inventory of this irratonal power which creates meanings and conveys them."[52] This power of giving significance, whether as speaker and author or as listener and reader, must be accepted as an ultimate fact, "since any explanation of it—whether empiricist, reducing new meanings to given ones, or idealist, positing an absolute knowledge immanent in the primary forms of knowledge—would amount to a denial of it."[53]

When we talk of the productive imagination we are talking about nothing less than "man's deepest essence."[54] Man is a subjunctive animal. As Merleau–Ponty writes in "From Mauss to Claude Lévi–Strauss," "The symbolic function ... finds reality only by anticipating it in imagination."[55] Or, as Robert Musil writes in *The Man without Qualities,* "If there is such a thing as a sense of reality, there must also be a sense of possibility." This sense of possibility is none other than what Heidegger—who, like Merleau–Ponty, was struck by Kant's theory of the imagination—calls Dasein's being ahead of itself. It is what Sartre—who wrote two books on the imagination—called, in memory of Hegel, the for-itself's being what it is not and not being what it is.[56] It is Hume's stress on man's imaginative animality that explains why Husserl sees Hume as a budding, albeit nipped in the bud, phenomenologist. The gap-filling propensities of the human imagination are given as significant a role in the writings of *le bon David* as they are given in Husserl's analyses of eidetic variation through aspects[57] and, we may add, as the gap-filling schematism of the imagination is given in Merleau–Ponty's analyses of sense-giving expression. It is this agreement with Husserl on the importance of the imagination that explains why the existential analyses developed by Heidegger and Sartre have the concrete *existenziell* point of departure where they and their readers are asking themselves about, wondering, what it means to be. It explains, too, why the whole of Merleau–Ponty's last work is an interrogation of or, more accurately, a wondering about interrogation and wonder.[58] In the work of Heidegger, Sartre, and Merleau–Ponty the question plays a part like that which the judgment plays in the *Critique of Pure Reason*. But while for Kant the logical forms of judgment are a clue to the categories of our understanding of the empirical world, for Heidegger, Sartre, and Merleau–Ponty the structure of the question is a clue to the existentials, that is, to the structures of being in the world. It is more accurate to describe what Merleau–Ponty is doing in *The Visible and the Invisible* as a wondering or meditation rather than an interrogation. We thereby avoid suggesting that he applies excruciating Baconian methods of inquisition to extort answers to clear and distinct questions. "What one too deliberately seeks one does not find."[59] He cites Gasquet's report of Cézanne's saying that in his youth he wanted to paint the white tablecloth likened in *La Peau de chagrin* to "a covering of newly fallen snow, from which rose symmetrically the plates and napkins crowned with pale yellow bread rolls." "I know now that one must try to paint only: 'the plates and napkins rose symmetrically,' and 'the pale yellow bread rolls.' I am done for if I try to paint 'crowned.'"[60] The painter, as Merleau–Ponty says elsewhere, is like the weaver who works on the wrong side of the rug. By the same indirection and by keeping himself at a respectful distance from his motif, the poet solicits *l'absente de tous bouquets*[61] and "frees the meaning captive in the thing." And so it is with the philosopher who wishes to bring the still silent experience of primordial being to "the pure expression of its own meaning."[62] He, too, is in need of negative capability. He, too, will do well to wait attentively for signs of synergic grace. Perhaps "the meaning is in the waiting."[63] Perhaps in this context too, to seek is already to have found. And if to this context we applied the text "by grace are ye saved through faith" (Eph. 2:8), that faith might be justified provided, as Heidegger says, *Sein* and *Dasein belong* together, or, as Merleau–Ponty says, echoing Bergson, *j'en suis*, "I am of it," "I belong."[64] Provided also we seek in the right way. But what is the right way? Seeking with patient attention? What sort of a way is that? A way that is not a method? The way of *Gelassenheit*, letting being and language speak? In any case, not through a too insistent questioning of particulars, deafening our sense of the wonder of it all. For

> the interrogative is not a mode derived by inversion or by reversal of the indicative and of the positive, is neither an affirmation nor a negation veiled or expected, but an original manner of aiming at something, as it were a *question-knowing [question-savoir]*, which in principle no statement or "answer" can go beyond and which perhaps therefore is the proper mode of our relationship with Being, as though it were the mute or reticent interlocuter of our questions. "What do I know?" is not only "what is knowing?" and not only "who am I?" but finally: "what is there?" and even "what is the *there is*?" These questions call not for the exhibiting of something said which would put an end to them, but for the disclosure of a Being that is not posited because it has no need to be, because it is silently behind all our affirmations, negations, and even behind all formulated questions, not that it is a matter of imprisoning it in our chatter, but because philosophy is the reconversion of silence and speech into each other.[65]

Into each other. Speech is the only way to the truth, which lies silently behind it. Perhaps even the chatter of this chapter questioning the particulars of empiricist and rationalist theories of meaning is, where it is most wanting, on the hermeneuticly circular way beyond the metaphysical concept of being to the meaning of Being disclosed when (see the end of section 3) we know what we do not want to say but do not know what we do, when (see part three) we let ourselves be struck by the thought that it is possible for language itself to be at a loss for words.

CHAPTER EIGHT
LÉVI–STRAUSS OR RICOEUR: STRUCTURAL OR HERMENEUTIC ANTHROPOLOGY?

Quand on veut étudier les hommes, il faut regarder près de soi; mais pour étudier l'homme, il faut apprendre à porter sa vue au loin: il faut d'abord observer les différences, pour découvrir les propriétés.

—Jean–Jacques Rousseau

Chapter 7 considered Merleau–Ponty's enlistment of Saussure to effect a reconciliation of structuralism with the phenomenologist's emphasis on historicity. The present chapter considers how from a structuralist point of view Claude Lévi–Strauss argues that structuralism embraces diachrony. It is not without philosophical significance that Lévi–Strauss begins *La Pensée sauvage* with a dedication to Merleau–Ponty. He ends it with a chapter giving the reasons for his own disagreement with Sartre. This does not mean that there are no important issues over which he is also in disagreement with Merleau–Ponty. There are also issues over which he is in agreement with Sartre. In the chapter entitled "History and Dialectic" in which he defines where he stands in relation to the position he believes Sartre occupies in the *Critique of Dialectical Reason*, he protests that structural anthropology is misconstrued by those who criticize it for being exclusively synchronic. This issue will be the chief topic of sections 2 and 3. Section 3 referees the debate between Lévi–Strauss and Paul Ricoeur over whether structural explanation in anthropology is more fundamental than hermeneutic understanding. But I shall first give a summary of Lévi–Strauss's theory of myth.

1. *Mythologicality*

It is chiefly primitive kinship systems and myths that Lévi–Strauss proposes to explain. The myths he records often deal at one level with antinomies connected with the rules of kinship practices. Not that there is explicit mention made of rules in these myths. They are usually alluded to through metonymy or metaphor made possible by the fact that the physical objects, birds, beasts, sensible qualities, etc., mentioned in them function as signs. This function derives from their being opposed to one or more contrary. The opposition is not always binary,[1] but there is some evidence that in Lévi–Strauss's opinion the ternary, quaternary, etc., oppositions are analyzed by mythic thinking into pairs like hot/cold, high/low, east/west, raw/cooked, wet/dry, sun/moon, day/night, near/far, and man/woman. The last four of these oppositions, for example, operate in the group of myths or rather (since a myth is the totality of its versions) in the myth from the Orenoco region described in the third volume of Lévi–Strauss's *Mythologiques*.

The axis of this complex story is the tension between the desire to perpetuate one's tribe and the desire to avoid promiscuity. This introduces the idea of what constitutes a proper distance a woman may travel. The tribes in question are river people, and according to their myths, a measure of the proper distance is sought by scratching pictures of the sun and moon on the face of the rocks along the river at points corresponding to the days and nights required for the journey by canoe. But the spatial measure thus obtained is out of kilter with the temporal experience of the travelers, since what is a proper distance in terms of the spatial criterion nonetheless takes a different time to cover according as one is traveling upstream or down. Different submyths narrate different episodes which on Lévi–Strauss's account are unconscious stratagems for overcoming or mediating these tensions. In one story occurs the idea of reversing the river's flow. In other versions the sun, a metaphor for man, and the moon, a metaphor for woman, are either halted in their course or set again in motion, the women's legs are broken to prevent their promiscuity, or characters are invoked who have only the upper half of a normal body. It seems to be Lévi–Strauss's view that these attempts at solution are never entirely successful, as is quite clear in the case of the one last mentioned, for it prevents promiscuity only by preventing procreation. Nevertheless, the dialectical proliferation of mythic attempts to overcome such contradictions has a kind of success. Lévi–Strauss maintains that "the purpose of myth is to provide a logical model capable of overcoming a ... contradiction,"[2] but since each would-be solution generates another contradiction, they fail in that purpose. However, this failure is *admitted* in the myths, "and there precisely lies their function."[3] The telling of a myth is a way of telling oneself that however far one pursues the dialectic, there are no grounds for expecting the quest will end in anything like a Hegelian apotheosis of absolute knowledge. Here is one respect in which Lévi–Strauss's picture of the human condition resembles the portrait drawn by Sartre.

Although the tellers and hearers of the myths are conscious of the surface sense of the words they use and the literal sense of the statements they are used to make, they need not be conscious, Lévi–Strauss holds, of the grammar, morphology, and phonology due to which these statements can be made. "We learn to speak before we learn how to speak." But the messages that the myths seem to convey have little apparent coherence. The primitive mind is a *bricoleur* improvising with odds and ends left over from half-forgotten stories to confect new stories which appear to have neither rhyme nor reason. Syntagmatically, that is, serially, considered only their parts in isolation have literal significance. As a whole they have no obvious sense. It is only when the structural analyst breaks the syntagmatic strings into elements and, instead of reading them and their variants and repetitions horizontally or melodically, directs our attention to their vertical, paradigmatic, or contrapuntal relations that we become conscious of the mythemes and their mytho-logicality.

In the structural linguistics of Saussure and Jakobson the phoneme, the morpheme, and the lexeme are constituted by oppositive differences like the difference between "let," "lot," and "lit," or "let," "met," and "pet." In the structural phonology of Jakobson the phoneme corresponding to, for example, the *l*, the *e*, or the *t* in "let" is an intersection of a selection of distinctive features generated by a comparatively small number of binary oppositions made use of by the large number of languages throughout the speaking world, for instance vowel/consonant, voiced/unvoiced, dental/labial, palatal/velar, acute/grave, open/closed. In the structural anthropology of Lévi–Strauss the mytheme, the element of mythological significance, is constituted by a binary relation between relations, a resemblance between differences. The differences are those between the contrary opposites that figure in the surface structure of the story. But it is only the analogies between these pairs that yield the structure thanks to which myths can perform the function

Lévi–Strauss ascribes to them. And these analogies hold between the binary oppositions figuring in the codes or universes of discourse at various levels. To illustrate, in the case of the Orenoco myth referred to earlier, the opposition between no moon and halted sun in the astronomic code is in apposition to the opposition between near and far in the geographic code, to that between woman without legs and vagabond woman in the anatomical code, to that between incest and exogamy in the sociological code, and to that between timidity and audacity in the ethical code. This makes it seem as though the relationship is one of simple analogy: A:B::C:D. It must not be overlooked that what Lévi–Strauss intends to bring out is not a simple relation but a relation between relations, and that these include inversions. He produces the formula

$$F_x(a):F_{y(b)}\simeq F_x(b):F_{a-1}(y)$$

which he explains as follows:

> Here, with two terms, *a* and *b*, being given as well as two functions, *x* and *y*, of these terms, it is assumed that a relation of equivalence exists between two situations defined respectively by an inversion of *terms* and *relations*, under two conditions: (1) that one term be replaced by its opposite (in the formula, *a* and *a − 1*); (2) that an inversion be made between the *function value* and the *term value* of two elements (above, *y* and *a*).[4]

He predicts that this formula will be satisfied by any myth considered as the totality of its variants.

2. *Diachronological structuralism*

In the first section of this chapter reference was made to Lévi–Strauss's description of the manner in which primitive mentality makes do with remnants of discarded stories to fabricate new ones. This is obviously a process through time and its recyclical pattern appears to reflect the patterns of retention-protention and recuperation or projective retrieval which play so large a part in phenomenology, fundamental ontology, and philosophical hermeneutics. On the face of it, the chapter in *La Pensée sauvage* called "History and Dialectic" concedes that writers like Merleau–Ponty and Sartre have been right to put so much stress on the significance for the social sciences of the diachronic and the historical. Lévi–Strauss goes as far as to say in this book that the anthropologist will fail to understand the institutions of so-called primitive peoples if he does not attend to both the synchronic structures and the diachronic events.[5] One obvious reason for this is that it is only because there is a structure acting as a selective grid that there can be identifiable events.[6] A second reason, one that relates more specially to structural anthropology, is that the historical transformations of societies have to be studied by anyone who reckons, as Lévi–Strauss does, that there is a structure that remains invariant through these transformations.[7]

Hence the synchronic is not to be confused with the static. Although it was useful to oppose the synchronic and the diachronic in the prototypical Saussurian phase of structuralism, that was because Saussure's predecessors had been too prone to assume that linguistics was a largely historical study of the origin and evolution of languages. Saussure was also wanting to focus interest on competence rather than performance, on the system, mastery of which is manifested in successful acts of speech as opposed to the acts of speech themselves. The latter take time. For ordinary mortals the temporal succession of the words that are uttered, heard, written, or read is a necessary condition for their having significance. This second kind of diachrony, too, falls outside the area Saussure is most concerned to investigate.

In spite of his wish to direct attention on the nonsuccessive structure of language, however, even Saussure allows that in any cross section of any natural language some forms will be in process of being replaced by others. But it is Jakobson who emphasizes most strongly that the static cross section is no more than a useful fiction. No doubt his stress on the teleonomic owes something to the contact he made during the 1920s in Prague with Hegelian modes of thought and with Husserl's theory of founding. The work of Lévi–Strauss takes on a new aspect if we see it as having, through Jakobson, this Husserlian lineage. In *Structural Anthropology* Lévi–Strauss quotes the sentences where Jakobson asserts the purely heuristic status of the idea of a static cross section of language.[8] Adjacent sentences he does not quote are no less seminal for his own thinking. The part of Jakobson's theory expressed there insists that obsolescent forms play a role in the synchronic structure of language, a view that is almost but not quite expressed even by Saussure. The synchronic is dynamic. The availability of a choice between an archaic and a modern form is one of the powers of language that a synchronist science of it must take into account. But a further principle of Jakobson's theory is that where a change that returns a language to a state of equilibrium in one area of it leads to the disruption of equilibrium in another, which in turn leads to a further corrective change, and so on, the question of the teleonomic order of these changes is a question that comes within the ambit of the synchronist science.[9]

In a similar vein Lévi–Strauss reminds the reader of *From Honey to Ashes* that he occasionally advances interpretations that imply an order between transformations of a particular myth which is either irreversible or reversible at too great cost. One example of this is his hypothesis that a certain myth of the Tacana, who permit coeducation, is derived from Bororo–Ge myths dealing with education for only one or the other sex. The Tacana myth is probably an adaptation of the myth associated with an Eastern tradition of male initiation or an adaptation of the myth belonging to a Western tradition that gives more importance to the education of females, these Eastern and Western myths themselves being derived probably from a still older myth. For another example, see the discussion in *The Raw and the Cooked* of the myths numbered M145 and M162 of which Lévi–Strauss writes:

> Although my analysis is concerned with form, it allows me to put forward a theory regarding the respective ages of the two myths and their primary or derivative function: for the syntagmatic sequences to be intelligible, M145 must be earlier than M162, and the second myth must appear to be the result of a kind of meditation, no doubt unconscious, on the first. The opposite theory would have no explanatory value whatsoever. Similarly, M175 would appear to be derivative in relation to M145 and M162, since it presupposes both of them.[10]

As I interpret these words they concern a question that is historical without ceasing to be formal. Their point is not to indicate that their author is making an exception by forsaking purely formal analysis in order to consider a historical question; it is rather to indicate, in the spirit of Jakobson, that he can deal with a certain historical question without going outside the limits of formal analysis. Whether we ought to agree with Lévi–Strauss on the unidirectionality of explanation cannot be decided unless we examine the myths in detail. For our purposes here it is sufficient if we agree that he has no intention of implying that structural anthropology can have nothing to do with matters historical. If our Jakobsonian reading of him is correct, Lévi–Strauss allows that the historical can be a part of the structural.

However, Lévi–Strauss has in mind also a different respect, external rather than internal, in which "structural analysis accords history a paramount place." This is

> the place that rightfully belongs to the irreducible contingency without which necessity would be inconceivable. In so far as structural analysis, going beyond the apparent diversity of human societies, claims to be reaching back to common and fundamental properties, it abandons the attempt to explain not of course particular differences which it can deal with by specifying in each ethnographical context the non-varying laws according to which they are being produced, but the fact that these differences, which are all potentially possible at the same time, do not all occur in practice and that only some of them actually occurred. To be valid, any investigation which is entirely aimed at elementary structures must begin by submitting to the powerful inanity of events.[11]

This, if I understand it, is a somewhat backhanded way of showing that structural anthropology "accords history a paramount place," since the place it accords it lies outside any system whose structure the anthropologist is competent to analyze. Incidentally, if he means that we cannot have the concept of necessity unless there is something contingent, what he says is open to question. If we have the concept of necessity we have the concept of contingency, but it is doubtful that something contingent must exist. This does not affect his main claim here, which is the claim Saussure made when, without using the word "structure," he observed that the causes of disturbance to the state of equilibrium obtaining in a cross section of a language are analogous to events that impinge from outside upon a celestial system and upset its state of equilibrium. Although Lévi–Strauss agrees with Jakobson—and indeed with Merleau–Ponty, for he, too, follows Jakobson on this matter—that there can be a structural analysis of the sequence of states of disequilibrium and equilibrium, he agrees with Saussure that the initial impinging event lies beyond the scope of structural analysis. This is because a structural explanation is not a causal explanation. And it is as well that this is so. For the nature of the material with which the anthropologist works is usually not written, and there is usually too little evidence on which to base hypotheses about historical events and their dating. Hence Lévi–Strauss's objection to diffusionist theories that they either lack empirical evidence or, in the case of alleged contact between very remote societies, fly in the face of it. As for first causes or origins, there seems to be a difficulty in principle in the way of establishing them. This is one of the grounds for Lévi–Strauss's objection to evolutionary anthropology.

Another reason he gives for his objection to evolutionism is that it imports value judgments in terms of which aboriginal societies are graded as more primitive than the so-called civilized society to which the anthropologist belongs. He also gives this as one of his reasons for objecting to Sartre. It deserves to be said that there can be existential and phenomenological analyses that do not make this particular evaluative assumption, for example the analysis proposed by Merleau–Ponty. It deserves to be said too that there can be evolutionary theories that do not make this ethnocentric assumption. But in practice many of them have done so. One case Lévi–Strauss mentions is the theory of Lévy–Bruhl according to which the aboriginal mentality is prelogical. This is precisely the kind of theory Lévi–Strauss is out to refute, thereby preserving for the modern anthropologist the scope to say something scientific about the infrastructure of aboriginal societies. For if that cannot be described in the logic to which the nonaboriginal anthropologist has access, his descriptions will be *ex hypothesi* misdescriptions. Lévi–Strauss's objection to Lévy–Bruhl's doctrine of prelogicality implies an objection to Bachelard's doctrine of the epistemological break. Although a critic of phenomenology and, as we shall soon see, of at least phenomenological hermeneutics, Lévi–Strauss is an ally of these movements in so far as he is a critic of Bachelard.

Hardly less embarrassing than Lévy–Bruhl's predicament, as seen by Lévi-Strauss, is that of functionalist theories. A consistent and interesting functionalism must concentrate, says Lévi-Strauss, on the details of particular societies, bringing out how the needs of each society are met by the institutions of that society. In so far as it is comparative it will describe the differences between societies. The only resemblances it can have empirical access to are likely to be commonplace ones based on the dogma that there is a causal connection between the psycho-physiological and the socio-cultural. Further, the functionalist neglects history.

> How shall we correctly estimate the role, so surprising to foreigners, of the *apéritif* in French social life if we are igno-

rant of the traditional prestige value ascribed to cooked and spiced wines ever since the Middle Ages? How shall we analyse modern dress without recognising in it vestiges of previous customs and tastes? To reason otherwise would make it impossible to establish what is an essential distinction between the primary function, which corresponds to a present need of the social body, and secondary function, which survives only because the group resists giving up a habit. For to say that a society functions is a truism; but to say that everything in a society functions is an absurdity.[12]

This leaves the reader in no doubt that we misunderstand the range of structural anthropology if we suppose it divorces itself from the historical.

3. *Ricoeur and hermeneutic historicity*

Let us look more closely at the historical partner in structural anthropology. "The distinctive features of historical knowledge," writes Lévi–Strauss, "are due not to the absence of a code, which is illusory, but to its particular nature: the code consists in a chronology. There is no history without dates."[13] The history whose relevance to structural analysis he emphasizes is the objective *Historie* of historiography and, especially, geology, the first of his "three mistresses."[14] He is no less emphatic about the irrelevance to structural analysis of what Heidegger calls *Geschichte*, "historicity," and what Gadamer calls effective or operatively historical consciousness, *wirkungsgeschichtliche Bewusstsein*. That this is so is evident from the replies Lévi–Strauss makes to Paul Ricoeur's thesis that anthropology, including structural anthropology, rests on hermeneutic understanding.[15]

Ricoeur does not argue, as earlier hermeneutic theorists like Schleiermacher and Dilthey do, that an understanding of texts or other artifacts can be achieved only if the interpreter uproots himself from his own preconceptions and transplants himself imaginatively in the life and times of the authors of these artifacts. In one respect Lévi–Strauss's position is closer to this classical hermeneutic theory than is the post-Heideggerian hermeneutics of Gadamer and Ricoeur. Schleiermacher holds that empathetic understanding of a historically remote people is facilitated by a shared human nature. And a crucial component of Lévi–Strauss's theory is that there is a shared human nature. Since this, in his view, exceeds any merely biological common denominator and extends to the structure of the unconscious mental principles according to which socio-cultural artifacts are constituted, he is well placed to defend a theory of empathetic understanding. Yet he does not believe such a theory would be part of structural anthropology. He takes the same attitude to post-Heideggerian hermeneutics. Not only is empathetic understanding of anthropological material irrelevant to structural analysis; so, too, is the self-understanding that Ricoeur maintains is the prerequisite of any understanding.

Like Gadamer, Ricoeur argues that whatever difficulties the anthropologist may have getting into the minds of the people he is studying, he cannot get outside his own mind. Consequently, Lévi-Strauss should acknowledge that the anthropologist's analysis of structures cannot be separated from the question of the relevance the anthropologist's discoveries have for the understanding of his own world and the situation he occupies in it. Lévi-Strauss concedes that although the anthropologist may take this interest in his material, it is not one he can have as structural anthropologist. The structural anthropologist is interested solely in "demonstrating the mechanism of objectivised thought."[16]

Ricoeur himself does not deny that the scientific attitude requires the scientist to disengage himself from his own involvement with the matter being investigated. What he denies is that the scientist can justifiably talk about *meaning* without plugging in to the hermeneutic circuit of his own self-understanding. Now, Lévi–Strauss does regard structural anthropology as an analysis of meaning. Ricoeur's inability to see how Lévi–Strauss can consistently do this stems from the former's unwillingness to make the Saussurian break between *langue* and *parole*. This is an unwillingness to acknowledge that "when we describe structures ... we are, as it were, in the realm of grammar and syntax, not of the spoken word," the same unwillingness that led Radcliffe-Brown to regard social structure as merely the sum total of social relations.[17] Does the fact that the meaning of expressions is constituted by individual acts of speech imply that there can be no scientific syntactico-semantics? Ricoeur must be willing to grant that individual acts of speech are possible only if the individual speaker has at his disposal a ready-made syntactico-semantic system about whose original historical constituting acts he raises no question. We have seen he is willing to grant that the scientist must abstract himself. Why then does he insist that the scientist must maintain the connection between the abstract and the concrete from which it is abstracted, and moreover forge a connection between the abstract and his own concrete life? Why does he say, referring to myths, "If I don't understand myself better in understanding them, can I still speak of meaning? If meaning is not a segment of self-understanding, I don't know what it is"?[18] There seems to be an assumption here that meaning attaches only to discovery, to the increase of understanding, and not to something we already understand. This is more radical than Bachelard's thesis, discussed above in chapter 5, that a concept has most meaning when its meaning is being changed. Understanding is not always coming to understand; and when we already understand, it is commonly the meaning of something, such as a word we have used correctly for many years.

It may be that Ricoeur is being misled by the Heideggerian idea that there is no understanding without interpretation. It is a short though not irresistible step from this idea to the belief that all meaning must lie below the surface and requires hard interpretative spade work to bring it to light. It is plainly false that all meaning is deep—but there is a lot to be said, and a lot has been said, for the idea that surface meaning has a deeper meaning underlying it. And Ricoeur knows that the structures that interest Lévi–Strauss are not the surface ones. That is one reason for Lévi–Strauss's dissatisfaction with Radcliffe–Brown's brand of functionalist "structuralism." Ricoeur knows, too, that Freudian theory is one of Lévi–Strauss's "three mistresses." It is therefore easy to appreciate why Ricoeur should expect Lévi–Strauss to be seeking an account of the deep meaning of what has surface meaning. Ricoeur is bound to judge that Lévi–Strauss fails in that search. This judgment is a corollary of the above-mentioned difficulty Ricoeur has in separating the societal fact of what something means from the individual fact of what something means for some person, the bearer of the myth or the scientific interpreter of the myth. This difficulty may arise in turn from endorsement of an extremely strong version of Gadamer's thesis that understanding is inseparable not only from interpretation but also from application, application being taken by Ricoeur in this context as application to one's own situation.

That all understanding in the social and natural sciences is self-understanding is uncontroversial if all that is meant is that the sciences furnish us with knowledge about matter, mind, and society, and the scientist himself has a mind and is a member of society. However, it appears not to be only this that Ricoeur intends. He believes structural analysis is inadequate to cope with the sense of destiny manifested by the stories and cults of certain peoples, like the Jews of the Old Testament with their consciousness that they were bearers of an eschatological message. For the myths and institutions of such peoples structural analysis is less revealing than hermeneutic analysis, he says. But structural analysis, he now agrees, may be more important than hermeneutic analysis with the totemic cultures to which Lévi–Strauss gives most of his attention. This is a constructive suggestion. If we are to determine whether it facilitates a reconciliation between Ricoeur's theory and the theory of Lévi–Strauss, we must ask how general the latter claims to be.

Bearing on this question is Lévi–Strauss's disarming confession that he decided he had better not try out his method, as Edmund Leach had done, on the mythic material of the Old Testament because there are so few ethnographical data accessible in the case of the dramatis personae of the Old Testament apart from the Bible itself.[19] This is disarming in the light of his later remark that it is because we know so little about the exotic societies he does study that they make eminently suitable subjects for structural analysis: The poverty of our knowledge compels us to consider only the essentials. These two remarks, whether or not they are more than apparently at odds with each other, underline the degree to which the material Lévi–Strauss bases his theories on is dependent on pragmatic methodological criteria. He claims nonetheless that the hypotheses he tests with this restricted material hold for all mankind. Lévi–Strauss concentrates on the relatively "cool" cultures, those like that of the Australian aborigines in which the thinking of the participants is marked by a timelessness that distinguishes them from the "hot" cultures like those of the Western world where life is predicated on calendars, timetables, etc.—and, presumably, from what one might call the intermediate "luke-warm" transitional cultures like those of Polynesia[20] and, perhaps, the Old Testament cultures concentrated on by Ricoeur. But Lévi–Strauss conjectures that wherever and whenever the human mind manifests itself it has the same fundamental logical structure. Totemism itself is "a *modus operandi* which can be discerned even behind social structures traditionally defined in a way diametrically opposed to totemism."[21] This allegedly scientific universalism is the most Lévi–Strauss offers to match the philosophical ecumenism of Ricoeur. It is reached by stages. He moves from a comparison of the myths or institutions of one cool culture to a comparison of those of contiguous and remote cool cultures to, ultimately, a comparison of those of cool and hot cultures. Comparisons of this last kind are infrequent, since his chief object as an anthropologist is to explain the working of primitive cultures. References to the anthropologist's own society are mainly limited to providing analogies to aid the understanding of primitive mentality, as in the following example.

> We know that among most primitive peoples it is very dif-
> ficult to obtain a moral justification or a rational explanation
> for any custom or institution. When he is questioned, the
> native merely answers that things have always been this way,
> that such was the command of the gods or the teaching of
> the ancestors. Even when interpretations are offered, they
> always have the character of rationalisations or secondary
> elaborations. There is rarely any doubt that the unconscious
> reasons for practising a custom or sharing a belief are remote
> from the reasons given to justify them. Even in our own soci-
> ety, table manners, social etiquette, fashions of dress, and
> many of our moral, political, and religious attitudes are scru-
> pulously observed by everyone, although their real origin
> and function are not often critically examined.[22]

Lévi–Strauss makes these appeals to our own society because he is
confident that "the savage mind is logical in the same sense as ours is,"[23]
the only difference being that whereas the savage mind starts with the
supremely concrete and sensible, the domesticated mind is supremely
abstract and formal.[24] That is, primitive mentality, *which is an aspect of
our own mentality*, is more responsive to the variegated hues, sounds,
smells, tastes, and textures of the world. But it is a mistake to infer, as
Lévy–Bruhl did, that the relation primitive mentality has to nature is
one of amorphous emotional participation. The mentality of primitive
cultures is no less intellectual than is our mathematico-scientific culture.
Fundamental to both is the principle of difference or opposition. The
pre-scientific mind gives primacy to the "secondary" sensible qualities
of matter, but it cannot dispense with form. The mathematical and scientific mind picks out the quantifiable "primary" qualities, but it cannot
dispense with sensible matter. Moreover, says Lévi–Strauss, wittingly
or unwittingly diverging still further from Bachelard and converging
with Bergson, recent developments in topological mathematics and the
theory of games show that form, structure, and necessity do not entail
quantity and measurability. And Saussure, followed by Jakobson and
Merleau–Ponty, has shown that the sensible and the conceptual are inseparable aspects of the sign. Lévi–Strauss wants to show that what
anthropologists have tended to regard as purely sensible and affective
items in the world of primitive man are instead socio-cultural signs

whose significative function must be understood in the same way as that of verbal signs, not on the model of a substantive sensible entity underlying it but on the model of oppositive relation exemplified by the way in which the phoneme represented by *e* is constituted by the contrast between, for instance, "let," "lit," and "lot." Lévi–Strauss perceives his task as the use of this diacritical model to bring to fruition the suggestion made by the third of his three main inspirers, Marx, that we should make explicit "the symbolic systems which underlie both language and man's relationship with the universe" as Jacob Grimm revealed the "etymological connection between the names of the precious metals and the relations of colours in the different Indo–European languages."[25] However,

> Marxism, if not Marx himself, has too commonly reasoned as though practices followed directly from *praxis*. Without questioning the undoubted primacy of infrastructures, I believe that there is always a mediator between *praxis* and practices, namely the conceptual scheme by the operation of which matter and form, neither with any independent existence, are realised as structures, that is as entities which are both empirical and intelligible. It is to this theory of superstructure, scarcely touched by Marx, that I hope to make a contribution.[26]

Lévi–Strauss cites Marx's statement that "it is only through the habit of everyday life that we come to think it perfectly plain and commonplace that a social relation of production should take on the form of a thing."[27] To think this is like falling under the illusion that with the kings, queens, and proletarian pawns in the game of chess what matters is the physical properties of each piece, whereas what really matters is their diacritical differences. So, too, for the science that seeks to explain primitive mentality, raw feelings and the purely sensory are without sense: as Kant said, blind; as Lévi–Strauss himself might say, the raw material of structural anthropology is precooked, only the grammatical powers of plants, animals, heavenly bodies, etc. have explanatory value; for the structural anthropologist the distinction between nature and culture is mainly methodological.[28] And like the grammar of a verbal language, the deep grammar of a kinship or mythological system is rarely, if ever, something of which the bearer is conscious.

Who or what is the bearer of the unconscious grammatical knowledge? In so far as we accede to Lévi–Strauss's request to be judged as a scientist, not as a philosopher, we should not expect him to answer this question. It is a question about performance and pragmatics rather than about competence and syntactico-semantics. Judged as science, there is every reason for saying, as Ricoeur does, that Lévi–Strauss's theory is a Kantianism without the transcendental self. So judged it is not incompatible with, because not an alternative to, any philosophical theory of the self, whether the transcendental theory of Kant, the phenomenological theory of Husserl, the existential theory of Sartre, or the hermeneutic theory of Ricoeur. And so judged it offers no foundation for philosophical declarations of the demise of man, any more than Saussure's decision to prosecute a science of *langue* sentenced speakers of *parole* to death. So judged it would, other things being equal, offer a foundation upon which to resolve the dispute between Ricoeur and Lévi–Strauss.

However, other things are not equal. This tidy reconciliation is ruled out because Lévi–Strauss, a philosopher by training, cannot, try as he may, cast off his old habits. He cannot resist talking philosophy, as he does, for example, when he scandalizes readers of *The Raw and the Cooked* by saying that myths think themselves.[29] We met something like this idea in Heidegger's later thoughts on language and in Gadamer's statement that "it is literally more correct to say that language speaks us, rather than we speak it." We alluded, in that connection, to Lichtenberg's "It thinks in me." This formula could be reserved for the grammatical and mythological workings of the unconscious, including the operations of metaphor and metonymy, leaving "I think," *cogito*, for consciousness. It would seem to suit also the passive synthesis of Husserl as adapted by Merleau–Ponty in his critique of Sartre. One should, however, avoid implying a contradiction between an It spoken in the passive voice and an I speaking in the active. What is needed, and what perhaps is being suggested by Lévi–Strauss, is the notion of a middle voice, though without the reflexive properties of the Greek middle voice. If this notion of a middle voice is what Heidegger, Gadamer, and Ricoeur would call the voice of destiny, *Geschicklichkeit*, we may have come upon another basis on which to effect a reconciliation between Ricoeur and Lévi–Strauss.

Before that reconciliation could be complete, some further tidying up would have to be done. For instance, we should have to distinguish two theses we have attributed to Ricoeur without so far separating them. First there is the thesis that a myth can have meaning for a bearer of it, that is, for a participant in the culture to which the myth belongs, only if understanding it contributes to his understanding of himself. Second, there is the more controversial thesis that a myth can have meaning for the anthropologist only if his understanding of it contributes to his understanding of himself.

Lévi–Strauss might charge Ricoeur with being guilty of what we could call the participant's fallacy when he advances the second, more radical, of the two theses just distinguished. The participant's fallacy would be the converse of what we could call the theoretician's fallacy. The latter supposes that to speak grammatically one must have a theoretical knowledge of the grammar. The participant's fallacy supposes that in order to have a theoretical knowledge of the grammar of a language one must be able to speak it.

The participant's fallacy is a fallacy. Although Ricoeur is guilty of other fallacies, I do not find him guilty of this one. I do take him to say, however, that in order to have a theoretical knowledge of the grammar of a language one must have a language of one's own. That is unexceptionable and is the basis for a last hope of reconciliation between himself and Lévi–Strauss. This was hinted at in my earlier comment on Lévi–Strauss's rejection of Lévy–Bruhl's theory of primitive prelogicality. If, as Lévi–Strauss says, primitive mentality is an aspect of our own, then indeed we cannot understand it without understanding ourselves. What is more, we observed above that Lévi–Strauss comes to regard the distinction between nature and culture as a largely methodological one. And (see note 28) his cultural interpretation of nature extends to inorganic nature. This implies that he should endorse an even more comprehensive version than we have so far entertained of the principle that the understanding of meaning is the understanding of oneself. It implies that this principle holds not only for the meaning of straightforwardly cultural phenomena like myths. It implies that it holds for the meaning of geological forms.

> Every landscape appears first of all as a vast chaos, which leaves one free to choose the meaning one wants to give it.... As I follow the traces of their age-old stagnation despite all obstacles—sheer cliff faces, landslides, scrub or cultivated land—disregarding paths and fences, I seem to be proceeding in a meaningless fashion. But the sole aim of this contrariness is to recapture the master-meaning, which may be obscure but of which each of the others is a partial or

distorted transposition.... When the miracle occurs ... I feel
myself to be steeped in a more dense intelligibility, within
which centuries and distances answer each other and speak at
last with one and the same voice.[30]

The middle voice in which there speaks a quite universal destiny?

To return to the two theses distinguished above, except on an unusually strict notion of meaning and of what it is to be a participant in a
culture, or on an extraordinarily liberal notion of understanding, both of
these theses are false, as I have argued earlier in this chapter and in the
chapter on Gadamer. The distinctions made in that chapter between
different kinds and different degrees of understanding should be made
again here. There is, it is true, a lack of understanding in the existential
sense if there is no fusion of horizons as described by Gadamer, Wittgenstein, and Winch. But there are many mansions in the house of
understanding. With regard to Ricoeur's first thesis, understanding a
myth may enrich one's sense of participating in a communal cultural
destiny and of being the bearer of a tradition. But, assuming we do not
make the first thesis true by giving an unusually narrow definition of
meaning and participation, a myth can mean something *for* a participant
even if it does not mean something, matter, *to* him. This is still more
clearly the case for the second thesis, that is, for the anthropologist. No
doubt neither the participant nor the anthropologist grasps the full force
of a myth unless he has entered wholeheartedly into the form of life of
which it is a part. That is a truism on which Lévi–Strauss and Ricoeur
must agree. Lévi–Strauss should agree, too, that the anthropologist's
understanding is deficient if he has no experience of participating in a
form of life. But that hypothesis is excluded by the hypothesis that he is
an anthropologist and therefore committed to at least the form of life of
an inquirer after anthropological knowledge. There is, however, no
reason why the knowledge he acquires should not be a detached epistemic understanding of the meaning of a myth without being a committed
existential understanding of its point. This is consistent with the truth of
the Heideggerian claim that epistemic, scientific, propositional understanding presupposes existential, pre-scientific, hermeneutic understanding. An anthropologist's detachment from a particular commitment, such as the commitment of those he is investigating, does not
entail detachment from all pre-scientific commitment. He will also, as a
scientist, aim to avoid being biased by his own prejudices. But, as
Gadamer convincingly argues, detachment from such epistemological

prejudice requires rather than rules out attachment to ontological pre-judgment. The hermeneutic circle remains unbroken.

PART THREE
META-ONTOLOGICAL
METAPHYSICS

CHAPTER NINE
RETROSPECT AND PROSPECT

*Il s'agit de poser expressément et systématiquement le prob-
lème du statut d'un discours empruntant à un héritage les
ressources nécessaires à la dé-construction de cet héritage
lui-même.*

—Jacques Derrida

1. *Science, poetry, and meta-metaphysics*

The Foreword of this book recalled the epistemological circle invoked
by Meno's paradox of inquiry and endorsed in Plato's theory of knowledge as anamnesis. That theory was in turn endorsed by later rationalist
philosophers. It was then adapted by Kant to provide a middle way
between classical rationalism and classical empiricism and between subjective idealism and transcendental realism. Kant's middle way was still
a theory of knowledge, in particular an answer to the questions How is
pure science of nature and how is metaphysics possible? Chapters 1 and
6 examined Heidegger's and Gadamer's grounds for saying that these
questions raise the prior question How is understanding possible? and
that more basic than any circle there may be in knowledge is the hermeneutic circle in understanding. This difference of level is the difference between beings and being, the ontic and the ontological, which
Heidegger calls the ontological difference. It was Husserl's thoughts about founding expressed in the *Logical Investigations* and elsewhere, and
his method of transcendental phenomenological reduction discussed
above in chapter 2, that prepared the way for Heidegger's thoughts on
the ontological difference and for an ontology, more fundamental than
questions about scientific and pre-scientific objects, processes, events,
or states of affairs, an ontology that circumvents the metaphysical
alternatives of rationalism or empiricism and idealism or realism.

173

If there had never been Husserl's essentialist phenomenology and Heidegger's fundamental ontology there could never have been the phenomenological existentialism of Sartre, which was the subject of chapter 3. There and in the following chapter on his Marxist existentialism it was argued that in spite of his mentors and in spite of himself, Sartre reverted to the level of the traditional metaphysical oppositions, succumbing to the temptation to imagine himself projected into a desituated position of Olympian survey. Merleau–Ponty avoids this *pensée de survol* in his synthesis of Husserl, Heidegger, Sartre, and Saussure. His adaptation of Saussure's semiology dealt with in chapter 7 and the exchange between Ricoeur and Lévi–Strauss analyzed in chapter 8 show how silly it would be to suppose that phenomenology and fundamental hermeneutic ontology are somehow against objective social science, even if by an objective science we mean a science that objectivizes, makes an object of, its subject matter. Chapter 2 demonstrated that Husserl's essentialist phenomenology aims to escape competition with physics and metaphysics. Its heirs, fundamental ontology and philosophical hermeneutics, are not in any way antagonistic to natural science or a philosophy of it like Bachelard's, which was expounded in chapter 5. What they call into question is a philosophy that takes as its model the framework of objectivising science yet takes itself to be fundamental and comprehensive. This point was made at the end of the chapter on Gadamer. It merits repetition here since some of the things Heidegger says about the relationship between science, poetry, and philosophical thinking give too little acknowledgment to the aspect of science that opens up a way to ontological thinking in his sense; and this is the aspect to which Bachelard gives full recognition. For example, in *An Introduction to Metaphysics* Heidegger writes:

> Only poetry stands in the same order as philosophy and its thinking, though poetry and thought are not the same thing. To speak of nothing will always remain a horror and an absurdity for science. But aside from the philosopher, the poet can do so—and not because, as common sense supposes, poetry is without strict rules, but because the spirit of poetry (only authentic and great poetry is meant) is essentially superior to the spirit that prevails in all mere science. By virtue of this superiority the poet always speaks as though the essent were being expressed and invoked for the first time. Poetry, like the thinking of the philosopher, has always so

much world space to spare that in it each thing—a tree, a mountain, a house, the cry of a bird—loses all indifference and commonplaceness.[1]

This fails to recognize the manner in which authentic and great scientific thinking, no less than authentic and great poetry, is poietic.

When Heidegger says that the scope of the concepts of Western philosophy and modern science is not grasped until we become aware of the hermeneutic circle which earths them in poetry, by poetry he means *Dichtung*, saying which is originative, projective and, as Gadamer uses the term, speculative. This is not the preserve of makers of poesy, *Gedichte*. Bachelard for one opposed science to poesy, but modern mathematical physics as he sees it is eminently poietic. This is because its essence is the formation of concepts. But when revolutionary science is on the way from an old to a new conceptual scheme, is it not in the no man's land of namelessness which, Heidegger says, is the way to the nearness of being?[2] Bachelard would have agreed with Wittgenstein's statement that concept formation is the limit of the empirical;[3] and he would have applied to modern science, because it is in his view mathematics, what Merleau–Ponty says of mathematics, that it is an emergence of meaning, a *devenir sens*.[4] Although, with reference to Bergson's statement that we should say not *homo sapiens* but *homo faber*,[5] Bachelard is fond of saying that *homo faber* must make way for *homo mathematicus*, on Bachelard's own account the modern mathematical scientist is an artificer of sense.

Science is no less poietic, therefore, than poetry or art. The contrast in respect of *poiesis* is not between science and poetry or art. It is between normal science and revolutionary science and between the prose of the world and its poetry. And these are differences only of degree. For the normal and prosaic supply the minimal common ground of convention on which the revolutionary and the poet must stand if their inventions are to have any sense; and however prosaic and orthodox one's us of language may be, if it is responsible use and not mere parrotry, it is adaptive; hence it is to some degree creative, to some degree poetry.

In other respect there are undeniable differences between science and art, for example the difference in the kinds of testability that are appropriate. Bachelard emphasizes the revolutionary nature of science, the manner in which it is a making of sense. Merleau–Ponty is keen to convince us that the prose Monsieur Jourdain was surprised to learn he had been speaking all his life had a penumbra of poetry; "dichterisch wohnet der Mensch." Further, although the testing appropriate in art is in various and varying ways different from that in science, and different from one genre of art or science to another, it is in all cases the attempt to achieve a more or less close contact between concepts or images and something taken for granted which comprises the norms of normal science and the prose of the world. This also comprises, however, the empirical base which is itself part of the culture, scientific or otherwise, not outside it. It is itself conceptually informed and not independent of the concepts and theories that are more liable to change. "What stands fast does so, not because it is intrinsically obvious or convincing; it is rather held fast by what lies around it."[6] It is therefore itself subject to reformation. Not so readily and not altogether at any one time. Something must stand fast where there is still understanding. Something must remain unquestioned. There is, however, no particular thing that must at any particular time. The realization of this can be extremely disconcerting. This, I guess, is the experience of dislodgement (*Umheimlichkeit*) that Heidegger hoped to provoke in the scientists who were in the audience at Freiburg when he delivered the inaugural lecture which asked "What is Metaphysics?"

If there is any truth in Bachelard's description of scientific thinking, science itself should be able to open the door to this breathtaking experience of ontological vertigo when we seem to hover in the space between concepts with no ground, no object, no thing, nothing on which to stand. I call this experience ontological since I see no reason for distinguishing it from the experience that may be evoked, according to Heidegger, by reflecting on the question Why is there something and not rather nothing? As Heidegger would have us ask this question, it is neither scientific nor metaphysical in the traditional sense,[7] for it is not simply a question about beings but raises a question about the meaning of being. It is not only ontic, but also ontological. Let us refer to it therefore as the ontic-ontological question.

Heidegger himself allows that the world view of modern science may be a route to the ontological experience when we reflect on the infinitely vast and infinitely small distances dealt with in space science and atomic physics, coming to see them as ontic portents of the ontologically stupendous.[8] When Heidegger says this he may have in mind Pascal's avowal of the terror struck into him by the eternal silence of space upon infinite space and Kant's celebration of the wonder and awe awakened in him by contemplation of the worlds upon worlds and systems upon systems revealed in the starry sky.[9] This regress of systems raises the question, treated in the Transcendental Dialectic of the first *Critique*, whether the regress from condition to condition in the sensible world points toward an unconditioned totality which we are compelled in practice to postulate. For Kant, however, this ultimate question is one about an extra special entity. The ultimate question for Heidegger is one concerning being. Not only does he add to Kant's table of categories the category of readiness to hand. Not only does he go beyond the universe of discourse of the *Critique of Pure Reason* by drawing up a table of existentials, he goes beyond the Ideas of reason, which are the ultimates in all three Critiques, to ask the question concerning the meaning of being without which the Ideas of reason and the formal concepts of the understanding are as blind as are the perceptions of sensibility without the concepts and the concepts without the Ideas.

In spite of these concessions, Heidegger gives science a raw deal. He underestimates the degree to which the work of science, like the work of poetic art, may be a route to fundamental ontology. This is not because science is one of the arts. Modern science, as both Bachelard and Heidegger agree, is mathematical representation and will to control. Its representation is itself an expression of that will to subjugate. Its concepts (*Begriffe*) are grasping (*begreifend*), its categories catechistic. Like science, the arts treat of beings. But it is natural for art to raise questions about beings without pressing for answers. Its questioning is not investigative research or inquisition. This may be why Heidegger considers the artist, and poetry in particular, closer to ontological thinking. Ontological thinking is not aggressive nor passive but patient anamnesis, remembrance of being (*Gedächtnis des Seins*).[10] It gives neither priority to the positive, as Bergsonism does, nor prominence to active negation, as do the ontologies of Bachelard and Sartre. Being cannot be posited or reified in Heidegger's ontology. Nor, therefore (and here there is a superficial similarity with both Bergson and Sartre), can nothingness. Although *das Nichts* and "nothingness" are nominal in form, to contend that Heidegger reifies nothingness is to confirm his contention that we forget the ontological difference. Being and nothingness are not names for entities, hence not names for anything whose existence can be affirmed or denied. The appropriate voice in which to speak of them would be not the passive nor the active voice, but a middle voice. The appropriate mood in which to address oneself to them is, as Merleau–Ponty observed in the passage cited at the end of chapter 7, not the indicative but the interrogative. Not interrogative, however, in the style of questions that can be equally well posed as imperative. The question

Why is there something and not far rather nothing? will not go over into "The reason why there is something and not far rather nothing is: ———. Fill in the blank."[11] To assume that the blank can be filled is to remain inside the onto-theo-logical universe of discourse governed by the principle of absolutely sufficient reason. The blank is essentially unfillable. For to fill it would be to supply a ground, whereas the heuristic force Heidegger ascribes to the question is that of raising the prior question concerning the meaning of being, which we so readily overlook. This ontological question is implicit within the ontic-ontological question and every ontic inquiry.[12] As was maintained in *Being and Time*, Dasein's way of being is to be concerned with the question of being even if we have only a pretheoretical understanding of this. Heidegger, Sartre, Gadamer, Merleau–Ponty, and Ricoeur can all agree that reduction regarded as *poiesis* is not cut off by a Bachelardian break from the estranging disruptions of the natural attitude brought about by the revelatory experiences of the revolutionary work of art or science and by the crises in one's personal life. Regarded as *poiesis*, fundamental hermeneutic ontology is rescued from the predicament in which Husserlian essentialist phenomenology found itself of being unable to explain how anyone adopting the naive natural attitude toward the world could be motivated to perform the transcendental phenomenological reduction. For "the *epoche* is no longer a miracle, an intellectual method, an erudite procedure; it is an anxiety which is imposed on us and which we cannot avoid; it is both a pure event of transcendental origin and an ever possible accident of our daily life."[13] The ontic question What is the meaning of life? which we may put to ourselves in situations that stretch us beyond the normal limit, is made possible by the ontological question What is the meaning of being?

It has been widely argued among twentieth-century philosophers that since What is the meaning of life? is a question without answer, it is a question without sense. So, it must finally be asked, can fundamental hermeneutic ontology be rescued from the predicament of asking a question that has no sense?

Fundamental hermeneutic ontology asks after the meaning of being. It was not this question, the ontological question, that was earlier said to be bound to remain without answer, but the ontic-ontological question Why is there something and not far rather nothing? asked as Heidegger would have us ask it, not asked in the onto-theo-logical way in which it presents itself to, for example, Leibniz and Schelling. He would have us think through this ontic-ontological question to the ontological question within it. There has been no suggestion on his part that this question is bound to remain without answer. The most we get is the confession that fundamental ontological thinking is at a serious disadvantage when attempts are made to conduct it in the medium of statements made in lectures or papers of the sort expected in learned periodicals. This is because, as John Austin and others have pointed out, we are inclined to take constative predication to be the basic use of words. But the question What is the meaning of being? apparently implies that being has a meaning, and if its meaning is something that can be predicated of it in a definition, we have still not gone beyond the domain of concepts and the predicate logic that, Heidegger asserts, may be adequate to what there is, but not to the "there is." Somehow we have to gain access, he further maintains, to the pre-predicative logic of the *logos* which had not yet been suppressed in the thinking of the early Greeks for whom, as Heidegger says in the metaphor commented upon above in chapter 1 (section 3) and unfolded in *An Introduction to Metaphysics* (chapter 4, sec. 3) and his essays on Heraclitus and Parmenides, *logos* is the shepherd, the gatherer, of being.

But is not this pre-Socratic way of thinking confined still to the ontic logic of predicates and propositions? For is not emergence a process, and are not processes among what is? Heidegger is not wishing to elicit only what underlies the logic of nouns and the physics and metaphysics of substance. Processes and events are also items in an ontic universe of discourse, as are actions and verbs—except the original verb to be. This last, along with the topics of language-*logos*, truth-*aletheia* and *Ereignis* which are inseparable from it, is the topic of fundamental hermeneutic ontology. But as soon as it gets talked about, the fundamental ontology threatens to collapse into a nonfundamental ontic ontology of process or life like the metaphysical accounts of what there is given by Bergson, Whitehead, and Lloyd Morgan. This threat is present in our own effort to grasp what Heidegger is after through the experience of concept formation as this is described in the writings of Bachelard, Gadamer, and Merleau–Ponty and in Lévi–Strauss's account of mythmaking *bricolage*. These writers are as keen as Saussure to escape what he calls nomenclature, a logic modeled on the apparent grammar of naming, the metaphysics of substance, and the epistemology of representation. By giving priority to relations, as does Bachelard's philosophy of physics, or to difference, as does Saussure's philosophy of language, we do not get beyond the ontic to fundamental ontology, and certainly not to the thinking of being beyond the fundamental ontology whose very claim to fundamentality suggests it is itself not beyond the onto-theo-logical metaphysics of the principle of sufficient ground.

That the means to this transcendence is an experience is suggested by certain of Heidegger's remarks about the ontic-ontological question. The danger, one Heidegger warns against, is that of turning fundamental hermeneutic ontology into a technique for obtaining a mystical or pseudomystical state of mind. That is one reason, I suggested, why the word he uses for the ontological experience is *Erfahrung*, not *Erlebnis*, intending to indicate that fundamental ontological thinking is always on the way, a *Fahren*. But a third danger (*Gefahr*) lurks here, that of conceiving this thinking to be a quest for a distant holy grail. This is a bad analogy, not only because being is not a thing, but also because this nonthing is not distant; one reason that it is overlooked is that it is nearer than any thing, *secretissime et praesentissime*.[14] We already understand the meaning of being, else we could not seek to articulate it. It is a question of something ordinary that may call for an extraordinary event to raise it.

Is the endeavor to articulate it destined to have a dead end? If being were a Platonic Form or Idea, a Husserlian noematic Object or concept, a Bachelardian super-object or super-concept, or a Lévi–Straussian super-relation, we could know in advance that its articulation or analysis was not impossible in principle. In *Being and Time* Heidegger himself articulates the structure of Dasein. When in his later work, however, he comes to dwell on *Sein*, his reader will ask himself what more there is left for Heidegger to do that is not done by the poets.

Yet, as we have seen, although Heidegger admits that a poem can assist ontological thinking in that both poem (*Gedicht*) and thought (*Denken*) are poietic (*Dichten*), poem and poietic thought do not coincide. If a poet has an aim, and does not just sing or cry without asking why, it is, at least in the view expressed in the passage from *An Introduction to Metaphysics* reproduced above, to return to things their pristine strangeness. Now, it may be said, "a tree, a mountain, a house, the cry of a bird" are beings, whereas the task of the thinker, as Heidegger sees it, is to return its pristine strangeness to being. However, the poet can assist the thinker in this task since strangeness is returned to being by returning strangeness to beings, by returning strangeness to words. The philosopher has traditionally been concerned with a relatively small group of key basic words, words for formal concepts or categories and transcendentals, most basic of all: being and truth. By taking a fresh look at the main figures in the history of philosophy,

Heidegger tries to show that, with the exception of a few poet-thinkers like Heraclitus and Parmenides, philosophers have become oblivious of the powers of these fundamental words. If he is right in saying this, it may not be futile to seek an anamnetic retrieval of these powers. This search will not be rendered vain from the start by the fact that our concepts and words are those of post-Platonic metaphysics and theory of knowledge. However comfortably this metaphysics may fit our grip, this is no guarantee that we shall never be at a loss for words or that they will not, like any other tool, break down under stress. Why could not that event be, not a chance merely to reproduce mechanically what was originally thought by the Greeks before the beginning of metaphysics, but an epoch-making moment in which we experience, as if for the first time, the belonging together of being and truth, returning full circle to where we belong and where, though we do not always bear this in mind, we *already are*—beyond metaphysics?

2. *Letting be*

So far in this book the word metaphysics has been used in the sense explained in the Foreword, a sense in which it is used by Heidegger. In this sense metaphysics is equivalent to epistemology and nonfundamental ontology: the theory of the beingness of beings. But the Greek *to on*, like the English "being" and the French *être*, is ambiguous. In some contexts it connotes a being, an entity or an "essent"; in others it connotes being, entity (entitivity) or essence. This ambiguity has made it possible for being to be equated with a being in general or God. In other respects, too, it has had more far-reaching consequences than has the multiplicity of the kinds of being treated by Aristotle and by Brentano in the study that played a part in the genesis of *Being and Time*. It is reflected in the amphibological title of *An Introduction to Metaphysics*, as befits a book about the history of the concealment of the ontological difference. In "What is Metaphysics?" and in "Overcoming Metaphysics," as in most of *An Introduction to Metaphysics*, metaphysics inquires about beings *as such*. Its topic is the beingness of beings. Its grounding question is the question about the ground. But, Heidegger notes, we cannot help asking after the ground of metaphysics itself, and this involves thinking both metaphysically and nonmetaphysically. The question that grounds metaphysics has implicit within it the prior question variously formulated How does it stand with being? What is the meaning of being? and What is the truth of being? Although this question is metaphysically incomprehensible,[15] the fact that it is implicit though overlooked in the founding question of metaphysics—and consequently in *all* questioning[16]—gives some point to Heidegger's resolve to play on the ambiguity of the word metaphysics in the title of a book that is largely occupied with the indeterminacy of the question of being and with the burden of bringing that ambiguity, and the ambiguity of all essential thinking, into the open.[17]

It might be supposed that if the word metaphysics retains this indeterminacy in the title of this present book, to move beyond the metaphysics of beingness is to move into a metaphysics of being. This inference might be encouraged by the knowledge that when Heidegger speaks of the "overcoming" of metaphysics by passing, in the Hegelian language that Heidegger retrieves, to the truth or the meaning of being, his *Überwindung* shares with Hegel's *Aufhebung* the idea that what is overcome or sublated is not left behind but is raised (*verwunden*) to a higher power.[18] This inference would not be valid. This Heidegger should with good reason use "metaphysics" in an indeterminate sense, and in the determinate sense in which metaphysics is equivalent to traditional ontology, is not a good reason why he should use it of his fundamental ontology or the thinking of the truth and meaning of being by which traditional ontology is overcome. Alluding to his earlier use of the term ontology for both traditional metaphysics and for his own fundamental ontology, he later decides that "it may be preferable to dispense in the future with the terms 'ontology' and 'ontological'. The two modes of questioning which, as we now see clearly, are worlds apart, should not bear the same name."[19] So it is only with scare quotes around the adjective that Heidegger now permits himself to refer to the prior question as "metaphysical."[20]

Perhaps the the distance that separates the traditional mode of asking the question Why is there anything and not rather nothing? and the mode appropriate to the prior question *Welches ist der Sinn von Sein?* would be more readily gauged if *Sinn* here were translated not by "meaning," but by "sense." Taking *von* both objectively and subjectively, we should have at least two questions to consider. On the one hand, understanding *Sinn* as orientation, the question at issue would be that of the history of being. On the other hand, the question at issue would be analogous to questions about someone's sense of humor, sense of right and wrong, or sense of wonder. The meaning of being is not a meaning such as one might expect to discover in a dictionary, but a sense, *Sinn*. In the words that appear in the title of one of Heidegger's essays, what is called for is not *Wissenschaft*, but *Besinnung*. It may seem that there is a good deal of *Wissenschaft* in the analysis of being-there undertaken in *Being and Time*. It may have come to seem so for its author. In what way is this existential analysis different in principle from the tabling of the categories of being carried out in the writings of Aristotle, Kant, or Hegel?

One difference is just this inclination to think that there is no difference in principle between existentials and categories. For example, we find ourselves supposing that meaning is always the sort of thing that a dictionary could give; that it is a concept or an Object, as is the Husserlian noematic *Sinn*. Whereas, Heidegger maintains, in the last analysis meaning is an existential, a way of Dasein's being, not a property of a word or any other entity.[21] Now, it is typical of our way of being that we forget this difference. It has been concealed throughout the history of philosophy. That the greatest of philosophers have been prone to make concepts or objects of what is neither is unlikely to reveal itself to an "oversight" which is purely conceptual, scientifically, or metaphysically objectivating, or a combination of these. Ontopathology, as we called it in chapter 1, whether the "destruction" of the history of philosophy or the analysis of the illusions of everyday life, needs *Besinnung*.

Although *Besinnung* plays a role in Heidegger's thinking similar to that which anamnesis performs in Plato's, what it brings to mind is not forms or formal concepts. Nor, on the other hand, is it a faculty of sensation. Rather are we in the vicinity of the productive imagination which, according to Kant, is the faculty of judgment. By judgment here he means not assertion with its logical forms, which are his clue to the categories of the understanding. He is thinking of judgment as he thinks of it in the third *Critique* and in the doctrine of schematism in the first. The transcendental schema is a temporalizing procedure to which Kant ascribes the amphibological status of "sensible concept." This procedure, he says, is "an art concealed in the depths of the human soul, whose real modes of activity nature is hardly likely ever to allow us to discover, and to have open to our gaze."[22] He also says, "There are two stems of human knowledge, namely, *sensibility* and *understanding*, which perhaps spring from a common, but to us unknown, root."[23] In *Kant and the Problem of Metaphysics* Heidegger argues that this hidden root is the transcendental productive imagination. It is this which he takes as his clue to the mode of thinking appropriate for the recollection of the meaning of being. What is at stake here is not information, but a stance, *Haltung*.[24] One of the words he adapts for this is Eckhart's word *Gelassenheit*.

The *lassen*, "letting be," of *Gelassenheit* is not mere passivity nor mere activity. It is both patiently vigilant lassitude and coolly passionate attention. This *Seinlassen* has affinities not only with the temporalizing poietic imagination,[25] but with what, taking further liberties with Kant, could be called the moral imagination that furnishes the quasi schemata or "typics" that enable practical reason to be applied in judgments about concrete states of affairs. According to Kant, practical reason is will. And according to Heidegger, the stance in which we may be granted a *recueillement* of being is one of will. However, as we pointed out in chapter 1, for Heidegger willing is resolve, *Ent-schlossenheit*, and resolve is to be understood as unclosedness, unconcealment, *Ent-borgenheit*. So the Kantian good will, for the Heidegger of *Being and Time*, is an ontic expression of the ontological willingness to have a conscience. And since conscience is the call of care, *Sorge*, and since to care is *in die Acht nehmen*, it is not far-fetched to compare the sense of being with Kant's *Achtung*, the sense of reverence or attentive respect. The latter, we and Heidegger might say, is made possible by the former.

Achtung in Kant is what others would call rational sympathy. And Kant's condemnation of morality based on what he calls pathological love does not prevent his allowing that *Achtung* is feeling. But it is a feeling with an object. That object is the moral law, the principle of the rationality of human and any superhuman being there may be. Heidegger relates *Sorge*, "care," to *cura*. The connecting of care with the Latin *cura* may be false etymology, as may be the connecting of care with *caritas*, "love." However, it is sufficient for our purpose now to observe that *Sorge* in *Being and Time* is "regard for being," and this is not an object or a being, though it manifests itself in *Besorgen*, "concern regarding nonhuman beings," and *Fürsorge*, "solicitude toward human beings." Our purpose now is to try to understand why Emmanuel Levinas reverses this order of priority, maintaining that not all the ways in which I stand with regard to others have any ontological condition such as care.

CHAPTER TEN
LEVINAS, DERRIDA, AND OTHERS VIS-À-VIS

He is Greek, and speaks Greek, does he not?

—Socrates

L'être n'arrive pas à être jusqu'au bout.

—Emmanuel Levinas

1. *Ethical metaphysics*

The physical, according to one notion of it, is that which has a natural origin and whose persistence toward its end is describable by natural laws. Heidegger frequently links this notion to a certain Greek conception of what it means to be. He also links it to the idea of emergence into the open and coming to light (*phos*). So the study of being, ontology, at the time of *Being and Time* is a phenomenology, a study of appearing (*phainesthai*) and dis-appearing. Husserl's phenomenology is no less an ontology, a study of essences, than Heidegger's fundamental ontology is a phenomenology. Both Heidegger and Husserl are describing what the Greeks called the physical, in the wide sense Heidegger finds this word to have had for them. If we understand the word in this wide sense we understand why Emmanuel Levinas says that the main topic of his thinking is metaphysical, though it is not metaphysical in either the determinate or the indeterminate sense of Heidegger explained in chapter 9, section 2. It is metaphysical because ethical. And it is ethical not because it is either a code of ethics or a metaphysics of ethics with which Levinas is concerned. Kant's groundwork of the metaphysics of ethics was appealed to above to allow an analogy to be drawn between Kantian respect and Heideggerian letting be. But it is being that is to be let be according to Heidegger, and it is the moral law that is to be respected according to Kant. The other person is to be respected, according to

185

Kant, only because the other person is a rational agent, and he is a rational agent only in so far as he personifies the moral law and is capable of exercising a freedom to refrain from following rules of behavior that could not be universally followed or willed. By the same standard the agent is entitled to respect himself. He respects the law which, without of course suspending them, transcends the laws of his physical nature. Kant's metaphysics of ethics describes the structures of inter-personality, a structure for which his analogy is that of the lawfulness of nature. It describes the foundation of justice.

The ethical, as Levinas describes it, is "older than" justice as conceived by Kant. It is a condition that is not a foundation of it; so it is more strictly speaking an un-condition which is pre-original and prior to the *inter-esse-ment* that is not less a feature of Kantian deontological morality than it is of the teleological morality of self- and general interest. Both of these models of morality are styles of being and being-with, *Mitsein*, notwithstanding the criteria they provide for distinguishing the immoral from the moral and the inauthentic from the authentic. They are both ontological. The ethical as Levinas would have us understand it is de-ontological, dis-ontological, *ent-ontologisch*. It is prior to all structures of being-with. It is prior to all structures, whether these are the categories of Greek philosophy, of Kant, of Hegel, of Husserl, or the structures of structuralism and of linguistic or economic exchange. Prior to system, to symmetry, to correlation, to the will, to freedom, and to the opposition of activity and passivity, the ethical is far more passive than the opposite of activity. It is the superlation of passivity. Because it is prior to the third person.

Without yet knowing what is, according to Levinas, prior to the third personal point of view, it is not difficult to see how he stands vis-à-vis certain of the authors whose work has been surveyed in previous chapters of this book. The surrationalistic structures of the natural sciences as conceived by Bachelard are third-personal objectivated systems. The disillusioning techniques prescribed in the critical theory of Habermas call for the same objectivation in the social sciences. This third-personal scientific objectivity is demanded by the theories and methods of interpretation advocated by Betti and Hirsch. As for the structuralist theories that Lévi–Strauss and others have developed from those of Saussure, they are predicated on a concept of language as a system of opposed terms regarded in isolation from the particular speech-acts performed by users of that system. *Langue*, as described by Saussure and his adaptors, fulfills the description Levinas gives of a system as a coexistence or agreement of different terms in the unity of a theme.[1]

Is Levinas, then, in the lineage of those who deny the primacy of *langue* over *parole*? And is he a champion of diachrony against synchrony? The answer to both of these questions is that he is, but in a way which sets him apart from all the thinkers whose writings have been looked at so far in this book. When Merleau–Ponty and Ricoeur re-emphasize the dependence of instituted language upon *parole*, they are stressing the intentionality of creative sense-giving speech-acts. When, following Husserl, Merleau–Ponty underlines the importance of anonymous, centri-petal intentionality, he is proposing nothing that transcends the general sphere of significance to which the structuralists apply their theories. He, like they, is talking about the universe of discourse in which one thing stands for another, the system of signifier and signified.[2] When the system of one thing with another and one thing standing for another is supplemented by the significative intentionality of a speaker, we are still short of the nonintentional, preintentional *signifiance* which, according to Levinas, is presupposed by all signification. And the diachrony of the speech-act is but a difference in the same time compared with the more radically dia-chronic difference of times Levinas ascribes to my responsibililty for the Other, *Autrui*, to whom I address my words—and myself. According to Husserlian essentialist phenomenology, utterance and all other signifying gestures are noetic-noematic, intentional projection of subjectivity toward an accusative. This holds for Husserl because *"all acts generally—even the acts of feeling and will—are 'objectifying' acts, original factors in the 'constituting' of objects,"* the necessary sources of different regions of being and of the ontologies that belong therewith.[3] For Husserl the prototype of even nontheoretical acts is perception and the co-relation of subjectivity and objectivity, of being with.

Levinas finds very much the same auto-affection at work in this prototype as is posited by the Kantians and neo-Kantians from whom Husserl was hoping to move away. These and Husserl are inheritors of the Cartesian tradition in which consciousness is egological. Another heir of this tradition is Sartre. Although in his existential phenomenology intentionality is interpreted as the for-itself's refusal of the in-itself with which it is correlated, a kind of "othering," consciousness remains a free recuperation. Its ideal is that of assumption, consumption, digestion, though, in contrast with the conceptual phenomenology of Hegel, achievement of the ideal is condemned to remain unfulfilled. In Husserl's essentialist phenomenology the Other, although my alter ego and an analogue of myself, resists assimilation because he is only ever appresented; I have no adequate consciousness of his consciousness. Sartre, for different reasons, agrees with this, yet he continues to see the for-itself as consciousness projected toward assimilation.

Somewhat the same assimilative character is ascribed by Gadamer to our efforts to understand each other and the texts and works of art and artifice that others have produced. Understanding is at the same time self-understanding and an interfusion of horizons. It is true that with Sartre cognition is secondary to consciousness and that with Gadamer and Heidegger consciousness is secondary to understanding as a structure of being. However, the Husserlian notion of horizon persists in the accounts Sartre, Gadamer, and Heidegger give of situation or environing world, *Umwelt*. This, Levinas maintains, is incommensurable with the for-the-other which, far from being the mere contingency that is Sartre's being-for-the-other, is an unavoidable and unvoidable human responsibility. Levinas would say that this ethical responsibility is also neglected in the hermeneutic co-responsibility of Gadamer's interpretation of understanding. He does say that it is beyond the reach of the ecstasis of *Verstehen* as described in *Being and Time*. It cannot be comprehended by comprehension. Like the infinite of Descartes's third Meditation, it cannot be comprehended. Levinas agrees with readers of the *Metaphysical Meditations* like Martial Gueroult, one of his teachers at Strasbourg, who take as provisional and artificial Descartes's distinction between the consciousness he has of his self and the consciousness he has of his finitude. "My nature is not only to be a thinking being, thinking itself as thought, but a being thinking itself as finite and consequently thinking the infinite."[4] The thought of the infinite is implicit in and logically prior to the thought of myself, to the *cogito*.

> In thinking the infinite—the self at once *thinks more than it can think*. The infinite does not enter into the *idea* of the infinite; it is not grasped; this idea is not a concept. The infinite is the radically, absolutely other.[5]

Whereas Descartes employs causal and ontological arguments to demonstrate that there is a God, the descriptions Levinas gives purport not to be ontological. They take as their cue the axiological function Descartes attributes to the idea of God's perfection, although, as Gueroult observes, Descartes does not make as clear a distinction as Malebranche does between judgments of truth or reality and judgments of value or perfection.[6] What Levinas refers to as the most high (*altus*) is the radically other (*alter*). The Other, *Autrui*, is not simply an alter ego, an appresented analogue of myself. He and I are not equals, citizens in an intelligible kingdom of ends. We are not relatives. We are not different as chalk and cheese. There is between us, in the Hegelian phrase Levinas adapts, an absolute difference. The Other is he to whom and in virtue of whom I am sub-ject, with a subjectivity that is heteronomy, not autonomy, hetero-affection, not auto-affection. The Other is not the object of my concern and solicitude. Beyond what Heidegger means by *Sorge* and *Fürsorge* is my being con-cerned, *con-cerné*, ob-sessed by the Other. He is not the accusative of my theoretical, practical, or affective intentionality or ecstasis. He is the topic of my regard (*il me regarde*) only because I am the accusative of his look (*il me regarde*).[7] The subject is an accusative, *me*, which is not a declension from a nominative but an accusative absolute like the pronoun *se* for which, Levinas says, Latin grammars acknowledge no nominative.[8] This latter accusative is not a case of the I which accuses itself. The accusative in question is beholden to the Other, but not for any services rendered. He is subpoenaed by the other, pursued and persecuted, but not on account of any crime or original sin.[9] The persecuted is himself responsible for the persecution to which he is subjected, but his responsibility is beyond free will; and the accusation is not one that he can answer or to which he can respond with an apology, for "persecution is the precise moment in which the subject is reached or touched without the mediation of the logos":[10] It is beyond the spoken word.

The accused self is categorized beyond free will and beyond the opposition of freedom and nonfreedom, where by freedom is understood freedom to choose and initiate. Original ontological freedom, according to Sartre, although prior to deliberation and will, is nonetheless an unreflective choice. It is also ontological because it is the choice of a way to be. The freedom Levinas attributes to ethical responsibility is preoriginal and beyond ontology. Sartrian fundamental choice founds the agent's situation. It is a descendent of Fichtean self-positing. Levinasian responsibility is nonfoundational and an-archic. It de-poses, exposes, and de-situates the self. This does not mean, however, that the self is alienated, "because the Other [*l'Autre*] in the Same is my substitution for the other [*l'autre*] through the *responsibility* for which I am summoned as the one who is *irreplaceable*."[11] This substitution is not a derivative of the intersubstitutability of *das Man*.

Through substitution for others, the oneself escapes *relation*. At the limit of passivity, the oneself escapes passivity or the inevitable limitation that the terms within relation undergo. In the incomparable relationship of responsibility, the other no longer limits the same, it is supported by what it limits. Here the overdetermination of the ontological categories is visible, which transforms them into ethical terms. In the most passive passivity, the self liberates itself ethically from every other and from itself. Its responsibility for the other, the proximity of the neighbour, does not signify a submission to the non-ego; it means an openness in which being's essence is surpassed in inspiration. It is an openness of which respiration is a modality or a foretaste, or, more exactly, of which it retains the aftertaste. Outside of any mysticism, in this respiration, the possibility of every sacrifice for the other, activity and passivity coincide.[12]

Since what Levinas here calls the most passive passivity and elsewhere the passivity of passivity is said to be a passivity that coincides with activity, it might be expected that he would refer to this also as a most active activity or the activity of activity. That he never does this marks off the superlative passivity Levinas does refer to not only from the Kantian rational will and Sartrian originative choice; it marks it off too from any respect and *Seinlassen* such as would lend itself to the middle voice. Levinas's beyond of passivity and activity is beyond being, whether being is that expressed by a noun, a verb, or by a verbal noun; in so far as it can be expressed by a word, it is more correct to call it a passivity than an activity. It follows that this passivity must not be construed as the taking on of suffering, suffering to suffer either a useful passion or a *passion inutile*. It is a passivity that is presupposed by any such assumption or undertaking. Contract, engagement, and commitment, whether entered into altruistically or from egoistic motives, are still at the level of egoity, and egoity has absolute passivity as its un-condition. Entering into a commitment is subscribing to a project, not something to which the accused self is sub-jected.

For Sartre even the adversity of that which limits my freedom is a function of my freedom,[13] as for Fichte is the resistance, *Anstoss*, of the not-I. He devotes several paragraphs of *Being and Nothingness* to describing the paradoxes of passivity.[14] These paradoxes arise, he says, from the supposition that passivity is a mode of being-in-itself, whereas both passivity and activity presuppose human beings and the instruments they use: "Man is active and the means which he employs are called passive." So activity and passivity presuppose being-for-itself, hence non-being. The self-consistency of being-in-itself is beyond both the active and the passive. The absolute passivity of which Levinas writes is indeed sub-jectivity, but subjectivity of the for-others not of the for-itself. Absolute passivity is also beyond being and nothingness. Levinas agrees with Hegel that meontology is the mirror image of ontology. They occupy the same logical space, the space of the Same. So too does the neutral third value between being and nothingness for which Levinas employs the expression *il y a*, "the there is." In *De l'existence à l'existant* this expression carries some of the force carried by the notions of facticity and thrownness in *Being and Nothingness* and *Being and Time*. But this sheer anonymous fact of one's existence is prior to the notions of world or situation. And prior to both the *il y a* and worldhood, availing an exit from them and an exile, is the absolute passivity of passivity.[15]

2. *Facial expression*

The absoluteness of my passivity answers the infinitude of the absolutely other. It fills the place Descartes gives to the infinitude of the freedom of my will, "that above all in respect of which I bear the image and likeness of God." For both Levinas and Descartes infinitude is the positive notion in terms of which the notion of man's finitude is understood. For this positive notion of infinity Kant substitutes a regulative idea required to give sense to scientific research. This notion of infinity is an ideal "ought." It is what Kant has to say about human finitude that Heidegger applauds, though where Kant interprets this as man's limitedness by the given, Heidegger interprets it as man's being toward death. Hegel opposes a good infinite to the interminable bad infinite of the Kantian "ought." To the finitude of man's being toward his term he opposes the negation of this finitude, the infinity of the end of history. Against this, Levinas says:

> We recognize in the finitude which the Hegelian infinite is opposed to and encompasses, the finitude of man before the elements, the infinitude of man invaded by the *there is*, at each instant traversed by faceless gods against whom labour is pursued in order to realize the security in which the "other" of the elements would be revealed as the same.[16]

That is to say, Hegel's good infinite is an infinite of goods. It is an economic infinity of need and the war of each in competition with all where my freedom is limited by the other. Levinas argues that room must be found also for an infinite of goodness, a peaceful infinite of desire which, instead of limiting my freedom and responsibility, extends and exalts it the more I respond to the Other's call: "The absolutely Other (*Autrui*) does not limit the freedom of the Same. In calling it to responsibility it renews and justifies it." The word Levinas uses for this renewal is *instauration*. This is the word one might use of the inauguration of a temple. It carries the idea that is conveyed by the word inspiration, which was met in sentences quoted above and which is the Levinasian hetero-affective counterpart to the Husserlian auto-affectively intentional animation of the body or the corporeal signifier. Husserl's egological sense-giving *Beseelung* is what Levinas doubtless has in view when he introduces his notion of heteronomous "psychism." In Levinas's account of Husserl's semiology, signs express meaning only within a horizon against which they are presented much after the manner of objects in a visual field. He gives a similar account of the ready to hand which is accorded priority over the present at hand in Heidegger's analysis of the everyday world as well as in the semiology of *Being and Time*. For Heidegger and Husserl, "To comprehend the particular being is to grasp it out of an illuminated site it does not fill."[17] For them there is no aspect of a being that is transcendentally foreign to being and comprehension, even if it may be temporarily hidden.

For Levinas the face of the Other is beyond being and comprehension. Beyond Husserlian expressive meaning and presupposed by it is the expression introduced into the world by the Other's face. This expression is not the expression that is seen. It is heard expression that is the discourse of Saying (*Dire*) and is presupposed by the Said (*Dit*). The face is not the countenance. It cannot be contained. Like the infinitude of Descartes's God, it cannot be comprehended. Unlike the Look of Sartre's being-for-the-other, the other's face is not a threat to my freedom before which I shrivel. It increases my responsibility and is welcomed.

> Under the eye of another, I remain an unattackable subject
> in respect. It is the obsession by the other, my neighbour,
> accusing me of a fault which I have not committed freely,
> that reduces the ego to a *self* on the hither side of my iden-
> tity, *prior to* all self-consciousness, and denudes me ab-

solutely. To revert to oneself is not to establish oneself at home, even if stripped of all one's acquisitions. It is to be like a stranger, hunted down even in one's home, contested in one's identity.... It is always to empty oneself anew of oneself, and to absolve onself, like in a haemophiliac's haemorrhage.[18]

The internal hemorrhage in my universe on Sartre's analysis results from my being seen by the other and is the foundation of my unreflective consciousness of myself.[19] The hemorrhage to which Levinas refers is not in the zone of self-consciousness, *Selbstbewusstsein*, or in any other region of consciousness, unconsciousness, or being, *Sein*. It is an emptying out of my self-consciousness commanded by the ethical word of the other which wounds, *blesse*, but is also a blessing, for it heals allergy.[20]

The first traumatic word that is the original expression of the face is "Thou shalt commit no murder."

> The epiphany of the face is ethical. The struggle this face can threaten *presupposes* the transcendence of expression. The face threatens the eventuality of a struggle, but this threat does not exhaust the epiphany of infinity, does not formulate its first word. War presupposes peace, the antecedent and non-allergic presence of he Other; it does not represent the first event of the encounter.[21]

By war Levinas means a resistance and counterresistance of energies, an allergy that is an opposition of powers analogous to the reciprocity of forces in the system of Newtonian mechanics. The ethical resistance is "the resistance of what has no resistance," since it is the weakness of the other that commands me. The other is the poor, the widow, and the orphan mentioned in the Book of Job. Paradoxically, it is the vulnerability of the other, the nakedness of the face, that wounds me. The ethical "thou shalt not" dominates the economic and political "I can." The "I can" and the philosophies of "I can" are not less egocentric than the philosophies of "I think," notwithstanding that the ego is correlated with an other. Although Levinas recognizes that in his later writings Husserl explores the limits of the correlation of subject and object, he insists that Husserl never relinquishes the idea that the ego—which Levinas equates with the Same—always has its correlative *cogitatum*;

that is to say, although, in the track of Brentano, Husserl holds that all intentionality, even nontheoretical intentionality, is the intending of a noematic Object, this other is assimilated into the Same. It is my concern. As with Heidegger, so with Husserl, on Levinas's reading of them, my ultimate concern is the unconcealment of the truth of being.[22] As with Hegel, so with Husserl, the Other is assimilated to the Same, to the identity of identity and difference. Hegel, Husserl, and Heidegger are all three philosophers of possibilities and powers. They are philosophers whose logics of *Aufhebung*, *Erinnerung*, and hermeneutic recycling recollect Plato's recollection but forget the *epekeina tes ousias*—which for Levinas is the singular plural *Autrui* rather than the neutral Good of the *Republic*. They forget that ontology presupposes metaphysics.[23]

3. *Paradoxical proximity*

In "Violence and Metaphysics" Jacques Derrida contends that Levinas forgets the ontological difference. He maintains that Heidegger's *Seinlassen* acknowledges the radical alterity that Levinas assigns to the ethical and metaphysical, and that this acknowledgement is already made in Husserl's conception of phenomenology.

In *Speech and Phenomena* Derrida plots the interplay between two themes of Husserl's phenomenology. On the one hand is the principle of all principles which demands that knowledge of any principle be based on "a primordial dator act," which is an intuition of essence analogous to perception.[24] This theme would lead one to expect an adequation of the act and its object. It is this theme that Levinas has in mind when he says that the model with which Husserl's phenomenological ontology works is that of satisfaction, hence of need rather than of desire as Levinas describes it.

On the other hand Husserl develops the theme that apodicticity of evidence is possible without its being adequate. Derrida cites Husserl's allusions to the infinite number of profiles of physical objects that are not presented to me but that are appresented with those that are. Then there are my retentions and protentions, experiences I remember or expect. The consciousness of my past and future ego, Husserl says, is an analogue of my consciousness of other selves. Which, if either, of these is prior is a question on which Husserl seems to have held different views at different times. In the *Cartesian Meditations* he takes the view that the consciousness of my past self is presupposed by my consciousness of other selves. He also takes the view there that the latter presupposes consciousness of physical things, in particular the other's body. But he insists that my consciousness of the other is different in principle from my consciousness of physical things in the sense that whereas I cannot have presentations of all of the profiles of the physical thing—although those that I do have will be presentations of profiles that the other person has or could have—I can have no presentations of his presentations. Is not this, Derrida asks, recognition of the infinite transcendence of the other, recognition of his positive infinitude, as against the negative infinitude involved in my inability to experience the totality of profiles of the physical thing? And is not this recognition of the infinite transcendence of the other possible only if, like Husserl, we conceive the other on analogy with the ego? If we do not, are not we conceiving the other on analogy with a stone? Does not the radical alterity of the other depend on his being another ego? And does not this otherness depend on this sameness, this dissymmetry on this symmetry? This dependence of his otherness on his being another ego does not make the other's ego a dependency of mine. It does not make him part of my real economy, because Husserl is describing a transcendental, not a real, economy.

Derrida is here saying about Levinas what was found necessary to say above in chapter 2 about those who contend that the author of the *Cartesian Meditations* espouses metaphysical realism and those who say he espouses metaphysical idealism. Transcendental phenomenological idealism is neutral in the debate between these contenders. The transcendental phenomenological reduction aims to suspend matters of empirical and metaphysical factuality. That is why it would be naive to equate Husserl's appeal to analogical appresentation with the argument from analogy to the existence of other minds. This would be a naivety comparable with the naivety of the supposition that there could be an ontological argument that proves the existence of God. This would be, in Husserl's sense, the naivety of the natural attitude in favor of the world the successful reduction suspends.

Now Levinas is no more intent than Husserl on producing ratiocinative proof of the existence of other minds or of God. We have noticed, however, that his parlance about others is at the same time parlance about God. It draws less on Descartes's fifth Meditation than on the third, but it abstracts from the causal terminology of the latter and from the theo*logicality* of both. It abstracts from causality because a cause and an effect are terms within a system. Their causal relation is their way of being together. But the proximity of the face to face is a "relation" of speaking (*langage*). This is why it can be neither theological nor analogical, hence not a topic of a theology of *analogia entis* or a *theologia negativa*. It is not logical. It is paralogical and paradoxical. That is to say, this strange speech-act is beyond the possibility Husserl ascribes to all theoretical and nontheoretical acts of being made the topic of doxic posting.[25] It cannot be named or nominalized. It cannot be said. It would seem, therefore, that it cannot be the topic of a phenomenology of the Husserlian kind, despite the indebtedness Levinas acknowledges to Husserl. This is the source of one of the difficulties Derrida warns us we shall find facing Levinas. Difficulties of which Levinas himself warns us, for example in his title *Difficult Freedom*.[26]

What sort of discourse can this be which is somehow beyond the scope of logic, exterior to what Derrida calls the logical and phenomenological *clôture*? How can there be any saying where what is said is not said within the framework of a language as systematic as that of cause and effect? And would not the description of the structures of that language be a science or a *logos* of the appearance of meaning: a semiology, to use Saussure's word, a phenomenology, to use Husserl's? Now, although part of the subject matter of phenomenology is the essence of facthood or facticity, empirical and any other factuality is excluded by reduction. Yet Levinas, Derrida suggests, seems to want to combine phenomenology with empiricism. A comparison with Descartes is again relevant. The idea of infinity for Descartes is not adventitious. It is not based on a sensible impression. Nor is it something I make; it is not my fiction, not inventitious. It is innate. But the innateness Descartes attributes to this idea goes along with a sort of adventitiousness in that it comes to me from my Maker—and in so far as Descartes and Malebranche allow that the idea is made by Him, it is to that degree also a fiction. Levinas's account of my idea of the Other draws upon Descartes's account of his idea of the infinite. Hence it is not surprising that on Levinas's account the idea of the Other is also a hybrid, an unstable amalgam of the phenomenological and the empirical. It is somewhat as though Aristotle, having told us that there is no science of the singular, nevertheless proceeded to present one. But somewhat as though only, because, according to Levinas,

> The neighbour concerns me with his exclusive singularity without appearing, not even as a *tode ti*. His extreme singularity is precisely his assignation: he assigns me before I designate him as *tode ti*.[27]

Levinas himself frequently says that by the standards of formal logic the instability and difficulty of his account would amount to contradiction.

As when "the Lord spake unto Moses face to face" (Ex. 33:11), and as when the Lord called Samuel and the latter replied, "Speak, Master, for they servant heareth," so does the Other command *me*, and I am ethically and religiously bound to answer, "Here am I," "Lo, here am I," "*me voici*," "*hineni*" (Ex. 3:4, Sam. 1, 3:4, 6, 8; cf. Gen. 22:1, 7,11). I am beholden. I am the One, as Levinas puts it, using the language of Parmenides. I am (On) It, as children say when playing hide-and-seek. I am uniquely responsible.[28] Levinas thinks that this empirical or, as he would prefer to say, ethical lopsidedness is in conflict with the symmetry Husserl ascribes to the relationship of the ego and the alter ego in the *Cartesian Meditations*. We have seen that Derrida denies there is conflict here. On the contrary, according to him the so-called empirical dissymmetry is possible only because of the transcendental symmetry. Levinas forgets that the ego described in the *Cartesian Meditations* is the transcendental ego, the ego in general. Levinas, though, *qua* philosopher wants to say something about the essence of the face to face. Perhaps there is little to be said about this, and what one says about it seems to leave out what is important. What is important in the discourse of the face to face either does not enter or slips through the net of the said, the *dit*. What is important is the *Dire*, the infinitive calling which is never said. Whatever is said about it calls to be unsaid or, better, dis-said, *dédit*. What is significant in the discourse of the face to face is not what is signified. It is not the meaning or the referent of a sign. Nor is it a sign. It is not and never was present and cannot be represented. To call it a trace is to give it not a name but a pro-name.

Maybe a trace of this pronominal trace can be picked up in the signature, and in the call sign a signaler transmits before his message begins. The call sign and the prefatory "I say" which beckons the person with whom one wants to speak are no more part of the message than is the autograph with which the author signs himself off. Even so, call signs and signatures can be faked, and no single one of them is indubitably authentic. The same applies to them as applies to any pronoun.

> The absolutely other (*Autre*) is the Other (*Autrui*). He and I do not form a number. The collectivity in which I say "you" or "we" is not a plural of the "I." I, you—these are not individuals of a common concept.... Alterity is possible only starting from *me*.[29]

That the most idiosyncratic of token reflexives is essentially imitable is something that has been maintained by philosophers as different as Hegel and Russell. "I" and "this" and "you" and "that," though not common names, are universal in their use. This is what Derrida demonstrates in his meditation on the various moments in *Otherwise than Being or Beyond Essence* when Levinas refers to what he is doing in that book "at this very moment".

4. *The back of beyond*

In his very philosophizing about what is beyond being the author is responding to an ethical call in the face to face with his reader. His reader is therefore, ethically speaking, his *magister*: his teacher and master. One reader, Derrida, comments on the difficulty of philosophizing about what is otherwise than being and beyond essence. Levinas himself comments on this difficulty. Is it a difficulty that amounts to paradox or incoherence? There is nothing paradoxical or incoherent in the idea of philosophical discourse about, say, incoherence or the illogical. The metalanguage may be perfectly coherent and logical. However, Levinas's predicament is different. His philosophical discourse purports to be about all discourse. So there is a self-referentiality that Levinas compares with that of the arguments for scepticicm regarding reason which depend on that very reason regarding which it is sceptical. Levinas's predicament is comparable too with Heidegger's embarrassment at having to assert propositions in order to distinguish the assertoric propounding of thoughts from monstrative saying. Heidegger needs to make this distinction in order to bring into the open the difference between the beingness of beings and the truth of being, in order, that is, to reveal that traditional metaphysics conceals the ontological difference. He sees that this difference is concealed again by its name and by his stating that his aim is to return metaphysics to fundamental ontology. Levinas states that his aim is to return so-called fundamental ontology to ethical metaphysics. It is to penetrate beyond the *logos*, beyond the propositional comprehension of metaphysical ontology, beyond the hermeneutic understanding of Heidegger's fundamental ontology, and beyond the coherent discourse of reason. Nonetheless, in seeking to achieve this aim

> one must refer—I am convinced—to the medium of all comprehension and of all understanding in which all truth is

reflected—precisely to Greek civilization, and to what it produced: to the logos, to the coherent discourse of reason.... One could not possibly ... arrest philosophical discourse without philosophizing.[30]

Levinas's discourse illustrates this. Whereas Heidegger, without denying that being is always being of a being, believes there is need to remind ourselves of the priority of being, Levinas aims to show "The philosophical priority of the existent [*étant*] over being."[31] Levinas's discourse is ontic, discourse about beings. It has that much in common with traditional metaphysical discourse on the being of beings and, despite their declared intentions, with the essentialist ontology of Husserl and the existentialist ontology of Sartre.

However, Levinas's metaphysics is ethical. The ethical would be a mode or region of the ontic as Heidegger uses this term, other modes being the psychological, the biological, and so on. But the ethical in Levinas's sense is not even remotely comparable with any natural or human science. And it is "more original" than fundamental ontology. Yet because the ethical "dimension" in which man ceases to be the measure of all things is a dimension of a being, albeit a dimension in which he transcends himself, one cannot help thinking of this as an ontological mode, as, in a phrase to which Levinas often has recourse, a way (*manière*) of being, a *Seinsweise*, to use Heidegger's word. Hence, notwithstanding Levinas's declared intention to convince his reader that "to exist has meaning in another dimension than that of the perduration of the totality; it can go beyond being,"[32] his rhetoric employs statements like "Being is exteriority."[33] That is, not only does Levinas, as Derrida points out, appear to confirm Heidegger's assertion that one tends to forget the ontological difference, it appears to confirm Heidegger's assertion that language is the house of being. Levinas does not wait for Derrida to tell him that the discourse of the face to face is inscribed within what they both call, following Bataille, the "general economy" of being. Of the many other examples of statements one could cite that, like "Being is exteriority," show that Levinas assumes a fore-understanding of being,[34] here is but one:

A relation whose terms do not form a totality can hence be produced within the general economy of being only as proceeding from the I to the other, as a *face to face*, as delineating a distance in depth—that of conversation (*discours*),

of goodness, of Desire—irreducible to the distance the synthetic activity of the understanding establishes between the
diverse terms, other with respect to one another, that lend
themselves to its synoptic operation.[35]

This is not a Levinasian version of what among English-speaking philosophers is known as the question whether "ought" can be derived
from "is." Rather, is it a denial that the *being* of alterity is the being of a
thought. It is a further contribution toward Heidegger's destruction of
the epistemological and perceptual tradition of metaphysics to which
those Greek-speaking philosophers Parmenides, Plato, Aristotle, Descartes, Kant, Hegel, and Husserl belong. It does not make the step
beyond being and beyond Heidegger announced in the title of the book
Levinas published in 1978 and already in a title of a section near the end
of *Totality and Infinity*. If the words just cited can be taken at their face
value, these titles canot be taken at theirs. Levinas's project must then
be interpreted in terms of the title of the essay that asks "Is Ontology
Fundamental?" He may go some distance toward showing, contrary to
Heidegger's earlier thoughts, that ontology is not fundamental. To this
extent he would be in agreement with Heidegger's later thinking. Indeed, Heidegger's reflections on the *Ab-grund* are foreshadowed in his
earlier reflections on the principle of sufficient reason. True, Levinas
stresses a different, ethical, kind of an-archy. But it is difficult to see how
this anarchy escapes being an anarchy in being rather than exterior to it,
epekeina tes ousias, or how this exteriority escapes being an exteriority
interior to being.

Derrida's estimate of Levinas's predicament is that his statements are
symptomatic of a general condition of all statement and thought. They
rest on or, rather, restlessly move between an exteriority that is an interiority and an interiority that is an exteriority. The trace of the other is
a trace of the trace of the general economy of being for which Derrida
also employs the pseudonyms spacing, differance, writing, and so on.
Levinas's predicament is our predicament. In contrasting exteriority
with a totalitarian system in which the past is resumed in the future
Levinas is forgetting that the time of that Hegelian and Husserlian re-
cuperative history is itself violated by the spacing of a nonphenomenological history which infinitely defers the achievement of absolute knowing
and self-identity in the living present of the "at this very moment."
Totality *is* Infinity. Because the "is" is always already erased, just as the
said is always already dis-said, intrinsically extrinsic, as though all words

were in scare quotes, in that unsteady state in which they are not obviously used or obviously mentioned, but neither and both. The idea that if a word can be mentioned, not used, it must be possible for it to be used and not mentioned is in order. But there is no way of telling of a particular word whether it is being mentioned or used. However clear a speaker may be about his intentions, neither he nor anyone else can state criteria sufficient to enable one to determine definitely what constitutes a use and what a mention. Derrida, no more than Wittgenstein, believes that this is "ordinarily" or "normally" necessary. But, no less than Wittgenstein, he believes that it is philosophically often thought to be so. And under pressure the most ordinary of us is liable to become a philosopher, to posit foundations, origins, and hidden roots. Preontologically, that is, pretheoretically, ontological as we are, endowed with the Gift of precomprehension of being, we are under the transcendental illusion that being is a metaphor behind which is a literal truth to which the philosopher would have us return. But the literal is a *pharmakon*, both poison and cure. Although the literal truth announces an Apocalypse Now in which the sign and its sense coincide, this coincidence is perpetually postponed.[36] The literal inside story turns out to be a figurative remark in the insecure space-time of nonphenomenological history: a figure of a figure of a face that has never shown itself and will only appear to appear. Literality is metaphor, not the place where metaphor, by backtranslation, comes to a stop, or where its *Bewegung* begins. Therefore not "the face to face ... where, absolutely present, in his face, the Other—without any metaphor—faces me."[37]

If we think, as we do, that metaphors have a natural home to which they can go back, like letters "returned to sender,"[38] we will be inclined to think that being is a metaphor whose origin it is the philosopher's duty to trace. We have seen that Levinas resists this idea of philosophy as homecoming. His Ulysses remains in exile. Yet even he indulges in the "etymological empiricism" that Derrida calls, with studied irony, the hidden root of all empiricism.[39] Space, exteriority, respiration, inspiration. These are well-worn metaphors for being. Levinas uses them as metaphors for alterity. We have now seen, however, that in spite of his declared intentions his rhetorical practice admits them at the same time as metaphors for and of being. Ontic metaphors too, as ontic as those that have led philosophers to overlook the ontological difference, including, in Derrida's view, the philosopher Emmanuel Levinas:

Because Being is nothing outside the existent, and beacuse

> the opening amounts to the ontico-ontological difference, it
> is impossible to avoid the ontic metaphor in order to articu-
> late Being in language, in order to let Being circulate in
> language.[40]

This ontic metaphorization

> explains everything except that at a given moment the
> metaphor has been thought *as* metaphor, that is, has been
> ripped apart as the veil of Being. This moment is the emer-
> gence of the thought of Being itself, the very movement of
> metaphoricity. For this emergence still, and always, occurs
> beneath an *other* metaphor.[41]

Put bluntly, space (and time), exteriority (and interiority), respiration
(and nonrespiration), inspiration (and expiration) *are*. To acknowledge
this is to let being be. At a given moment in the history of thought,
which is the history of being, this letting be of being may call for the
thinking of new metaphors—whether they are "poetic" or "scientific"
makes no difference (see chapter 9, section 1, above)—while thinking
the metaphor *as such*.

Derrida's way of letting being be and thinking the metaphor as such is
to play one against the other and the other against the one. This con-
trariness is exemplified in the difference between the treatment a writer
receives from him in one place and the treatment he receives in another.
We have already seen how in *Speech and Phenomena* Derrida questions
the compatibility of the principle of all principles, Husserl's "empiricism," and Husserl's admission of fundamental alterity. But faced with
Levinas's questioning of Husserl, Derrida springs to the latter's defense.
This is an illustration of the peaceful violence he asks Levinas to acknowledge when the only violence the latter seems to see is the bellicose
violence of totality.

Similarly, when faced with Levinas's charge that Heideggerian ontology is one of totalitarian violence, Derrida contends that Heidegger
shows respect to radical alterity. Being can be oppressive and domineer-
ing only if being is a category. But as early as the introduction to *Being
and Time*, notes Derrida, Heidegger begins to "destroy" the traditional
idea that being is a transcendental concept and to show that it is as
"refractory to the category" as is Levinas's Other.

If to understand Being is to be able to let be (that is, to respect Being in essence and existence, and to be responsible
for one's respect), then the understanding of Being always
concerns alterity, and par excellence the alterity of the Other
in all its originality: one can have to let be only that which
one is not. If Being is always to be let be, and if to think is to
let Being be, then Being is indeed the other of thought. But
since it is what it is only by the letting be of thought, and
since the latter is thought only by virtue of the presence of
the Being which it lets be, then thought and Being, thought
and the other, are the same: which, let us recall, does not
mean identical, or one, or equal.[42]

If Levinas were to reply that respect for radical alterity is accorded only
when it is acknowledged that I am ethically responsible to the Other,
Derrida could say that this acknowledgment is perhaps implicit in
Heidegger's inclusion of conscience in his table of existentials. Yet in
"The Ends of Man" Derrida himself emphasizes the degree to which
Heidegger is a philosopher of total presence, of nostalgia for uninter-
rupted proximity, a philosopher of *hiraeth* for one's ownmost home.[43]
This countersuggestibility on Derrida's part is not a childish whim to be
different. It is a levity with serious intent: that of showing respect for the
texts he faces, for instance for both the *Heimlichkeit* and the *Unheimlichkeit* that are in Heidegger's text at one and the same place and
time—and for the sameness and difference that are in the texts of Levinas *en ce moment même*. Where one is inclined to see only sameness, an
effort must be made to show that difference is ubiquitous too; and vice
versa. Derrida's apparently *ad hominem* polemics are, he would say,
excused, if not justified, by the *polemos* of sameness and difference
which is the disconcerting condition of thought about either. *Logos* is
already outside itself, like being.

And like the book. In *Of Grammatology* Derrida says of Hegel that
although, like Plato and Husserl, he is par excellence a philosopher of
Erinnerung and the living self-presence of speech, he is "*also* the thinker
of irreducible difference"; and that although he is "the last philosopher
of the book," he is also "the first thinker of writing."[44] Derrida says this
in a chapter headed "The End of the Book and the Beginning of Writing." However, as he makes clear elsewhere, the Book, whether this is
Hegel's *Encyclopaedia* or *Science of Logic* or a metaphor for any
volume that closes on itself, has no end; and writing does not begin.[45]

The *viva voce* is less safe and sound than Socrates believes when, because of that belief, he accords it priority over writing in the *Phaedrus*, a book that both Derrida and Levinas draw on and draw out. The conceptual grip of speech is less securely maintained than he thinks. Its apparently self-enclosed now is at a distance from itself, doubly *ent(–)fernt*, like the spacing of phonetic script. There is no *nunc stans*.

Nor is there the totality. This is one of the lessons Derrida reads in and into the professions of *Totality and Infinity*. What does Levinas find when the roles of professor and reader are reversed?

> What stays constructed after de-construction is surely the severe architecture of the discourse which deconstructs and which employs in predicative propositions the present tense of the verb "to be." Discourse in the course of which, at the very moment when it is shaking the foundations of truth, in face of the evidence of a lived present which appears to offer a last refuge to presence, Derrida still has the strength to say "Is that certain?", as if anything could be certain at that moment, and as if certainty and uncertainty should still matter.
>
> It would be tempting to appeal to this use of logocentric language against that very language as an objection to the resulting de-construction. An approach often made in the refutation of scepticism which, nevertheless, having been knocked down and trampled under foot, gets up again to become once more the legitimate child of philosophy. An approach which perhaps Derrida himself has not always disdained to follow in his polemics.
>
> But in following this approach there is a risk of failing to recognize the signification effected by the very inconsistency of this procedure; of failing to recognize the incompressible non-simultaneity of the Said and the Saying, the dislocation of their correlation: a minimal dislocation, but wide enough for the words of the sceptic to pass through without being strangled by the contradiction between what is signified by what is *said* in them and what is signified by the very fact of uttering something *said*. As if the two significations lacked the simultaneity needed for contradiction to be able to break the knot in which they are tied. As if the correlation of the *Saying* and the *Said* were a dia-chrony of what cannot be united; as if the situation of the *Saying* were already a "mem-

ory of retention" for the *Said*, but without the *lapsed* moments of Saying allowing themselves to be retrieved in this memory.[46]

Otherwise said: Derrida has a keen eye for the diachrony of the said. He locates that diachrony in the dead time of writing with which the living present of the spoken word is engraved. But beyond this diachrony and/or supplementary to it is a radical diachrony which Derrida runs the risk of failing to recognize: a diachrony that is due to the paradoxical tie between the said and the fact of someone's saying something. The paradoxicality, as explained earlier, is the recalcitrance of the uttering to formulation as a proposition that is said. It is because the saying and the said are in this way "refractory to the category" that it and the said are *inassemblable*; they are so incomparable that they resist every attempt to bring them together. They resist *Ereignis*. They resist even the togetherness of logical contradictories. Statements that contradict each other logically are *mutually* contradictory. They are contradictory only because they are posited together at the same time. The contradiction is resolved by asserting them at different times. But the saying and the said are neither at the same time nor at different times. They are *in* different times. So the saying cannot be retrieved in the said.

How does this bode for beyondness and the hermeneutic circle?

The hermeneutic circle, as announced in the Foreword, is "the ontological condition of understanding." More precisely, it is the priority of the existential over the apophantic, the recalcitrance of the existential to the category. Assuming that saying is existential and the said categorial, Heidegger, Gadamer, and Levinas agree that the categorial cannot retrieve the existential without a residual existential trace—and they would agree with Merleau–Ponty's judgment that the lesson the reduction teaches us is the impossibility of a complete reduction. But the Heideggerian existentials are ontological conditions of understanding, whereas saying, Levinas alleges, is beyond ontology and beyond understanding. Further, the Heideggerian existentials constitute time, and although existential temporality is not the same kind of time as the time of the categorized objects about which we assert propositions, the latter is in the former, which is somehow prior. Admittedly, there remains the difficulty of giving an account of this inclusive priority, the difficulty with which Heidegger is occupied in his extrapolation of Kant's doctrine of schematism. This difficulty has not been resolved. It is not resolved by Heidegger, nor has it been resolved in the deconstructions of Heidegger's doctrines undertaken by Derrida and Levinas. Indicative of this difficulty is Levinas's need to have it both ways: to affirm the radical alterity of the time of the other's saying while granting that irretrievable moments of saying are nonetheless, *as it were*, immemorial memories retained in the same memory with the said. Metaphorically speaking, so to speak.

The difficulty is the difficulty with metaphor. If, as Derrida says, all metaphors are ontic, they will present a difficulty for anyone, like Heidegger, trying to get beyond ontic metaphysics to fundamental ontology, and for anyone, like Levinas, trying to get beyond ontology to ethical metaphysics. "The extraordinary word *beyond*" transmits an ontic metaphor.[47] So too does the word "prior."[48] Therefore, when Derrida and Levinas have begun deconstructing these metaphors we can expect to have difficulty deciding what is prior to what. The apparently secure notion of logical priority will begin to quake, and we may consequently fail to find our feet with Levinas when he says, "The neighbour concerns me outside every a priori—but perhaps *prior to every a priori*"[49] When faced with the question whether ontology is beyond metaphysics or metaphysics is beyond being, we may be at a loss for words.

Notes to the Foreword

1. Martin Heidegger, "Overcoming Metaphysics," in *The End of Philosophy*, trans. Joan Stambaugh (London: Souvenir Press, 1975), pp. 88–89 [*Vorträge und Aufsätze* (Pfullingen: Neske, 1967), vol. 1 p. 67].
2. Martin Heidegger, "What is Metaphysics?" trans. R. F. C. Hull and Alan Crick, in *Existence and Being* (London: Vision, 1949), p. 382 [*Was ist Metaphysik?* (Frankfurt am Main: Klostermann, 1955), p. 44].
3. Josef Bleicher, *Contemporary Hermeneutics* (London: Routledge and Kegan Paul, 1980), p. 267.

Notes to Chapter 1

1. Martin Heidegger, *Existence and Being* (London: Vision, 1949), p. 382 [*Was ist Metaphysik?* (Frankfurt am Main: Klostermann, 1955), p. 44].
2. Martin Heidegger, "My way to Phenomenology," in *On Time and Being*, trans. Joan Stambaugh (New York: Harper and Row, 1972) [*Zur Sache des Denkens* (Tübingen: Niemeyer, 1969)]. See also Walter Biemel, *Martin Heidegger*, trans. J. L. Mehta (London, Routledge and Kegan Paul, 1977), chap. 2.
3. Martin Heidegger, *On the Way to Language*, trans. Peter Hertz and Joan Stambaugh (New York: Harper and Row, 1971), p. 10 [*Unterwegs zur Sprache* (Pfullingen: Neske, 1959), p. 96].
4. Martin Heidegger, "Letter on Humanism," trans. Edgar Lohner, in *Philosophy in the Twentieth Century*, ed. William Barrett and Henry D. Aiken (New York: Random House, 1962), p. 279 (Heidegger, *Basic Writings*, ed. David Farrell Krell [London: Routledge and Kegan Paul, 1978], p. 207) [*Platons Lehre von der Wahrheit, mit einem Brief über den "Humanismus"* (Bern: Francke, 1947, 1954), p. 71].
5. Ibid., pp. 293–94; (pp. 229–30) [pp. 101–03].
6. *The Piety of Thinking: Essays by Martin Heidegger*, trans. James G. Hart and John C. Maraldo (Bloomington: Indiana University Press, 1976), pp. 22ff [*Phänomenologie und Theologie* (Frankfurt am Main, Klostermann, 1970), pp. 37ff].
7. See note 1.
8. Martin Heidegger, *Being and Time*, trans. John Macquarrie and Edward Robinson (Oxford: Blackwell, 1962) [*Sein und Zeit*, 7th ed. Tübingen: Niemeyer, 1953), pp. 9–10]. The page references are those of the German edition and are given in the margins of the translation by John Macquarrie and Edward Robinson. They are henceforth included in the text of this chapter.
9. See note 4.
10. Heidegger, *On the Way to Language*, p. 29 [*Unterwegs zur Sprache*, p. 121].
11. Cf. *Being and Time*, p. 180.
12. *An Introduction to Metaphysics*, trans. Ralph Manheim (New York: Doubleday, 1961), p. 68 [*Einführung in die Metaphysik* (Tübingen: Niemeyer, 1953), p. 62].
13. Cf. *Being and Time*, p. 211: "If the *cogito sum* is to serve as the point of departure for the existential analytic of Dasein, then it needs to be turned around, and furthermore its content needs new ontologico-phenomenal confirmation. The *sum* is then asserted first, and indeed in the sense that 'I am in a world.'"
14. See Kant's references to "common knowledge" at the end of the preface to his *Fundamental Principles of the Metaphysic of Morals*.
15. There is a close study of problems arising from Heidegger's modal distinctions in Klaus Hartmann, "The Logic of Deficient and Eminent Modes in Heidegger," *Journal of the British Society for Phenomenology* 5, 1974.

16. W. B. Macomber, *The Anatomy of Disillusion* (Evanston, Ill.: Northwestern University Press, 1967), p. 87.
17. See Heidegger, "A Dialogue on Language," in *On the Way to Language.*
18. Heidegger, "Letter on Humanism," p. 279 (*Basic Writings*, p. 206) [*Platons Lehre von der Wahrheit*, p. 70].
19. Ludwig Wittgenstein, *Philosophical Investigations*, trans. G. E. M. Anscombe (Oxford: Blackwell, 1967), par. 24. I do not know whether Wittgenstein ever read *Being and Time*, but there is evidence, to which reference is made below, that in 1929, a critical year for the development of his thinking, he was aware of some of the things Heidegger was saying.
20. Immanuel Kant, *Critique of Practical Reason*, pt. 1, bk. 1, chap. 2.
21. See Ludwig Wittgenstein, *Tractatus Logico-Philosophicus*, trans. D. F. Pears and B. F. McGuinness (London: Routledge and Kegan Paul, 1961), 6.4311. Cf. Paul Edwards, "Heidegger and Death as 'Possibility,'" *Mind* 74, 1975, and "Heidegger and Death: A Deflationary Critique," *Monist* 59, 1975. A modified version of these papers is *Heidegger on Death: A Critical Evaluation* (La Salle: The Hegeler Institute, 1979). See too J. E. Llewelyn, "The 'Possibility' of Heidegger's Death," *Journal of the British Society for Phenomenology* 14, 1983.
22. Martin Heidegger, *Kant and the Problem of Metaphysics*, trans. James S. Churchill (Bloomington: Indiana University Press, 1962) [*Kant und das Problem der Metaphysik*, 2d ed. (Frankfurt am Main: Klostermann, 1951)]; and Heidegger, *What is a Thing?* trans. W. D. Barton and Vera Deutsche (Chicago: Regnery, 1967) [*Die Frage nach dem Ding* (Tübingen: Niemeyer, 1962)]; see also Heidegger, "Kant's Thesis about Being," *The Southwestern Journal of Philosophy* 4, 1973 [*Kants These über das Sein* (Frankfurt am Main: Klostermann, 1963)], and *Phänomenologische Interpretation von Kants Kritik der reinen Vernunft* (Frankfurt am Main: Klostermann, 1977).
23. See note 78.
24. Martin Heidegger, *Poetry, Language and Thought*, trans. Albert Hofstadter (New York: Harper and Row, 1971), p. 67 [*Holzwege* (Frankfurt am Main: Klostermann, 1950, 1972), p. 55].
25. These notions along with hearing and speech are discussed against their theological background in Augustine and Luther by Manfred Stassen, *Heideggers Philosophie der Sprache in "Sein and Zeit"* (Bonn: Bouvier, 1973).
26. See Heidegger, *Zur Sache des Denkens*, p. 21. See also Otto Pöggeler, "Sein als Ereignis," *Zeitschrift für philosophische Forschung* 13, 1959, pp. 597–632.
27. Heidegger, *On the Way to Language*, p. 127 [*Unterwegs zur Sprache*, p. 258]. We go on to bring out the connection between *Ereignis* and *es gibt*, "there is"; see "Letter on Humanism," pp. 283–84 (*Basic Writings*, p. 214) [*Platons Lehre von der Wahrheit*, p. 80]: "The *gibt* names, however, the essence of being; the giving itself and the imparting of its truth. The giving itself into the open with this self is being [*Sein*] itself." One could go on to bring out the connection between *Ereignis*, *es gibt*, and *Geschick*, "destiny" or "dispensation."
28. Heidegger, *Zur Sache des Denkens*, p. 38
29. Heidegger, *On the Way to Language*, p. 127 [*Unterwegs zur Sprache*, p. 258].
30. *Poetry, Language and Thought*, p. 86 = *Holzwege*, p. 99.
31. Heidegger, *On the Way to Language*, p. 129 [*Unterwegs zur Sprache*, p. 260].
32. John Locke, *An Essay Concerning Human Understanding*, II, 13, 19.
33. Heidegger, "The Thinker as Poet," in *Poetry, Language and Thought* [*Aus der Erfahrung des Denkens* (Pfullingen: Neske, 1954). With reference to this English title it should be noted that Heidegger distinguishes the thinker from the poet. "The thinker utters being. The poet names what is holy" ("Der Denker sagt das Sein. Der Dichter nennt das Heilige"). But cf. *On the Way to Language*, p. 136 [*Unterwegs zur Sprache*, p. 267]: "All reflective thought is poetic: all poetry, however, is thought" ("Alles sinnende Denken ist ein Dichten, alle Dichtung aber ein Denken"). *Existence*

and Being, p. 391 [*Was ist Metaphysik?* p. 51]. Cf. Heidegger, *What is Called Thinking?* trans. Fred D. Wieck and J. Glenn Gray (New York: Harper and Row, 1968,
1972), pp. 128–34 [*Was heisst Denken?* (Tübingen: Niemeyer, 1954, 1971), pp. 87f.
and 154]. *Gedachtes, Cahiers de l'Herne* 15, 1971, pp. 169–87.

34. Heidegger, *Poetry, Language and Thought*, p. 194 [*Unterwegs zur Sprache*, p. 16].
35. Martin Heidegger, *Identity and Difference*, trans. Joan Stambaugh, (New York: Harper and Row, 1969), pp. 32 and 95 [*Identität und Differenz* (Pfullingen: Neske, 1957),
p. 23].
36. Ibid., pp. 31 and 94 [p. 22].
37. Ibid., pp. 38f. and 103f. [pp. 31f].
38. Heidegger, *On the Way to Language*, p. 5 [*Unterwegs zur Sprache*, p. 90].
39. Heidegger, "Letter on Humanism," p. 302 (*Basic Writings*, p. 242) [*Platons Lehre von
der Wahrheit*, p. 119]. Cf. Meister Eckhart, *Werke*, vol. 2 (Stuttgart: Kohlhammer,
1936), pp. 274–75: "Created things have being the way air has light."
40. Heidegger, "Letter on Humanism," p. 300 [p. 115].
41. Heidegger, *An Introduction to Metaphysics* [*Einführung in die Metaphysik*], *Poetry,
Language and Thought*, pp. 145ff. [*Vorträge und Aufsätze* (Pfullingen: Neske, 1967),
vol. 2 pp. 19ff.].
42. Heidegger, *On the Way to Language*, pp. 107 and 135 [*Unterwegs zur Sprache*, pp. 215
and 267].
43. Heidegger, *On Time and Being*, p. 22 [*Zur Sache des Denkens*, p. 23].
44. Ibid., p. 23 [p. 24].
45. Ibid., p. 20.
46. Heidegger, *Poetry, Language and Thought*, p. 86, cf. p. 72 [*Holzwege*, p. 99, cf.
p. 82].
47. Heidegger, *On Time and Being*, p. 24 [*Zur Sache des Denkens*, p. 25].
48. Heidegger, *Vorträge und Aufsätze*, vol. 3, pp. 53ff.
49. Ibid., pp. 13ff. See also Magda King, "Truth and Technology," *The Human Context*
5, 1973.
50. Heidegger, *Identity and Difference*, pp. 52 and 118 [*Identität und Differenz*, p. 48].
51. Heidegger, *On the Way to Language*, p. 10 [*Unterwegs zur Sprache*, p. 96].
52. Ibid., p. 12 [p. 99].
53. Ibid., p. 38 [p. 133].
54. Ibid., p. 39 [p. 134].
55. Ibid., pp. 114–15 [pp. 244–45].
56. J. L. Austin, *Philosophical Papers* (Oxford: Clarendon, 1961), p. 219.
57. On p. 103, quoted below, Heidegger says "closeness" (*Nähe*) is a mode of *Entfern-
theit*. My hendiadys is intended to record the connection of *Ent-fernung* with what is
zunächst und zumeist, "proximal and for the most part." "'Proximally' signifies the
way in which Dasein is 'manifest' in the 'with-one-another' of publicness, even if 'at
bottom' everydayness is precisely something which, in an existentiell manner, it has
'surmounted.' 'For the most part' signifies the way in which Dasein shows itself for
Everyman, not always, but 'as a rule'" (370).
58. Sec. 7 of "On the Essence of Truth," in *Existence and Being* (also *Basic Writings*)
[*Vom Wesen der Wahrheit*, (Frankfurt am Main: Klostermann, 1943, 1954)].
59. See *Hegel's Concept of Experience*, trans. Kenley Dove, (New York: Harper and
Row, 1970) [*Holzwege*, pp. 105ff.].
60. Heidegger, *The Piety of Thinking*, p. 25 [*Phänomenologie und Theologie*, p. 41].
61. Heidegger, *On the Way to Language*, p. 163 [*Unterwegs zur Sprache*, p. 41]: "The
German *fremd*, the Old High German *fram*, really means: forward to somewhere
else, underway toward ..., onward to the encounter with what is kept in store for it."
62. Heidegger, *Poetry, Language and Thought*, pp. 213ff. [*Vorträge und Aufsätze*, vol. 2,
pp. 61ff.]
63. Heidegger, *Identity and Difference*, p. 33 [*Identität und Differenz*, p. 97].

64. Heidegger, *Poetry, Language and Thought*, p. 74 [*Holzwege*, p. 61].
65. Heidegger, *Poetry, Language and Thought*, p. 194 [*Unterwegs zur Sprache*, p. 16].
66. Ibid., p. 208 [p. 31].
67. Heidegger, *On the Way to Language*, p. 59 [*Unterwegs zur Sprache*, p. 161].
68. Cf. W. B. Macomber, *The Anatomy of Disillusion*, p. xiii.
69. For *ohne es recht zu bedenken* the translator has "without giving it thought."
70. Heidegger, *On the Way to Language*, p. 51 [*Unterwegs zur Sprache*, p. 149].
71. Ibid., p. 47 [p. 145].
72. Ibid., p. 25 [p. 115].
73. Ibid., pp. 129–30 [p. 261].
74. "Letter on Humanism," p. 280 (*Basic Writings*, p. 208) [*Platons Lehre von der Wahrheit*, p. 72].
75. See especially "The Thing," in *Poetry, Language and Thought*, pp. 165ff [*Vorträge und Aufsätze*, vol. 2, pp. 37ff. 163ff.].
76. See especially "The Question Concerning Technology," in *The Question Concerning Technology and Other Essays*, trans. William Lovitt (New York: Harper and Row, 1976) [*Vorträge und Aufsätze*, vol. 1, pp. 5ff.]; *Identity and Difference*, pp. 35ff. and 99ff. [*Identität und Differenz*, pp. 27ff.]. Cf. note 49 above.
77. F. P. Ramsey, *The Foundations of Mathematics* (London: Kegan Paul, Trench and Trubner, 1931), p. 238: "But what we can't say we can't say, and we can't whistle it either." Not even if we are virtuosi at whistling, as was Wittgenstein.
78. Heidegger, *Existence and Being*, p. 380 [*Was ist Metaphysik?* p. 42. Cf. *An Introduction to Metaphysics* [*Einführung in die Metaphysik*, chap. 1], and *The Essence of Reasons*, trans. Terrence Malick (Evanston, Ill.: Northwestern University Press, 1969), pp. 115 and 123ff. [*Vom Wesen des Grundes* (Frankfurt am Main: Klostermann, 1955), pp. 48 and 51ff.]. F. Waismann and B. F. McGuiness, *Ludwig Wittgenstein und der Wiener Kreis* (Oxford: Blackwell, 1967), p. 68.
79. Wittgenstein, *Philosophical Investigatons*, 89.
80. See the exergue of this chapter and Edmund Husserl, *Logical Investigations*, trans. J. N. Findlay (London: Routledge and Kegan Paul, 1970), Investigation 6, sec. 44.

Notes to Chapter 2

1. The page references given in the text of this chapter are to the first volume of Husserliana as reproduced in the *Cartesian Meditations*, trans. Dorion Cairns (The Hague: Nijhoff, 1960).
2. Franz Brentano, *Psychology from an Empirical Standpoint*, trans. L. L. McAlister, A. C. Rancurello and D. B. Terrell (London: Routledge and Kegan Paul, 1973), pp. 88ff. [*Psychologie vom empirischen Standpunkt* (Leipzig: von Duncker und Humblot, 1874), vol. 1, pp. 115f.
3. G. E. Moore, "The Subject-Matter of Psychology," *Aristotelian Society Proceedings* vol. 10, 1909–10.
4. G. E. Moore, "The Refutation of Idealism," *Mind* n. s. vol. 12, 1903, reprinted in G. E. Moore, *Philosophical Studies* (London: Routledge and Kegan Paul, 1922). See also J. N. Findlay, "Some Neglected Issues in the Philosophy of G. E. Moore," in *G. E. Moore: Essays in Retrospect*, ed. Alice Ambrose and Morris Lazerowitz (London: Allen and Unwin, 1970), pp. 73–74.
5. Ludwig Wittgenstein, *Philosophical Investigations*, Oxford, Blackwell, 1953, p. 230.
6. The translator uses "Ego" where Husserl has *Ich* and "ego" where Husserl has *Ego*.
7. In *Formal and Transcendental Logic*, trans. Dorion Cairns (The Hague: Nijhoff, 1969) [*Formale und transzendentale Logik*, Halle: Niemeyer, 1929] (Husserliana 27), Husserl says that judgments have a sense-history (*Sinnesgeschichte*) (p. 184).

8. Edmund Husserl, *Ideen zu einer reinen Phänomenologie und phänomenologischen Philosophie* 3, (Husserliana 5) (The Hague: Nijhoff, 1952), pp. 152–53.
9. Wittgenstein, *Philosophical Investigations*, 90.
10. Ibid., 124.
11. J. N. Findlay, "Phenomenology and the Meaning of Realism," in *Phenomenology and Philosophical Understanding*, ed. E. Pivčević (Cambridge: Cambridge University Press, 1975), p. 157.
12. Husserl, *Formal and Transcendental Logic*, p. 222 [*Ideen* 3, p. 153].
13. Edmund Husserl, *Ideas*, trans. W. R. Boyce Gibson (London: Allen and Unwin, 1931) [*Ideen* 1 (Husserliana 3), (The Hague: Nijhoff, 1950), sec. 46].
14. Husserl, *Ideen* 3, p. 153.
15. Husserl, *Ideas* 1, sec. 55.
16. Cf. David Carr, *Phenomenology and the Problem of History* (Evanston, Ill.: Northwestern University Press, 1974), p. 15; Robert Sokolowski, *The Formation of Husserl's Concept of Constitution* (The Hague: Nijhoff, 1970), passim; Roman Ingarden, *On the Motives which Led Husserl to Transcendental Idealism*, trans. Arnór Hannibalsson (The Hague, Nijhoff, 1975).
17. Martin Heidegger, *Being and Time*, trans. John Macquarrie and Edward Robinson (Oxford: Blackwell, 1962), p. 212.

Notes to Chapter 3

1. J.–P. Sartre, *Being and Nothingness*, trans. Hazel Barnes (London: Methuen, 1969) [*L'Etre et le néant* (Paris: Gallimard, 1943)]. The twinned references in the text of this chapter are to these books.
2. John Locke, *An Essay Concerning Human Understanding*, II, 8, 9 and IV, 3, 13–14.
3. Ibid., II, 8, 17, and IV, 3, 26.
4. Gilbert Ryle, review of Heidegger's *Sein und Zeit* reprinted from *Mind*, 1929, in *The Journal of the British Society for Phenomenology* 1, 3 (October 1970): 10.
5. A. G. N. Flew, "Is there a "Problem of Freedom'?" in *Phenomenology and Philosophical Understanding*, ed. E. Pivčević (Cambridge: Cambridge University Press, 1975), p. 209.
6. Hazel Barnes uses "utility" in this chapter to translate *ustensilité*, the word for which she uses "instrumentality" when it occurs in the chapter on Transcendence.
7. Cf. p. 550 [p. 635]: "Each person realises only one situation—*his own.*"
8. My emphasis.
9. See note 10.
10. The distinction is marked in English by "meaning" that admits of a natural plural and "meaning" that does not. The connection is exploited and explored by many philosophers, e.g., by Frege in "The Thought," by Wittgenstein, particularly in his remarks on point and purpose, by philosophical pragmatists, by Bergson, and by many writers in the phenomenological tradition, not least Husserl himself, in spite of his antipathy for anything that might smack of psychologism. Gilbert Ryle once confessed that he became less interested in the works of Husserl when they began using "meaning" in a butter-spreading way. Wittgenstein is fairly lavish in his use of the word in his phenomenology of aspects. But the champion philosopher of ambiguity, Merleau–Ponty, smears "meaning" so extravagantly as to be willing to cite as a motto for his chapter on Temporality Claudel's gloss on time as "le *sens* de la vie (*sens*: comme on dit le sens d'un cours d'eau, le sens d'une phrase, le sens d'une étoffe, le sens de l'odorat)." The common idea present or in the offing here is directionality—though this idea takes in the sense of smell best if one is a dog, and it could be that that is why in his text Merleau–Ponty chooses to refer to the sense of sight. Directionality is central to

Sartre's analysis of adversity and utility, for the tie between these "coefficients" and importance derives from the project toward an ultimate Value in a manner not totally unlike what one finds in Hume, e.g., his statement in appendix 1 of the *Enquiry Concerning the Principles of Morals* that "utility is only a tendency to a certain end; and were the end totally indifferent to us, we should feel the same indifference towards the means." For both Hume and Sartre indifference is the null limiting case of instrumentality and detrimentality, the disrelatedness on to which necessity and obligation are superimposed by passion. But while Hume sees this passion as a sentimental journey the traveler undergoes, Sartre sees it as a freely chosen though ultimately frustrated pilgrimage, a *passion inutile*.

11. Ludwig Wittgenstein, *Philosophical Investigations*, 219.
12. J.-P. Sartre, *Nausea*, trans. R. Baldick (London: Penguin, 1965), pp. 182ff.
13. Locke, *Essay*, II, 23, 10.
14. Maurice Merleau–Ponty, *Phenomenology of Perception*, trans. Colin Smith (London: Routledge and Kegan Paul, 1962), p. 432 [*Phénoménologie de la perception* (Paris: Gallimard, 1945), p. 494.].
15. My emphasis.
16. Martin Heidegger, *Being and Time*, trans. John Macquarrie and Edward Robinson (Oxford: Blackwell, 1962), pp. 156–57.

Notes to Chapter 4

1. J.-P. Sartre, *Being and Nothingness*, trans. Hazel Barnes (London: Methuen 1969), p. 7 [*L'Etre et le néant* (Paris: Gallimard, 1943), p. 42].
2. Ibid., p. 297 [pp. 358–59].
3. J.-P. Sartre, *Critique of Dialectical Reason*, trans. Alan Sheridan-Smith (London: New Left Books, 1976) [*Critique de la raison dialectique* (Paris: Gallimard, 1960)]. The twinned references in the text of this chapter are to these books.
4. Sartre, *Being and Nothingness*, p. 378 [p. 447].
5. Ibid., p. 363 [p. 430].
6. J.-P. Sartre, *The Problem of Method*, trans. Hazel Barnes (London: Methuen, 1964), p. 84 [*Critique de la raison dialectique*, p. 59].
7. J.-P. Sartre, *Situations* 3 (Paris: Gallimard, 1949).
8. See Marjorie Grene, *Sartre* (New York: New Viewpoints, 1973), p. 216.
9. Not, according to Marjorie Grene's *lapsus calami*, Georges Lefebvre.
10. Kant, *Prolegomena*, sec. 4, and *Fundamental Principles*, preface.
11. Sartre, *The Problem of Method*, pp. 134–35 [*Critique de la raison dialectique*, pp. 86–87].
12. Sartre, *The Problem of Method*, p. 131 [*Critique de la raison dialectique*, p. 91].
13. Sartre, *The Problem of Method*, p. 34 [*Critique de la raison dialectique*, p. 32].
14. Sartre, *Being and Nothingness*, p. 282 [p. 342].
15. J.-P. Sartre, *Existentialism and Humanism*, trans. Philip Mairet (London: Methuen, 1948), pp. 51–52 [*L'Existentialisme est un humanisme* (Paris: Nagel, 1946), p. 83].
16. J.-P. Sartre, *The Transcendence of the Ego*, trans. Forrest Williams and Robert Kirkpatrick (New York: Noonday, 1957), pp. 56, 58 [*La Transcendance de l'Ego* (Paris: Vrin, 1972), pp. 39, 42].
17. Sartre, *Being and Nothingness*, pp. 495–96 [p. 576].
18. Ibid., p. 373 [p. 441].
19. Ibid., p. 372 [p. 440].

20. Ibid., p. 520 [p. 603].
21. My emphasis.
22. Sartre, *Being and Nothingness*, p. 408 [p. 479].
23. Ibid., pp. 518–19 [p. 601].

Notes to Chapter 5

1.. Gaston Bachelard, *La Dialectique de la durée* (Paris: Presses Universitaires de France, 1936, 1950), p. 19.
2. Ibid., p. 14.
3. Ludwig Wittgenstein, *Notebooks 1914–1916* (Oxford: Blackwell, 1961), p. 93.
4. Gaston Bachelard, *Le Nouvel esprit scientifique* (Paris: Presses Universitaires de France, 1934, 1946), p. 51.
5. Bachelard, *La Dialectique de la durée*, p. 15.
6. Ibid., p. 9.
7. Bachelard, *Le Nouvel esprit scientifique*, p. 16.
8. Gaston Bachelard, *L'Activité rationaliste de la physique contemporaine* (Paris: Presses Universitaires de France, 1951), p. 26.
9. Ibid., pp. 25–26.
10. Gaston Bachelard, *Le Rationalisme appliqué* (Paris: Presses Universitaires de France, 1949), p. 54.
11. Bachelard, *Le Nouvel esprit scientifique*, p. 162.
12. Ibid., p. 164. Cf. Gaston Bachelard, *La Philosophie du non* (Paris: Presses Universitaires de France, 1940, 1949), p. 9.
13. Bachelard, *La Philosophie du non*, p. 85.
14. Bachelard, *Le Rationalisme appliqué*, p. 36. Cf. Friedrich Nietzsche, *The Will to Power*, trans. Walter Kaufmann and R. J. Hollingdale (London: Weidenfeld and Nicolson, 1967), p. 230: "One must not take one's morality too seriously and not let oneself be deprived of a modest right to its opposite." Paul Feyerabend, *Against Method* (London: New Left Books, 1975), p. 189: "To be a true dadaist, one must also be an anti-dadaist," cited in Roy Bhaskar, "Feyerabend and Bachelard: Two Philosophies of Science," *New Left Review* 94, 1975, p. 41. Dominique Lecourt, *L'Epistémologie historique de Gaston Bachelard* (Paris: Vrin, 1972), p. 63.
15. Bachelard, *La Philosophie du non*, p. 85.
16. Bachelard, *Le Nouvel esprit scientifique*, pp. 55 and 97; *La Philosophie du non*, p. 70; Gaston Bachelard, *Le Pluralisme cohérent de la chimie moderne* (Paris: Vrin, 1932), pp. 230–31.
17. *Le Nouvel esprit scientifique*, p. 51.
18. François Dagognet, *Bachelard* (Paris: Presses Universitaires de France, 1972), p. 10.
19. Henri Bergson, *Time and Free Will*, trans. F. L. Pogson (London: Sonnenschein, 1910), chap. 2 [*Essai sur les données immédiates de la conscience* (Paris: Presses Universitaires de France, 1970) chap. 2].
20. Often, it has to be admitted, Bachelard expresses himself carelessly, so that instead of the interesting point we have been discussing here he makes one that could be mistaken for it, one that is no more than a triviality. For instance, in *Le Nouvel esprit scientifique*, he writes:

> People have been in too much of a hurry to say that the conception of the photon reinstated Newton's early idea of light corpuscles. Such reinstatement is possible only at the inception of a scientific outlook, where first impressions seem to be of equal weight; but corrected thoughts never return to their point of departure. (p. 93)

Later in the same book he observes that

> there are thoughts that never have a second start; these are thoughts which have
> been corrected, broadened, completed. They don't retrace their steps to the
> narrow home ground they ventured to leave. (p. 173)

This is only a colorful way of saying that corrected thoughts are different from their uncorrected forerunners.

21. Gaston Bachelard, *La Valeur inductive de la relativité* (Paris: Vrin, 1929), p. 241.
22. Bachelard, *La Philosophie du non*, p. 82. John Locke, *Essay Concerning Human Understanding*, II, 23, 8.
23. Wittgenstein, *Notebooks 1914–1916*, p. 85: "... idealism leads to realism if it is strictly thought out."
24. Bachelard, *Le Nouvel esprit scientifique*, p. 5.
25. Ibid., pp. 44–45.
26. Ibid., p. 149.
27. Bachelard, *La Philosophie du non*, p. 33.
28. Bachelard, *Le Nouvel esprit scientifique*, p. 45.
29. Ibid., p. 139
30. Ibid., p. 54. Hence mathematics is not just a notation, *langage*, according to Bachelard in *L'Activité rationaliste de la physique contemporaine*, p. 29.
31. Bachelard, *Le Nouvel esprit scientifique*, p. 55.
32. Ibid. Cf. pp. 99, 108, 110, 136, 173.
33. ibid., p. 139.
34. Ibid. Cf. Ludwig Wittgenstein, *Philosophische Bemerkungen* (Oxford: Blackwell, 1964), 27: "Tell me *how* you seek and I will tell you *what* you seek."
35. Bachelard, *La Philosophie du non*, p. 55. Cf. Einstein: "How a magnitude is measured is what it is."
36. Gaston Bachelard, *La Formation de l'esprit scientifique* (Paris: Vrin, 1972), p. 61.
37. Ibid.
38. See Thomas S. Kuhn, *The Structure of Scientific Revolutions* (Chicago: University of Chicago Press, 1962).
39. Bachelard, *La Philosophie du non*, pp. 139–40.
40. Emile Meyerson, *Identity and Reality*, trans. Kate Loewenberg (New York: Dover, 1962), chap. 11.
41. Bachelard, *L'Activité rationaliste de la physique contemporaine*, p. 25.
42. Gaston Bachelard, *L'Air et les songes* (Paris: Corti, 1943), p. 298.
43. Bachelard, *Le Nouvel esprit scientifique*, p. 53.
44. Bachelard, *L'Activité rationaliste de la physique contemporaine*, p. 192.
45. J.-P. Sartre, *Being and Nothingness*, trans. Hazel Barnes (London: Methuen, 1969), p. 601 [*L'Etre et le néant* (Paris: Gallimard, 1943), p. 692].
46. Bachelard, *Le Nouvel esprit scientifique*, p. 15.
47. Bachelard says that in his *Lautréamont* (Paris: Corti, 1951) he gives an "interprétation non-lautréamontienne du lautréamontisme."
48. Bachelard, *Le Nouvel esprit scientifique*, p. 91. Cf. the sentence from Nietzsche cited above in note 14.
49. Bachelard, *L'Activité rationaliste de la physique contemporaine*, p. 139.
50. Bachelard, *Le Nouvel esprit scientifique*, p. 16.
51. Ibid., p. 51.
52. Bachelard, *La Formation de l'esprit scientifique*, p. 237.
53. Ludwig Wittgenstein, *Philosophical Investigations*, trans. G. E. M. Anscombe (Oxford: Blackwell, 1967), 242.
54. Bachelard taught sciences in the *lycée* of his native town Bar-sur-Aube before going on to posts at the University of Dijon and the Sorbonne.

Notes to Chapter 6

1. Martin Heidegger, *Being and Time*, trans. John Macquarrie and Edward Robinson (Oxford: Blackwell, 1962), p. 148. Cf. Hans–Georg Gadamer, *Philosophical Hermeneutics*, trans. David E. Linge (Berkeley: University of California Press, 1976), p. 32 [*Kleine Schriften*, vol. 1 (Tübingen: Mohr, 1967), p. 123].

2. E. D. Hirsch, *Validity in Interpretation* (New Haven: Yale University Press, 1967). Emilio Betti, *Die Hermeneutik als allgemeine Methodik der Geisteswissenschaften* (Tübingen, Mohr, 1962); *Teoria generale della interpretazione* (Milan: Giuffré, 1955) (*Zur Grundlegung einer allgemeinen Auslegungslehre* [Tübingen: Mohr, 1954]). The single page references in this chapter are to Hirsch. The most relevant part of Hirsch's book was first published in *The Review of Metaphysics* 18, 1965.

3. The twinned references in this chapter are to Hans–Georg Gadamer, *Truth and Method*, trans. Garrett Barden and John Cumming (London: Sheed and Ward, 1975) [*Wahrheit und Methode*, 3d ed. (Tübingen: Mohr, 1972)].

4. See also Ludwig Wittgenstein *Philosophical Grammar*, trans. Anthony Kenny, p. 41, and *The Blue and Brown Books* (Oxford: Blackwell, 1958) p. 167. Charles Darwin remarks that the person who understands every note of a piece of music will best appreciate the overall effect.

5. Jürgen Habermas, *Knowledge and Human Interests*, trans. Jeremy J. Shapiro (London: Heinemann, 1972), p. 172. Cf. Wolfhart Pannenberg, *Theology and the Philosophy of Science*, trans. Francis McDonagh (London: Darton, Longman and Todd, 1976), pp. 199–201.

6. Edmund Burke, *Reflections on the Revolution in France* (London: Penguin, 1968), p. 183.

7. See above chapter 1, section 1.

8. Habermas, *Zur Logik der Sozialwissenschaften* (Frankfurt am Main: Suhrkamp, 1970), p. 279.

9. Wolfhart Pannenberg, *Basic Questions in Theology* trans. George H. Kehm (London: SCM, 1970), pp. 134–36.

10. Gadamer, *Philosophical Hermeneutics*, p. xxix.

11. Ibid., p. xxv.

12. Heidegger, *Being and Time*, p. 158.

13. Ibid., p. 161.

14. Martin Heidegger, "Letter on Humanism," in *Philosophy in the Twentieth Century*, ed. William Barrett and Henry D. Aiken (New York: Harper and Row, 1971). Also in Heidegger, *Basic Writings*, ed. D. F. Krell, (London: Routledge and Kegan Paul, 1977).

15. *Truth and Method* contains a discussion of Collingwood's logic of question and answer.

16. Hans Lipps, *Hermeneutische Logik* (Frankfurt am Main: Klostermann, 1976).

17. Hans–Georg Gadamer, *Hegel's Dialectic*, trans. P. Christopher Smith (New Haven: Yale University Press, 1976), p. 99. The published translation has "valid" for *verbindende*. Although in some contexts that is possible (see, for example, *Being and Time*, p. 156), in this context the word is being used as it is used when a telephone operator is said to "connect" two speakers, to put them *in Verbindung*.

18. Hegel, *Science of Logic*, the beginning of Book 1. Cf. Ludwig Feuerbach, *Zur Kritik der Hegelschen Philosophie*, in *Gesammelte Werke* (Berlin: Akademie Verlag, 1970), Kleinere Schriften 2, pp. 16ff.

19. Aristotle, *Posterior Analytics*, II, 19.

20. Gadamer, *Hegel's Dialectic*, p. 109.

21. Gadamer, *Philosophical Hermeneutics*, p. 64 [*Kleine Schriften*, vol. 1, p. 97.].

22. Georg Christoph Lichtenberg, *Vermischte Schriften* (Göttingen, 1844 etc.), vol. 1, p. 99. *Es denkt in mir*.

23. Gadamer, *Philosophical Hermeneutics*, p. 80 [*Kleine Schriften*, vol. 1, p. 68].
24. Ibid., pp. 77–81 [pp. 67–69].
25. See chapter 5 section 3.

Notes to Chapter 7

1. Maurice Merleau–Ponty, *Signs*, trans. Richard C. McCleary (Evanston, Ill: Northwestern University Press, 1964), p. 82 [*Signes* (Paris: Gallimard, 1960), p. 102].
2. Ibid. Also, Maurice Merleau–Ponty, *The Visible and the Invisible*, trans. Alphonso Lingis (Evanston, Ill.: Northwestern University Press, 1968), pp. 94, 128–29, 175 [*Le Visible et l'invisible* (Paris: Gallimard, 1964), pp. 130, 170–71, 229].
3. Merleau–Ponty, *Signs*, p. 39 [p. 49].
4. Ferdinand de Saussure, *Course in General Linguistics*, trans Wade Baskin (London: Fontana-Collins, 1974), pp. 16, 68 [*Cours de linguistique générale* (Paris: Payot, 1971), pp. 33, 100]. Cf. Roland Barthes, *Elements of Semiology*, trans. Annette Lavers and Colin Smith (London: Cape, 1967), pp. 9–11 [*Eléments de sémiologie* (Paris: Seuil, 1964), pp. 1–3.].
5. Hans–Georg Gadamer, *Truth and Method*, trans. Garrett Barden and John Cumming (London: Sheed and Ward, 1975), p. 359 [*Wahrheit und Methode*, 3d ed. (Tübingen: Mohr, 1972), p. 376]. Cf. above, chapter 6, section 3.
6. Barthes, *Elements*, p. 10 [pp. 1–2].
7. Saussure, *Course*, p. 66 [p. 98]. But cf. p. 119 [p. 164].
8. Barthes, *Elements*, p. 11 [p. 2].
9. Gilbert Ryle, "Ordinary Language," *Philosophical Review* 62, 1953. Husserl writes of the game-meaning (*Spielbedeutung*) of chess pieces in *Logical Investigations*, Investigation 1, sec. 20. Cp. Gottlob Frege, *Grundgesetze der Arithmetik* (Jena: Pohle, 1903) vol. 2 sec. 107ff.
10. Saussure *Course*, pp. 118, 120 [pp. 164, 166]. Cf. Nicolai Trubetzkoy, *Actes du premier congrès international des linguistes*, 1928, p. 10, and Merleau–Ponty, *Signs*, p. 117 [p. 146]. The apparent indecision of Saussure may be explained away as an inaccuracy on the part of his editors. His own view seems to have been not that phonemes or morphemes are purely differential, but that their elements are. This is the view stated in *Course*, p. 120 [p. 166]. Cf. Roman Jakobson, *Essais de linguistique générale*, vol. 2 (Paris: Minuit, 1973), pp. 131–166, and Elmar Holenstein, *Jakobson* (Paris, Seghers, 1974), pp. 149–50.
11. Saussure *Course*, p. 120 [p. 166].
12. James M. Edie, foreword to Maurice Merleau–Ponty, *Consciousness and the Acquisition of Language* trans. H. J. Silverman (Evanston, Ill.: Northwestern University Press, 1973), pp. xxxi–ii. Cf. Paul Ricoeur, *Le Conflit des interprétations* (Paris: Seuil, 1969), p. 245.
13. Merleau–Ponty, *Signs*, pp. 43, 90 [pp. 55, 112]
14. Maurice Lagueux, "Merleau–Ponty et la linguistique de Saussure," *Dialogue* 4, 1965.
15. Saussure *Course*, p. 115 [p. 160].
16. Ibid., p. 98 [p. 138].
17. Merleau–Ponty, *Signs*, p. 86 [p. 107].
18. Saussure *Course*, p. 89 [p. 127].
19. Merleau–Ponty, *Signs*, p. 87 [p. 108]. Cf. Claude Lévi–Strauss on *bricolage* in *L'Esprit sauvage*, a book dedicated to the memory of Merleau–Ponty.
20. H.–J. Pos, "Phénoménologie et linguistique," *Revue internationale de philosophie* 1, 1939.
21. Merleau–Ponty, *Consciousness and the Acquisition of Language*, p. 29.
22. Pp. 244–46.

23. Pos, "Phénoménologie," p. 360.
24. Merleau–Ponty, *Signs*, p. 86 [p. 108].
25. Ibid., p. 87 [p. 109].
26. Saussure *Course*, p. 89 [p. 127].
27. Maurice Merleau–Ponty, *Phenomenology of Perception*, trans. Colin Smith (London: Routledge and Kegan Paul, 1962), p. 178 [*La Phénoménologie de la perception* (Paris: Gallimard, 1945), p. 208].
28. Ibid., p. viii [p. III].
29. Merleau–Ponty, *Signs*, p. 44 [p. 56].
30. Ibid.
31. Edmund Husserl, *Logical Investigations*, trans. J. N. Findlay (London: Routledge and Kegan Paul, 1970), Investigation 6, sec. 8 and 14.
32. See H. B. Acton, *Kant's Moral Philosophy* (London: Macmillan, 1970), pp. 37–39.
33. Merleau–Ponty, *Signs*, pp. 90–91, [p. 113].
34. Ibid., p. 92 [p. 115].
35. Merleau–Ponty, *Phenomenology of Perception*, pp. 178–79, 389, 391 [pp. 207–08, 446, 449].
36. Merleau–Ponty, *Signs*, p. 45 [pp. 56–57.]
37. Stéphane Mallarmé, *Crise de vers*, Oeuvres complétes (Pléiade) (Paris: Gallimard, 1945), p. 366.
38. Paul Valéry, "Rhumbs," *Tel Quel* II (Pléiade 2, p. 163), cited by Roman Jakobson, *Essais de linguistique générale*, vol. 1 (Paris: Minuit, 1963), p. 233.
39. Merleau–Ponty, *Signs*, pp. 46–47 [pp. 58–59].
40. Ibid., p. 90 [p. 113]. Cf. Jakobson's remarks on equivalence in the essay referred to in note 38.
41. Merleau–Ponty, *Phenomenology of Perception*, p. 391 [p. 448].
42. Ibid., p. 188 [p. 219].
43. Maurice Merleau–Ponty, *The Structure of Behaviour*, trans. Alden L. Fisher (Boston: Beacon, 1963), pp. 39–40 (*La Structure du comportement* (Paris: Presses Universitaires de France, 1967), pp. 39–40].
44. For some comments see J. E. Llewelyn, "Bennett's Words and Deeds," *Inquiry* 21, 1978, pp. 120–29.
45. See chapter 3, section 1.
46. Husserl is adapting the term after Brentano. See his *Ideas* I (London: Allen and Unwin, 1931), sec. 47, footnote. Cf. Husserl, *Logical Investigations*, Investigation 1, sec. 3.
47. Merleau–Ponty, *Phenomenology of Perception*, p. 192.
48. Edmund Husserl, *Experience and Judgement*, trans. James S. Churchill and Karl Ameriks (London: Routledge and Kegan Paul, 1973), secs. 8 and 26. Cf. *Cartesian Meditations*, trans. Dorion Cairns (The Hague: Nijhoff, 1960), Edmund Husserl, sec. 38. Cf. also Mary Warnock, *Imagination* (London: Faber, 1976), pp. 144.–49. She says Merleau–Ponty's theory is "a theory of perception which has no rooms for imagination." I see it as a theory of perception pervaded by the productive imagination.
49. Husserl, *Logical Investigations*, Investigation 1, sec. 4.
50. Merleau–Ponty distinguishes between *le prosaïque* and *la grande prose* in "Un Inédit de Maurice Merleau–Ponty," *Revue de métaphysique et de morale* 67, 1962, p. 407.
51. Immanuel Kant, *Critique of Pure Reason*, A 141 [B 180].
52. Merleau–Ponty, *Phenomenology of Perception*, p. 189 [p. 221].
53. Ibid., pp. 389–90 [pp. 446–47]. Cf. pp. 194, 197 [pp. 226, 230].
54. Ibid., p. 196 [p. 228].
55. Merleau–Ponty, *Signs*, p. 122 [p. 154].
56. Merleau–Ponty, *Phenomenology of Perception*, pp. 197–98 [p. 230–31].
57. See G. E. Davie, "Edmund Husserl and 'The As Yet, in Its Most Important Respect,

Unrecognised Greatness of Hume,'" in *David Hume: Bicentenary Papers*, ed. G. P. Morice (Edinburgh: Edinburgh University Press, 1977).

58. Cf. Eugen Fink, "The Phenomenological Philosophy of Edmund Husserl and Contemporary Criticism," in *The Phenomenology of Husserl*, ed. R. O. Elveton (Chicago: Quadrangle, 1970) ["Die phänomenologische Philosophie Edmund Husserls in der gegenwartigen Kritik," *Kantstudien* 38, 1933].
59. Merleau–Ponty, *Signs*, p. 83 [p. 104].
60. Merleau–Ponty, *Phenomenology of Perception*, pp. 197–98 [p. 230].
61. Stéphane Mallarmé, "Avant dire au *Traité du Verbe* de René Ghil," misquoted in Merleau–Ponty, *Signs*, p. 44 [p. 56].
62. Husserl, *Cartesian Meditations*, p. 77, quoted in Merleau–Ponty, *The Visible and the Invisible*, p. 129 [p. 171].
63. R. S. Thomas, "Kneeling," *Selected Poems* (London: Hart-Davis, MacGibbon, 1973).
64. Merleau–Ponty, *The Visible and the Invisible*, pp. 137, 248 [pp. 181, 302].
65. Ibid., p. 129 [p. 171].

Notes to Chapter 8

1. Claude Lévi–Strauss, *The Savage Mind (La Pensée sauvage)* (London: Weidenfeld and Nicolson, 1966), p. 140, 142.
2. Claude Lévi–Strauss, *Structural Anthropology*, trans. Claire Jacobson and Brooke Grundfest Schoepf (London: Penguin, 1972), p. 229.
3. Claude Lévi–Strauss, "The Story of Asdiwal," in *The Structural Study of Myth and Totemism,* ed. Edmund Leach (London: Tavistock, 1971), p. 28.
4. Lévi–Strauss, *Structural Anthropology*, p. 228.
5. Lévi–Strauss, *The Savage Mind*, pp. 73–74.
6. Ibid., pp. 257–58.
7. Lévi–Strauss, *Structural Anthropology*, p. 21.
8. Ibid., p. 89.
9. Roman Jakobson, *Selected Writings*, vol. 1 (The Hague: Mouton, 1962), pp. 218–19.
10. Claude Lévi–Strauss, *The Raw and the Cooked*, trans. John and Doreen Weightman (London: Cape, 1970), pp. 308ff.
11. Claude Lévi–Strauss, *From Honey to Ashes*, trans. John and Doreen Weightman (London: Cape, 1973), pp. 474–75.
12. Lévi–Strauss, *Structural Anthropology*, pp. 12–13.
13. Lévi–Strauss, *The Savage Mind*, p. 258.
14. Claude Lévi–Strauss, *Tristes Tropiques*, trans John and Doreen Weightman (London: Penguin, 1976), chap. 6. On p. 69 he writes: "Unlike the history of the historians, that of the geologist is similar to the history of the psychoanalyst in that it tries to project in time—rather in the manner of a *tableau vivant*—certain basic characteristics of the physical or mental universe."
15. Claude Lévi–Strauss, Paul Ricoeur, etc., "Réponses à quelques questions," *Esprit*, 322, 1963.
16. Ibid., p. 640.
17. Lévi–Strauss, *Structural Anthropology*, p. 303.
18. Ricoeur, "Réponses," pp. 636, 641.
19. Lévi–Strauss, "Réponses," p. 632.
20. Lévi–Strauss, *The Savage Mind*, pp. 232–33, 262.
21. Ibid., p. 129.
22. Lévi–Strauss, *Structural Anthropology*, pp. 18–19.
23. Lévi–Strauss, *The Savage Mind*, p. 268.

24. Ibid., p. 269.
25. Lévi–Strauss, *Structural Anthropology*, p. 95.
26. Lévi–Strauss, *The Savage Mind*, p. 130.
27. Lévi–Strauss, *Structural Anthropology*, p. 95.
28. Lévi–Strauss, *The Savage Mind*, p. 247. Cf. Claude Lévi–Strauss, *L'Homme nu* (Paris: Plon, 1971), pp. 611ff., and "Philosophie et anthropologie," *Cahiers de philosophie*, vol. 1, 1966, p. 50: "Models which could be thought to be purely cultural already exist at the level of nature"; "There's much more culture in nature than we are inclined to think." Lévi–Strauss has in mind cybernetics and the genetic code. His declarations of allegiance to materialism must be understood in the context of remarks like these and like his statement on page 248 of *The Savage Mind* that "when we finally succeed in understanding life as a function of inert matter, it will be to discover that the latter has properties very different from those previously attributed to it." We are not far from the "idealism" of that notorious *mot* by the dedicatee of *The Savage Mind*: "Laplace's nebula is not behind us, at our remote beginnings, but in front of us in the cultural world" (Maurice Merleau–Ponty, *The Phenomenology of Perception*, trans. Colin Smith [London: Routledge and Kegan Paul, 1962] p. 432). Nor is Lévi–Strauss far from the idealist superrationalism of Bachelard. Compare Bachelard's statement "Le métal appartient vraiment au règne humain" in *Le Matérialisme rationnel* (Paris: Presses Universitaires de France, 1963, p. 73)—a title Lévi–Strauss might have chosen to describe his own position—with the statements from Lévi–Strauss cited at the beginning of this note and with the following passage from pages 70–71 of *Tristes Tropiques*: "At a different level of reality, Marxism seemed to me to proceed in the same manner as geology and psychoanalysis (taking the latter in the sense given it by its founder). All three demonstrate that understanding consists in reducing one type of reality to another; that the true reality is never the most obvious; and that the nature of truth is already indicated by the care it takes to remain elusive. For all cases, the same problem arises, the problem of the relationship between feeling and reason, and the aim is the same: to achieve a kind of *superrationalism*, which will integrate the first with the second, without sacrificing any of its properties." This "reduction" is also an *Aufhebung*. Is this *Aufhebung* also a discontinuous transition across an epistemological break?
29. Lévi–Strauss, *The Raw and the Cooked*, p. 12.
30. Lévi–Strauss, *Tristes Tropiques*, pp. 68–69.

Notes to Chapter 9

1. *An Introduction to Metaphysics* (New York: Doubleday, 1961), pp. 21–22 [*Einführung in die Metaphysik* (Tübingen: Niemeyer, 1953), p. 20].
2. Martin Heidegger, "Letter on Humanism", trans. Edgar Lohner, in *Philosophy in the Twentieth Century*, ed. William Barrett and Henry D. Aiken (New York: Random House, 1962), p. 274 [*Platons Lehre von der Wahrheit, mit etnem Brief über den "Humanismus"*: (Bern: Francke, 1947, 1954), p. 60].
3. Ludwig Wittgenstein, *Remarks on the Foundations of Mathematics*, trans. G. E. M. Anscombe (Oxford: Blackwell, 1956), p. 121.
4. Maurice Merleau–Ponty, *The Prose of the World*, trans. J. O'Neill (London: Heinemann, 1974), pp. 126–27 [*La Prose du monde* (Paris: Gallimard, 1969), pp. 177–79].
5. Henri Bergson, *Creative Evolution*, trans Arthur Mitchell (London: Macmillan, 1911), p. 146 [*L'Evolution créatrice* (Paris: Alcan, 1911), p. 151].
6. Ludwig Wittgenstein, *On Certainty*, trans. D. Paul and G. E. M. Anscombe (Oxford: Blackwell, 1969), 144.

7. Martin Heidegger, *Kant and the Problem of Metaphysics*, trans. James S. Churchill (Bloomington: Indiana University Press, 1962) [*Kant und das Problem der Metaphysik*, (Frankfurt am Main: Klostermann, 1951), sec. 1].

8. Martin Heidegger, "The Age of the World Picture," in *The Question of Technology and Other Essays*, trans. William Lovitt (New York: Harper and Row, 1977), pp. 135–36 ["Die Zeit des Weltbildes," in *Holzwege* [Frankfurt am Main: Klostermann, 1950, 1972), pp. 87–88].

9. Blaise Pascal, *Oeuvres* (Paris: Hachette, 1925), p. 127. Immanuel Kant, *Critique of Practical Reason*, conclusion.

10. Martin Heidegger, *The Question of Being*, trans. Jean T. Wilde and William Kluback (New Haven: College and University Press, 1958), pp. 82–83 ["Zur Seinsfrage," in *Wegmarken* (Frankfurt am Main, Klostermann, 1967), p. 239; 1976, p. 411].

11. Cf. J. E. Llewelyn, "What is a Question?" *Australasian Journal of Philosophy* 42, 1964.

12. Heidegger, *An Introduction to Metaphysics*, pp. 27ff. [pp. 25ff.].

13. J.–P. Sartre, *The Transcendence of the Ego*, trans. Forrest Williams and Robert Kirkpatrick (New York: Noonday, 1957), pp. 102–03 [*La Transcendance de l'Ego* (Paris: Vrin, 1972), pp. 83–84.] Eugen Fink, "The Phenomenological Philosophy of Edmund Husserl and Contemporary Criticism," in *The Phenomenology of Husserl*, ed. R. O. Elveton (Chicago: Quadrangle, 1970) ["Die phänomenologische Philosophie Edmund Husserls in der gegenwartigen Kritik," *Kantstudien* 38, 1933]. Maurice Merleau–Ponty, "The Philosopher and His Shadow," in *Signs*, trans. Richard C. McCleary (Evanston, Ill.: Northwestern University Press, 1964) [*Signes* (Paris: Gallimard, 1960)].

14. As Augustine said in a different connection in *Confessions*, bk. 1, chap. 4. I am grateful to Noel O'Donoghue for drawing my attention to this phrase. It would be dangerously misleading in the present connection, of course, if *praesentissime* were taken to mean a superlative way of being present at hand.

15. Martin Heidegger, "Overcoming Metaphysics," in *The End of Philosophy*, trans. Joan Stambaugh (London: Souvenir Press, 1975), p. 91 [*Vorträge und Aufsätze* (Pfullingen: Neske, 1954), vol 1, p. 70].

16. Heidegger, *An Introduction to Metaphysics*, pp. 34–35 [pp. 32–33].

17. Ibid., p. 8 [p. 7].

18. Heidegger, *The End of Philosophy*, pp. 84–85 [pp. 63–64]; Heidegger *The Piety of Thinking: Essays by Martin Heidegger*, trans. James G. Hart and John C. Maraldo (Bloomington: Indiana University Press, 1976), p. 18 [*Phänomenologie und Theologie* (Frankfurt am Main: Klostermann, 1970), p. 29].

19. Heidegger, *An Introduction to Metaphysics*, p. 34 [p. 31].

20. Ibid., p. 36 [p. 33].

21. Martin Heidegger, *Being and Time*, trans. John Macquarrie and Edward Robinson (Oxford: Blackwell, 1962), p. 150.

22. Immanuel Kant, *Critique of Pure Reason*, A141 [B180–81].

23. Ibid., A15 [B29].

24. Heidegger, *An Introduction to Metaphysics*, pp. 17, 35 [pp. 16, 32].

25. Heidegger, *The End of Philosophy*, p. 68 [Heidegger, *Nietzsche* (Pfullingen: Neske, 1961), vol. 2, p. 473. Some of the topics treated in this chapter are explored further in John Llewelyn, "Heidegger's Kant and the Middle Voice," in *Time and Metaphysics*, ed. David Wood and Robert Bernasconi (University of Warwick, Parousia Press, 1982), pp. 87–120.

Notes to Chapter 10

1. Emmanuel Levinas, *Otherwise than Being or Beyond Essence*, trans. A. Lingis (The Hague: Nijhoff, 1981), p. 165 [*Autrement qu'être ou au-delà de l'essence* (The Hague: Nijhoff, 1978), p. 210].
2. Ibid., and p. 148 [p. 188].
3. Edmund Husserl, *Ideas*, I (London: Allen and Unwin, 1931), sec. 117.
4. Martial Gueroult, *Descartes selon l'ordre des raisons* (Paris: Aubier, 1953), I, L'Ame et Dieu, p. 229.
5. Emmanuel Levinas, *En découvrant l'existence avec Husserl et Heidegger* (Paris: Vrin, 1974), p. 172.
6. Gueroult, *Descartes selon l'ordre des raisons*, p. 224.
7. Levinas, *Otherwise than Being*, p. 116 [p. 147].
8. Ibid., p. 112 [p. 143].
9. Ibid., p. 121 [p. 156].
10. Ibid., (the translation has "with").
11. Ibid., p. 114 [p. 146].
12. Ibid., p. 115 [p. 146].
13. J.-P. Sartre, *Being and Nothingness*, trans. Hazel Barnes (London: Methuen, 1969), pp. 83, 92 [*L'Etre et le néant* (Paris: Gallimard, 1943), pp. 125–26, 135–36].
14. Ibid., pp. xxxivf., xl–xli [pp. 24f., 31–32].
15. Emmanuel Levinas, *Existence and Existents*, trans. A. Lingis (The Hague: Nijhoff, 1978), p. 21 [*De l'existence à l'existant* (Paris: Vrin, 1981), p. 26], Levinas, *Ethique et Infini* (Paris: Fayard, 1982) pp. 45ff.
16. Emmanuel Levinas, *Totality and Infinity*, trans. A. Lingis (The Hague: Nijhoff, 1969), p. 197 [*Totalité et Infini* (The Hague: Nijhoff, 1961), p. 171].
17. Ibid., p. 190 [p. 164].
18. Levinas, *Otherwise than Being*, p. 92 [p. 117].
19. Sartre, *Being and Nothingness*, pp. 257–60 [pp. 315–18].
20. Levinas, *Totality and Infinity*, p. 197 [p. 171].
21. Ibid., p. 199 [pp. 173–74].
22. Emmanuel Levinas, *De Dieu qui vient à l'être* (Paris: Vrin, 1982), p. 239.
23. Levinas, *Totality and Infinity*, p. 48 [p. 18].
24. Husserl, *Ideas*, 1, sec. 24.
25. Ibid., sec. 117.
26. Emmanuel Levinas, *Difficile liberté: Essais sur le Judäisme* (Paris: Albin Michel, 1963 and 1976).
27. Levinas, *Otherwise than Being*, p. 86 [p. 109].
28. Ibid., pp. 159, 161 [pp. 124, 126].
29. Levinas, *Totality and Infinity*, pp. 39–40 [pp. 9–10]; *Otherwise than Being*, p. 159 [p. 202].
30. Levinas, *Difficile liberté*, cited at Jacques Derrida, *Writing and Difference* trans. Alan Bass (London: Routledge and Kegan Paul, 1978), p. 152 [*L'Ecriture et la différence* (Paris: Seuil, 1967), p. 226].
31. Levinas, *Totality and Infinity*, p. 51 [p. 52].
32. Ibid., p. 301 [p. 278].
33. Ibid., p. 290 [p. 266].
34. Some of these are cited by Derrida in *Writing and Difference*, p.141 [p. 208].
35. Levinas, *Totality and Infinity*, p. 39 [p. 9].
36. See Jacques Derrida, "D'un ton apocalyptique adopté naguère en philosophie," in *Les Fins de l'homme*, ed. Philippe Lacoue–Labarthe and Jean–Luc Nancy (Paris: Galilée, 1981).
37. Levinas, *En découvrant l'existence avec Husserl et Heidegger*, p. 196; Derrida, *Writing and Difference*, p. 100 [p. 149].

38. Jacques Derrida, *La Carte postale de Socrate à Freud et au-delà* (Paris: Flammarion, 1980).
39. Derrida, *Writing and Difference*, p. 139 [p. 203].
40. Ibid., p. 138 [p. 203].
41. Ibid., p. 139 [p. 204].
42. Ibid., p. 141 [p. 207]. See also Heidegger, *Identity and Difference*, and chapter 1, section 3, above.
43. Jacques Derrida, *Margins of Philosophy*, trans. Alan Bass (Chicago: University of Chicago Press, 1982), pp. 129ff. [*Marges de la philosophie* (Paris: Minuit, 1972), pp. 155ff.].
44. Jacques Derrida, *Of Grammatology*, trans. Gayatri Chakravorty Spivak (Baltimore: Johns Hopkins, 1974), p. 41 [*De la grammatologie* (Paris: Minuit, 1967), p. 26].
45. Jacques Derrida, *Positions*, trans. Alan Bass (London: Athlone, 1981), p. 14 [*Positions* (Paris: Minuit, 1972), p. 23].
46. Emmanuel Levinas, "Tout autrement," *L'Arc: Jacques Derrida*, 54, 1973, p. 35 [*Noms propres* (Montpellier: Fata Morgana, 1976), pp. 85–86].
47. Levinas, *Otherwise than Being*, p. 19 [p. 16].
48. Derrida, *Writing and Difference*, p. 141 [p. 208].
49. Levinas, *Otherwise than Being*, p. 192, note 20 [p. 109, note 20]. See John Llewelyn, *Derrida on the Threshold of Sense* (London: The Macmillan Press, forthcoming).

BIBLIOGRAPHY

A selection from the works referred to in this book.

Gaston Bachelard, *L'Activité rationaliste de la physique contemporaine* (Paris: Presses Universitaires de France, 1951).

Gaston Bachelard, *La Dialectique de la durée* (Paris: Presses Universitaires de France, 1936, 1950.

Gaston Bachelard, *La Formation de l'esprit scientifique* (Paris: Vrin, 1972).

Gaston Bachelard, *Le Matérialisme rationnel* (Paris: Presses Universitaires de France, 1963).

Gaston Bachelard, *Le Nouvel esprit scientifique* (Paris: Presses Universitaires de France, 1934, 1946).

Gaston Bachelard, *La Philosophie du non* (Paris: Presses Universitaires de France, 1940, 1949).

Gaston Bachelard, *Le Pluralisme cohérent de la chimie moderne* (Paris: Vrin, 1932).

Gaston Bachelard, *Le Rationalisme appliqué* (Paris: Presses Universitaires de France, 1949).

Gaston Bachelard, *La Valeur inductive de la relativité* (Paris: Vrin, 1929).

Roland Barthes, *Elements of Semiology*, trans. Annette Lavers and Colin Smith (London: Cape, 1967) [*Eléments de sémiologie* (Paris: Seuil, 1964)].

Henri Bergson, *Creative Evolution*, trans. Arthur Mitchell (London: Macmillan, 1911) [*L'Evolution créatrice* (Paris: Alcan, 1911)].

Henri Bergson, *Time and Free Will*, trans. F. L. Pogson (London: Sonnenschein, 1910) [*Essai sur les données immédiates de la conscience* (Paris: Presses Universitaires de France, 1970)].

Emilio Betti, *Die Hermeneutik als allgemeine Methodik der Geisteswissenschaften* (Tübingen: Mohr, 1962).

Emilio Betti, *Teoria generale della interpretazione* (Milan: Giuffrè, 1955) [*Zur Grundlegung einer allgemeinen Auslegungslehre* (Tübingen: Mohr, 1954)].

Walter Biemel, *Martin Heidegger*, trans. J. L. Mehta (London: Routledge and Kegan Paul, 1977).

Josef Bleicher, *Contemporary Hermeneutics* (London: Routledge and Kegan Paul, 1980).

Franz Brentano, *Psychology from an Empirical Standpoint*, trans. L. L. McAlister, A. C. Rancurello and D. B. Terrell (London: Routledge and Kegan Paul).

François Dagognet, *Bachelard* (Paris: Presses Universitaires de France, 1972).

Jacques Derrida, *La Carte postale de Socrate à Freud et au-delà* (Paris: Flammarion, 1980).

Jacques Derrida, *Of Grammatology*, trans. Gayatri Chakravorty Spivak (Baltimore: Johns Hopkins, 1974) [*De la grammatologie* (Paris: Minuit, 1967)].

Jacques Derrida, *Margins of Philosophy*, trans. Alan Bass (Chicago: University of Chicago Press, 1982) [*Marges de la philosophie* (Paris: Minuit, 1972)].

Jacques Derrida, *Positions*, trans. Alan Bass (London: Athlone, 1981) [*Positions* (Paris: Minuit, 1972)].

Jacques Derrida, "D'un ton apocalyptique adopté naguère en philosophie," in *Les Fins de l'homme; à partir du travail de Jacques Derrida*, ed. Philippe Lacoue–Labarthe and Jean–Luc Nancy, (Paris: Galilée, 1981) [*D'un ton apocalyptique* (Paris: Galilée, 1982)].

Jacques Derrida, *Writing and Difference*, trans. Alan Bass (London: Routledge and Kegan Paul, 1978) [*L'Ecriture et la différence* (Paris: Seuil, 1967)].

Eugen Fink, "The Phenomenological Philosophy of Edmund Husserl and Contemporary Criticism," in *The Phenomenology of Husserl*, ed. R. O. Elveton (Chicago: Quadrangle, 1970) ["Die phänomenologische Philosophie Edmund Husserls in der gegenwartigen Kritik," *Kantstudien*, 38, 1933].

Hans-Georg Gadamer, *Hegel's Dialectic*, trans. P. Christopher Smith (New Haven: Yale University Press, 1976) [*Hegels Dialektik* (Tübingen: Mohr, 1971)].

Hans-Georg Gadamer, *Kleine Schriften* (Tübingen: Mohr, 1962 etc.).

Hans-Georg Gadamer, *Philosophical Hermeneutics*, trans. David E. Linge (Berkeley: University of California Press, 1976).

Hans-Georg Gadamer, *Truth and Method*, trans. Garrett Barden and John Cumming (London: Sheed and Ward, 1975) [*Wahrheit und Methode* (Tübingen: Mohr, 1972)].

Jürgen Habermas, *Knowledge and Human Interests*, trans. Jeremy J. Shapiro (London: Heinemann, 1972).

Jürgen Habermas, *Zur Logik der Sozialwissenschaften* (Frankfurt am Main: Suhrkamp, 1970).

Martin Heidegger, *Basic Writings*, ed. David Farrell Krell (London: Routledge and Kegan Paul, 1978).

Martin Heidegger, *Being and Time*, trans. John Macquarrie and Edward Robinson (Oxford: Blackwell, 1962) [*Sein und Zeit* (Tübingen: Niemeyer, 1953)].

Martin Heidegger, *The End of Philosophy*, trans. Joan Stambaugh (London: Souvenir Press, 1975).

Martin Heidegger, *Aus der Erfahrung des Denkens* (Pfullingen: Neske, 1954).

Martin Heidegger, *Existence and Being*, trans. Alan Crick, R. F. C. Hull and Douglas Scott (London: Vision, 1949).

Martin Heidegger, *Gedachtes, Cahiers de l'Herne*, 15, 1971.

Martin Heidegger, *Hegel's Concept of Experience*, trans. Kenley Dove (New York: Harper and Row, 1970).

Martin Heidegger, *Holzwege* (Frankfurt am Main: Klostermann, 1950, 1972).

Martin Heidegger, *Identity and Difference*, trans. Joan Stambaugh (New York: Harper and Row, 1969) [*Identität und Differenz* (Pfullingen: Neske, 1957)].

Martin Heidegger, *An Introduction to Metaphysics*, trans. Ralph Manheim (New York: Doubleday, 1961) [*Einführung in die Metaphysik* (Tübingen: Niemeyer, 1953)].

Martin Heidegger, *Kant and the Problem of Metaphysics*, trans. James S. Churchill (Bloomington: Indiana University Press, 1962) [*Kant und das Problem der Metaphysik* (Frankfurt am Main: Klostermann, 1951)].

Martin Heidegger, *Kants These über das Sein* (Frankfurt am Main: Klostermann, 1963)].

Martin Heidegger, *Nietzsche* (Pfullingen: Neske, 1961).

Martin Heidegger, *Phänomenologie und Theologie* (Frankfurt am Main: Klostermann, 1970).

Martin Heidegger, *Phänomenologische Interpretation von Kants Kritik der reinen Vernunft* (Frankfurt am Main: Klostermann, 1977).

Martin Heidegger, *The Piety of Thinking*, trans. James G. Hart and John C. Maraldo (Bloomington: Indiana University Press, 1976).

Martin Heidegger, *Platons Lehre von der Wahrheit, mit einem Brief über den "Humanismus"* (Bern: Francke, 1947, 1954).

Martin Heidegger, *Poetry, Language and Thought*, trans. Albert Hofstadter (New York: Harper and Row, 1971).

Martin Heidegger, *The Question of Technology and Other Essays*, trans.

William Lovitt (New York: Harper and Row, 1977).

Martin Heidegger, *Zur Sache des Denkens* (Tübingen: Niemeyer, 1969).

Martin Heidegger, *On Time and Being*, trans. Joan Stambaugh (New York: Harper and Row, 1972).

Martin Heidegger, *Vorträge und Aufsätze* (Pfullingen: Neske, 1967).

Martin Heidegger, *Was ist Metaphysik?* (Frankfurt am Main: Klostermann, 1955).

Martin Heidegger, *On the Way to Language*, trans. Peter Hertz and Joan Stambaugh (New York: Harper and Row, 1971) [*Unterwegs zur Sprache* (Pfullingen: Neske, 1959)].

Martin Heidegger, *Wegmarken* (Frankfurt am Main: Klostermann, 1967).

Martin Heidegger, *Vom Wesen der Wahrheit* (Frankfurt am Main: Klostermann, 1943, 1954).

Martin Heidegger, *What is Called Thinking?*, trans. Fred D. Wieck and J. Glenn Gray (New York: Harper and Row, 1968, 1972) [*Was heisst Denken?* (Tübingen: Niemeyer, 1954, 1971)].

Martin Heidegger, *What is a Thing?*, trans. W. D. Barton and Vera Deutsche (Chicago: Regnery, 1967) [*Die Frage nach dem Ding* (Tübingen: Niemeyer, 1962)].

E. D. Hirsch, *Validity in Interpretation* (New Haven: Yale University Press, 1967).

Elmar Holenstein, *Jakobson* (Paris: Segbers, 1974).

Edmund Husserl, *Cartesian Meditations*, trans. Dorion Cairns (The Hague: Nijhoff, 1960).

Edmund Husserl, *Experience and Judgment*, trans. James S. Churchill and Karl Ameriks (London: Routledge and Kegan Paul, 1973).

Edmund Husserl, *Formal and Transcendental Logic*, trans. Dorion Cairns (The Hague: Nijhoff, 1969).

Edmund Husserl, *Ideas*, trans. W. R. Boyce Gibson (London: Allen and Unwin, 1931).

Edmund Husserl, *Ideen zu einer reinen Phänomenologie und phänomenologischen Philosophie* (The Hague: Nijhoff, 1950, 1952, 1971).

Edmund Husserl, *Logical Investigations*, trans. J. N. Findlay (London: Routledge and Kegan Paul, 1970).

Roman Jakobson, *Essais de linguistique générale* (Paris: Minuit, 1963 etc.).

Roman Jakobson, *Selected Writings* (The Hague: Mouton, 1962).

Thomas S. Kuhn, *The Structure of Scientific Revolutions* (Chicago: University of Chicago Press, 1962).

Dominique Lecourt, *L'Epistémologie historique de Gaston Bachelard* (Paris: Vrin, 1972).

Emmanuel Levinas, *En découvrant l'existence avec Husserl et Heidegger* (Paris: Vrin, 1974).

Emmanuel Levinas, *Difficile liberté: essais sur le judäisme* (Paris: Albin Michel, 1963, 1976).

Emmanuel Levinas, *Ethique et Infini* (Paris: Fayard, 1982).

Emmanuel Levinas, *Existence and Existents*, trans. Alphonso Lingis (The Hague: Nijhoff, 1978) [*De l'existence à l'existant* (Paris: Vrin, 1947, 1981)].

Emmanuel Levinas, *Otherwise than Being or Beyond Essence*, trans. Alphonso Lingis (The Hague: Nijhoff, 1981) [*Autrement qu'être ou au-delà de l'essence* (The Hague: Nijhoff, 1978)].

Emmanuel Levinas, *Totality and Infinity*, trans. Alphonso Lingis (The Hague: Nijhoff, 1969) [*Totalité et Infini* (The Hague: Nijhoff, 1961)].

Emmanuel Levinas, "Tout autrement," *L'Arc: Jacques Derrida*, 54, 1973 (*Noms propres* [Montpellier: Fata Morgana, 1976)].

Claude Lévi–Strauss, *L'Home nu* (Paris: Plon, 1971).

Claude Lévi–Strauss, *From Honey to Ashes*, trans. John and Doreen Weightman (London: Cape, 1973).

Claude Lévi–Strauss, *The Raw and the Cooked*, trans. John and Doreen Weightman (London: Cape, 1970).

Claude Lévi–Strauss, *The Savage Mind (La Pensée sauvage)* (London: Weidenfeld and Nicolson, 1966).

Claude Lévi–Strauss, "The Story of Asdiwal," in *The Structural Study of Myth and Totemism*, ed. Edmund Leach (London: Tavistock, 1977).

Claude Lévi–Strauss, *Structural Anthropology*, trans. Claire Jacobson and Brooke Grundfest Schoepf (London: Penguin, 1972).

Claude Lévi–Strauss, *Tristes Tropiques*, trans. John and Doreen Weightman (London: Penguin, 1976).

Claude Lévi–Strauss, Paul Ricoeur, etc., "Réponses à quelques questions," *Esprit*, 322, 1963.

Hans Lipps, *Hermeneutische Logik* (Frankfurt am Main: Klostermann, 1976).

W. B. Macomber, *The Anatomy of Disillusion* (Evanston, Ill.: Northwestern University Press, 1967).

Maurice Merleau–Ponty, *Consciousness and the Acquisition of Language*, trans. H. J. Silverman (Evanston, Ill.: Northwestern University Press, 1973).

Maurice Merleau–Ponty, *Phenomenology of Perception* trans. Colin Smith (London: Routledge and Kegan Paul, 1962) [*Phénoménologie de la perception* (Paris: Gallimard, 1945)].

Maurice Merleau–Ponty, *The Prose of the World*, trans. J. O'Neill (London: Heinemann, 1974) [*La Prose du monde* (Paris: Gallimard, 1969)].

Maurice Merleau–Ponty, *Signs*, trans. Richard C. McCleary (Evanston, Ill.: Northewstern Unitersity Press, 1964) [*Signes* (Paris: Gallimard, 1960].

Maurice Merleau–Ponty, *The Structure of Behavior*, trans. Alden L. Fisher (Boston: Beacon, 1963) [*La Structure du comportement* (Paris: Presses Universitaires de France, 1967)].

Maurice Merleau–Ponty, *The Visible and the Invisible*, trans. Alphonso Lingis (Evanston, Ill.: Northwestern University Press, 1968) [*Le Visible et l'invisible* (Paris: Gallimard, 1964)].

Emile Meyerson, *Identity and Reality*, trans. Kate Loewenberg (New York: Dover, 1962).

Wolfhart Pannenberg, *Basic Questions in Theology*, trans. George H. Kehm (London: SCM, 1970).

Wolfhart Pannenberg, *Theology and the Philosophy of Science*, trans. Francis McDonagh (London: Darton, Longman and Todd, 1976).

H.–J. Pos, "Phénoménologie et linguistique", *Revue internationale de philosophie*, 1, 1939.

Paul Ricoeur, *Le Conflit de interprétations* (Paris: Seuil, 1969).

Jean–Paul Sartre, *Being and Nothingness*, trans. Hazel Barnes (London: Methuen, 1969) [*L'Etre et le néant* (Paris: Gallimard, 1943)].

Jean–Paul Sartre, *Critique of Dialectical Reason*, trans. Alan Sheridan–Smith (London: New Left Books, 1976) [*Critique de la raison dialectique* (Paris: Gallimard, 1960)].

Jean–Paul Sartre, *Existentialism and Humanism*, trans. Philip Mairet (London: Methuen, 1948) [*L'Existentialisme est un humanisme* (Paris: Nagel, 1946)].

Jean–Paul Sartre, *Nausea*, trans. R. Baldick (London: Penguin, 1965).

Jean–Paul Sartre, *The Problem of Method*, trans. Hazel Barnes (London: Methuen, 1964).

Jean–Paul Sartre, *The Transcendence of the Ego*, trans. Forrest Williams and Robert Kirkpatrick (New York: Noonday, 1975) [*La*

Transcendance de l'Ego (Paris: Vrin, 1972)].

Ferdinand de Saussure, *Course in General Linguistics*, trans. Wade Baskin (London: Fontana–Collins, 1974) [*Cours de linguistique générale* (Paris: Payot, 1971)].

INDEX

activity, 40, 186, 190–191
analogy, 38
analytic reason, 71–72
anamnesis, xiii, 28, 147, 177, 181
an-archy, 200
Anaximander, 25
anthropology, 67, 75, 153, 157–
162, 165–166, 168–169
anxiety (*Angst*), 15, 18
apperception, 38–39
application, 91, 95, 99–101, 111
appresentation, 37, 188, 195
Aristarchus, 87
Aristotle, xiii, 3, 24, 31, 46, 110,
118, 120, 181, 183, 200
art, 104, 117, 126, 130, 175–176
"as", 12–13, 113
assertion (proposition), 12, 25, 28,
113, 115, 205
Augenblick, 17–18, 26
Augustine, 28, 115, 144
Austin, J., 24, 115, 179
authenticity, 7, 16–17, 19, 22, 75,
174, 186

Bachelard, G., xiv, 54, 83–95, 99,
116, 118, 125, 163, 165, 174–
180, 186
Bacon, F., 90, 115, 150
bad faith, 68
Barthes, R., 129–130, 143
Bataille, G., 199
Beaufret, J., 26
behaviourism, 145
being, 3, 23, 29, 46, 49, 66, 77, 81,
151, 173, 179–181, 184, 194,
198–199, 202–203; meaning of,

xiii, 4–5, 11, 20, 25, 45, 66, 151,
178–181
being-in-the-world, 11, 13, 25
Bennett, J., 145
Bergson, H., 4, 75, 78, 83–85, 87–
88, 94–95, 134–135, 151, 165,
175, 177, 179
Berkeley, Bishop, 40, 52, 66, 128
Betti, E., xiv, 100, 110, 186
beyond, 198, 206
biblical exegesis, 100, 109–110,
113, 163–164
Biran, M. de, 84
Blackett, P. M. S., 90
Braig, C., 3
Brentano, F., 3, 33, 194
bricolage, 155, 179
Bultmann, R., 117
Burke, E., 104
Butler, Bishop, 75

care (*Sorge*), 9, 11, 15, 46, 184
categories, xiii, 3, 50, 65–66, 150,
176, 183, 202, 205
Cézanne, P., 150
chess, 136
choice, 54, 58–60, 66
Chomsky, N., 137, 146
circle, 6, 49–53, 59, 63, 70, 73, 79,
81
coefficient of adversity, 54, 68
cogito, 7, 33–34, 37
collectives, 69–70
community, 65, 73–81 (see also
Mitsein)
Comte, A., 89
concepts, 6, 29, 35, 37, 42, 66, 83,

231